Jean-Paul Sartre: The Philosopher as a Literary Critic

BY BENJAMIN SUHL

COLUMBIA UNIVERSITY PRESS
NEW YORK & LONDON

To the one,
and to the many,
everywhere,
Morts sans sépulture.

Library of Congress Catalog Card Number: 71-116377
ISBN 0-231-03338-9 *Cloth*
ISBN 0-231-08319-x *Paperback*

PRINTED IN THE UNITED STATES OF AMERICA

PREFACE

This is to date the only survey and appraisal of Sartre's literary criticism in any language. Yet the contribution Sartre continues to make in this field is original and considerable. To him literary criticism is a dynamic correlation between literature, based on experience, and systematic philosophy.

In a widening spiral, from his early reviews to his works on Baudelaire, Flaubert, and Genet, he developed his positions on the significance of stylistic techniques, on the complexity of aesthetic pleasure, on a definition of beauty valid in any art, on a method of analysis in which the literary product appears as the synthesis of an author's life; and what has emerged, linked indeed to Sartre's aesthetics, is a radically new point of departure for an existentialist ethics.

The reader not acquainted with all Sartre's philosophy and critical writing of the last thirty years will find a descriptive presentation of the material, including the *Critique de la raison dialectique* and recent articles such as those on Flaubert, as yet unavailable in English. A correlation of Sartre's evolution as a philosopher and a literary critic (and creative writer) was mandatory. This has been done here in a manner which should be accessible even to those not conversant with philosophy.

PREFACE

In such a presentation, quotation rather than paraphrase was often necessary to elucidate the precise meanings of Sartre's ideas and the polemics they provoked. Authorized translations were used, giving an unavoidable variation in style. My own translations are indicated by the retention of the French or German title of an as yet untranslated book or article.

I am happy to have this opportunity to thank Jean-Albert Bédé, personally acquainted already with the young Sartre and thoroughly familiar with his thought, for his informed and sympathetic reading of my manuscript. I am also indebted to Robert D. Cumming, Robert Gorham Davis, and Léon Roudiez for their scholarly and encouraging comments. Regretfully, my appreciation to Justin O'Brien, a *vingtièmiste* who was a personal link to many an author and many a literary event of our time, must be expressed posthumously. Finally, I should credit my wife, Giovanna delle Donne, with whatever clarity there may be in this exposition; hers was the difficult task of being my first reader.

ACKNOWLEDGMENTS

To all the publishers and individuals who granted permission to quote, I wish to acknowledge my gratitude, specifically: George Allen & Unwin Ltd., Edmund Husserl, *Ideas.* L'Arc, Jean-Paul Sartre, "Jean-Paul Sartre Répond," No. 30, 1966. George Braziller, Inc., from *Situations* by Jean-Paul Sartre, translated from the French by Benita Eisler, reprinted with the permission of George Braziller, Inc. English translation copyright © 1965 by George Braziller, Inc., and from *Saint Genet* by Jean-Paul Sartre, translated from the French by Bernard Frechtman, reprinted with the permission of the publisher. English translation copyright © 1963 by George Braziller, Inc. La Librairie José Corti, Robert Ellrodt, *Les Poètes métaphysiques anglais* (Paris, Les Editions José Corti, 1960). Les Editions Gallimard, Jean-Paul Sartre, *Situations* I (1947) and II (1948), and *Critique de la raison dialectique* (1960), © by Editions Gallimard. Grove Press, Inc. and Anthony Blond Ltd., Jean Genet, *Our Lady of the Flowers,* translated by Bernard Frechtman, copyright © 1963 by Grove Press, Inc., published by Grove Press, Inc., and Jean Genet, *The Thief's Journal,* translated from the French by Bernard Frechtman, copyright © 1964 by Grove Press, Inc., published by Grove Press, Inc. Hamish Hamilton, Ltd., from *Baudelaire,* copyright © 1949 by Jean-Paul Sartre, translation copyright © 1949 by Martin Turnell (Hamish Hamilton, London). Alfred A. Knopf, Inc., Jean-Paul Sartre, *Search for a Method,* copyright © 1963 by Alfred A. Knopf, Inc. The Macmillan Company, Edmund Husserl, *Ideas,* first Collier Books Edition 1962. Methuen

& Co. Ltd., Jean-Paul Sartre, *Problem of Method.* New Directions Publishing Corporation, Jean-Paul Sartre, *Baudelaire,* translated by Martin Turnell, copyright 1950 by New Directions Publishing Corporation. S. G. Phillips, Inc. and Hutchinson Publishing Group Ltd., reprinted by permission of S. G. Phillips, Inc., from *Literary and Philosophical Essays* by Jean-Paul Sartre, copyright © 1955 by S. G. Phillips, Inc. Used by permission of Philosophical Library, Inc., *Being and Nothingness* by Jean-Paul Sartre, Copyright 1956 by The Philosophical Library, Inc., New York; *What is Literature?* by Jean-Paul Sartre, Copyright 1949 by The Philosophical Library, Inc., New York; and *The Psychology of Imagination* by Jean-Paul Sartre, Copyright 1948 by The Philosophical Library, Inc., New York. Presses Universitaires de France, Léopold Sédar Senghor, *Anthologie de la nouvelle poésie nègre et malgache* (Paris, 1948). Random House, Inc., Robert D. Cumming, *The Philosophy of Jean-Paul Sartre,* copyright © 1965. The Rutgers University Press, Germaine Brée and Margaret Guiton, *An Age of Fiction: The French Novel from Gide to Camus* (New Brunswick, N.J., 1957). Bulletin de la Société Française de Philosophie, passages by Jean-Paul Sartre (April–June 1948). Les Temps Modernes, passages from articles on Flaubert by Jean-Paul Sartre, in Nos. 244 and 245 (1966). Andre Deutsch Ltd., and The World Publishing Company, reprinted by permission of The World Publishing Company from *The Prime of Life* by Simone de Beauvoir, copyright © 1960 by Librairie Gallimard. English translation © 1962 by The World Publishing Company.

CONTENTS

JEAN-PAUL SARTRE: THE PHILOSOPHER AS A LITERARY CRITIC

Introduction

PHILOSOPHY AND LITERATURE

It has been said that literature is latent existentialism. Indeed, the subjective, the particular and the specific experience of individuals is the primary concern of both. And both are distinctly nonscientific and nonaprioristic in their approach to their experience of life. Deliberately, they run counter to the prevailing *Zeitgeist:* the social "sciences," and for that matter most British and American philosophy, have tried to account for man's behavior and the validity of his thinking through the use of statistics and of mathematical logic. Also much of the arts and even of music attest to the dominance of the scientific spirit through the pursuit of geometric forms and of arithmetic patterns and a pervading cerebrality. Already early in the century a reaction had set in with the emergence of the phenomenological movement, which constituted a radical turning-away from the "natural world,"[1] from science, from aprioristic

[1] "The DISCONNEXION from Nature was for us the methodological means whereby the direction of the mental glance upon the pure transcendental consciousness becomes at all possible. . . . With the suspending of the natural world . . . *all the sciences natural and mental,* with the entire knowledge they have accumulated, *undergo disconnexion* as sciences which require for their development the natural standpoint" (Edmund Husserl, *Ideas,* paragraph 56).

philosophy [2] and from common-sense reasoning. This "pure" phenomenology—reflecting on consciousness in a new way and thus giving philosophy a point of departure as fresh as had been that of Descartes—now focused its attention on the concrete aspect of existence, which is, by and large, also the perennial subject of literature.

The phenomenological movement, spearheaded by Husserl, had thereby led to a rapprochement between philosophy and literature; a rapprochement which, while considerably furthered by Heidegger, Merleau-Ponty and other philosophers, has certainly so far been best accomplished in the systematic writings of Jean-Paul Sartre, a considerable body of work still in progress.

Sartre had early made Husserl's reduction [3] and phenomenological description [4] his own. The purpose of the method was

[2] "We have not been arguing academically from a philosophical standpoint fixed in advance, we have not made use of traditional or even of generally recognized philosophical theories, but on lines which are in the strictest sense *fundamental* have *shown up* certain features, i.e., given true expression to distinctions which are directly given to us in *intuition.* We have taken them exactly as they present themselves, without any admixture of hypothesis or interpretation, and without reading into them anything that might be suggested to us by theories handed down from ancient or modern times. Positions so laid down are real 'beginnings' . . ." (*Ideas,* paragraph 18).

[3] "The *philosophic epoché* [abstention, reduction] . . . should consist, when explicitly formulated, in this, that *in respect of the theoretical content of all previous philosophy, we shall abstain from passing any judgment at all, and that our whole discussion shall respect the limits imposed by this abstention*" (*Ideas,* paragraph 18).

[4] "The most perfect geometry and its most perfect practical control cannot help the descriptive student of nature to express precisely (in exact geometric concepts) that which in so plain, so understanding, and so entirely suitable a way he expresses in the words: notched, indented, lens-shaped, umbelliform, and the like—simple concepts which are *essentially and not accidentally inexact,* and are *therefore* also unmathematical.

"Geometrical concepts are *'ideal' concepts,* they express something which one cannot 'see'; their 'origin,' and therefore their content also, is essentially other than that of the *descriptive concepts* as concepts which express the essential nature of things as drawn directly from simple intuition, and not anything 'ideal.' Exact concepts have their correlates in essences, which have the character of *'Ideas' in the Kantian sense.* Over against these Ideas or ideal essences stand the *morphological essences,* as correlates of descriptive concepts" (*Ideas,* paragraph 74).

to reach incontrovertible, apodictic evidence through one's own reflection, unprejudiced by any kind of aprioristic reasoning, and to reveal knowledge inaccessible to the scientific method, which can only be applied to the mechanistic that is causal relationships between things.

Between 1936 and 1940, Sartre wrote four phenomenological studies [5] describing the structures of perception and of imagination and of the emotions, a series of articles of literary criticism, several short stories and *Nausea,* in which he clarified his understanding of his experiences. In the process Sartre was led to realize the ultimate implication of Husserl's major innovation: the concept of intentionality, that is, of consciousness as consciousness of something. By the time he came to write *Being and Nothingness* (1943), consciousness appeared to him as nothing in itself but as an awareness of something *outside* of itself, and entirely in the world. Furthermore, Descartes's *cogito* was, one might say, "reduced": an immediate, prereflective consciousness was uncovered—the one which perceives and imagines—underlying the *cogito* considered to be the reflective consciousness. At this point, therefore, consciousness was seen at once to exist in the world and at the same time to be free to endow the world with meaning.

Sartre, who had begun by giving his attention to specialized studies of the structures of consciousness, now found himself confronted with existence. In his monumental yet well-proportioned and rigorously structured "phenomenological ontology," he—unlike Heidegger—took as his point of departure, and as his tool of investigation, this consciousness on two levels in order to achieve a description of our being in the world. Existence precedes essence: the phenomena of our freely chosen acts constitute our essence (which can only be evaluated in

[5] *The Transcendence of the Ego: An Existentialist Theory of Consciousness* (1936–37). *Imagination. A Psychological Critique* (1936). *The Emotions. Outline of a Theory* (1939). *The Psychology of Imagination* (1940).

retrospect as what we have been). The biological, historical, social and psychological determinisms of the nineteenth and twentieth centuries were still acknowledged, but only as determining environmental factors in relation to which reflective consciousness freely assumes a position, always transcending them by "tearing itself away" from them. Sartre attempted to define an individual's "project"—the aim of his ontological freedom—which is always in the final analysis a distinctive attempt to have consciousness coincide with being. In so doing, he worked out principles of an existentialist psychoanalysis. As in the earlier studies, no place could be found for the subconscious, but there was a differentiation of pure from impure reasoning, of acts in good faith from those in bad faith. The ground seemed cleared for the next stage, the promised work on ethics.[6]

Responding to the political revival and division taking place in France after the war and to the upheaval caused by the Algerian events at home, Sartre committed himself ever more fully to specific public issues. If it may be permitted to simplify still further in order to obtain a first over-all view of complex developments and a key to the analysis that is to follow: Sartre was to center his ethics and aesthetics and politics, as well as his plays—closely related to them—around the exercise of freedom. It is this period, from 1943 to 1960, which also saw the major outpouring of his literary criticism: the *Baudelaire* and the *Saint Genet,* a number of programmatic and occasional articles in *Les Temps Modernes* and other magazines, several

[6] Simone de Beauvoir did publish a monograph, *Pour une morale de l'ambiguïté* (1947), which, however, was hardly intended to represent the expected ethical treatise. She was herself to disavow much of her earlier attempt when explaining that "the fact remains that on the whole I went to a great deal of trouble to present inaccurately a problem to which I then offered a solution quite as hollow as the Kantian maxims." And that primarily because "I was in error when I thought I could define a morality independent of a social context. I could write an historical novel without having a philosophy of history, but not construct a theory of action" (Beauvoir, *Force of Circumstance,* p. 67).

prefaces and essays, many of them subsequently collected in *Situations* (so far numbering Vols. I through VII).

The publication of the *Critique* in 1960 aroused widespread disappointment. Those who had expected an ethics of freedom felt themselves confronted with a sociology of necessity. One critic of the book even entitled his review "Metaphysical Stalinism."[7] This review and many others were written with the easy conviction of first impressions. This very difficult work represents more than its author claims, namely, the exposition of an existentialist ideology within Marxism, primarily designed to correct post-Marxism distortions of Marx and to make the latter's sociology intelligible. For this attempt at the "reintegration of man in the heart of an anthropology[8] has led Sartre to elaborate an original method of research, meticulously developed through phenomenological descriptions and fully defined in the two parts of the *Critique.* Indeed, in a dialectical process of acting and being acted upon, man's freedom in the realm of "rareté" (scarcity) and therefore of "nécessité" (compulsion) can readily become alienated to the "other"; however, it is man's project[9] which remains the point of departure. In the period from the appearance of *The Condemned of Altona* (1960) to *The Words* (1964) and a number of critical essays contemporary to or following the *Critique de la raison dialectique*—Sartre's latter period, which might be called one of existentialist anthropology—one finds in the multiple and intricate pursuits of these writings a fundamental consistency with the earlier phenomenological and ontological stages of Sartre's development as a philosopher, an author and a critic.

Sartre's criticism and his creative writing do not simply fol-

[7] Abel, *Dissent* (Spring 1961).

[8] *Search for a Method* (a translation of the first part of the *Critique*), p. 179. (Henceforth: *Search.*)

[9] The project *is* man, as man *is* his aims. His way to react to a given situation depends on his interpretation of this situation, which interpretation is dependent on his point of view embodied in his project. Thus compulsion can only be defined as such from the vantage point of one's goals.

low in logical sequence his advances in philosophy. While it is true that the latter often precede the former, they are all interrelated as parts of an ever-widening spiral. "A life develops in spirals; it passes again and again by the same points but at different levels of integration and complexity" (*Search,* p. 106).

Let us examine this ascension and growth of Sartre's endeavor, especially as it affects his literary criticism. My purpose and interpretative procedure will be to render Sartre's literary criticism explicit from the vantage point of his philosophy. A chronological analysis of Sartre's work should permit an understanding of the correlation between his evolution as a philosopher and as a literary critic. Sartre's philosophy provides the unity of development in his total work, given the coherent nature of philosophy as compared to that of literary criticism. Hence an outline of his philosophical development has been traced above, while that of Sartre's literary criticism can best follow in the conclusion of this study.[10]

[10] See below, pp. 266–71.

Chapter 1

PHENOMENOLOGICAL AND EXISTENTIALIST DESCRIPTION IN LITERATURE: THE EARLY REVIEWS

Ease, spontaneity, a freedom of attack bordering on willfulness are the surprising characteristics of Sartre the critic. There is none of the methodological exposition of his monographs; his creative writing also, even the ironical *The Childhood of a Leader,* is much more subdued and somewhat conventional in its manifest structure. It is as if the author—now speaking to us from across the table—is formulating his immediate reactions to a first reading of a book. A closer analysis of the reviews will show, however, that it is the entire Sartre who is behind this seemingly freewheeling voicing of opinion.

It was after some public recognition as the author of *Nausea* and of a few short stories that Sartre was asked by Paulhan, Parain and Cassou to write some "chroniques" for the *Nouvelle Revue Française, Mesure,* and *Europe.* Thus, while engrossed in the early stages of his own *Roads to Freedom,* Sartre took to literary criticism. It concerned for the most part French fiction recently published or American authors then not widely known in France. The latter must have seemed particularly attractive to Sartre because of their spontaneity and new techniques, comparatively free from tradition.

It is impossible to undertake an appraisal of Sartre's early criticism—if this appraisal is to have as its point of departure Sartre's own understanding of it—without considering his phenomenological monographs[1] and his creative writing, which are interwoven with his literary criticism. One of Sartre's early encounters with phenomenology is vividly described by Simone de Beauvoir:

> Sartre was coming to realize that in order to give the ideas dividing his mind some coherent organization, help was essential. The first translations of Kierkegaard appeared about this time: we had no particular incentive to read them, and left them untouched. On the other hand, Sartre was strongly attracted by what he had heard about German phenomenology. Raymond Aron was spending a year at the French Institute in Berlin and studying Husserl simultaneously with preparing a historical thesis. When he came to Paris he spoke of Husserl to Sartre. We spent an evening together at the Bec de Gaz in the Rue Montparnasse. We ordered the specialty of the house, apricot cocktails; Aron said, pointing to his glass: "You see, my dear fellow, if you are a phenomenologist, you can talk about this cocktail and make philosophy out of it!" Sartre turned pale with emotion at this. Here was just the thing he had been longing to achieve for years—to describe objects just as he saw and touched them, and extract philosophy from the process. Aron convinced him that phenomenology exactly fitted in with his special preoccupations: by-passing the antithesis of idealism and realism, affirming simultaneously both the supremacy of reason and the reality of the visible world as it appears to our senses. On the Boulevard Saint-Michel Sartre purchased Lévinas's book on Husserl, and was so eager to inform himself on the subject that he leafed through the volume as he walked along, without even having cut the pages. . . . Sartre decided to make a serious study of him,

[1] The major shortcoming of Iris Murdoch's *Sartre, Romantic Rationalist* (1953) is her total disregard of Sartre's phenomenological point of departure. She thus makes short shrift of what she calls Sartre's "very persuasive descriptions" when berating him because he "offers nothing like a convincing deduction of his categories" (pp. 91–92). (Another flaw is her insistence on Sartre's trilogy *Roads to Freedom* which is perhaps the weakest part of his work. We shall have occasion to return to Miss Murdoch's highly interesting book.)

and took the necessary steps to succeed Aron at the French Institute in Berlin for the coming year—this on Aron's own instigation.[2]

Corroborating Simone de Beauvoir's account, and broadening its relevance, Merleau-Ponty flatly states that "several of our contemporaries had the feeling of recognizing what they were waiting for rather than that of meeting a new philosophy." [3] Indeed, in France, Valéry [4] and—as often as not—Proust [5] had prepared the ground for the new point of departure.

Sartre, in his drive to "touch" reality, already in his first monograph, *The Transcendence of the Ego* (1936–37), drops the last vestiges of idealistic philosophy still clinging to Husserl, who, somewhat despairingly, called himself near the end of his life "ein ewiger Anfänger nur"—an eternal beginner. Sartre would not conceive of any content to consciousness, finding it transparent through and through, nothing but experience of the world. With this one step beyond Husserl he even more radically than the former turned his back on the endless epistemological concern and paradox from Zeno to Ayer.[6] It is no

[2] Beauvoir, *The Prime of Life*, p. 112. (Henceforth: *Prime*.)

[3] Merleau-Ponty, *Phénoménologie de la perception*, p. ii.

[4] See for instance his statement that "education in depth consists in undoing one's first education" (*Introduction à la méthode de Léonard de Vinci* [1919], Pléiade, I, 1165–66). Valéry has indeed reeducated himself and his readers.

[5] Sartre will give credit to certain aspects of Proust all through his writing; for example, when mentioning "Proustian immediacy" (*Situations* I, 309).

[6] Ayer himself, in a sense, throttled epistemology at the other end, when stating: "The philosopher must be content to record the facts of scientific procedure" (*Language, Truth and Logic*, p. 98).

As for most of contemporary Anglo-American philosophy, which is so severely limiting itself, it may be interesting to quote Hazel E. Barnes: "Both existentialist and Oriental believe that philosophy can and should perform tasks more significant than the analysis of the language of propositions. They take issue with the idea that only those questions which are scientifically or logically verifiable are legitimate material for the philosopher. They feel such verification is important only for scientific and logical problems. They blame the analytic philosophers, not only for limiting the subject matter of philosophy to the structure of the language but for tending to limit experience itself" ("The Optimism of World Denial," p. 8).

longer what we can see but what we do see that concerns us. For that which we can describe as existing in our perception does exist in the world, provided we take care to withhold—to "bracket"—any and all conceptualizing which precedes our perception and may falsify it. To this pure consciousness, when reflective, the ego appears as an object, more intimate than other objects but still an object. Therefore, there is no self which self-analysis might yield.

It becomes obvious that already now Sartre would consider illusory that part of literature and literary criticism dealing with the inner life of its heroes, with the self as the locus of an idealistic point of view.

In his first article [7] for an audience primarily interested in literary criticism, the readers of the *Nouvelle Revue Française,* Sartre says in a mere four pages much that is understandable only in the light of his later voluminous writings. It is as if this early lightning discovery that consciousness, while it is everything (the world it perceives), is nothing (without any content of its own), had at once opened up to him the outlines of his future work. The immediate critical result is seen here in his outcry: "We are freed from Proust. Freed at the same time from the 'inner life.' " In later writings we find very positive appreciations of Proust, but here the rejection is obviously that of his subjective analyses. Indeed, one might say that in their very lengthiness and sinuosity they express at times their innate futility. Contrary to Proust, Sartre makes the lapidary statement that "if we love a woman, it is because she is lovable."

Sartre, who had begun work on *Nausea,* had to "abandon" Roquentin because Alcan, the editor, had asked him to write on imagination, the subject of his "diplôme d'études supérieures." [8] The resultant treatise, *Imagination,* provides us

[7] "Une Idée fondamentale de la phénoménologie de Husserl: L'Intentionnalité" (Intentionality: A Fundamental Idea of Husserl's Phenomenology). *NRF,* January 1939.

[8] See Beauvoir, *Prime,* p. 163.

with a good example of the phenomenological method. Sartre describes in detail what happens *in his mind* when looking at a piece of paper on his desk and when looking away from it at an image of the paper.

> Unprejudiced self-examination would disclose that I distinguish quite spontaneously between what exists as a thing and what exists as image. . . . The recognition of an image as such is an immediate datum of inner sense, of inner experience [p. 3].

While there is no mathematical or logical proof for the above statement—nor can there be—everyone may find in the workings of his own mind an intuitive verification. And yet

> wholly *a priori* speculation has turned the image into a thing. . . . All have built *a priori* their theories of the image. And when finally they took to consulting experience, it was too late. Instead of allowing themselves to be guided by experience, they have forced experience to answer yes or no to leading questions [p. 5].

After having thus freed himself from the theories of Descartes, Leibniz and Hume, who do not clearly distinguish perception from imagination, he disposes characteristically of more recent French predecessors. Of Ribot, who was "no more concerned to describe the facts than Taine was. He began with explanations" (p. 36). And of Bergson: "He never *looked at* his images" (p. 56). And of recent methodology:

> Instead of going right to the point and shaping the method on the object, *first* method has to be defined (the analysis of Taine, the synthesis of Ribot, the experimental introspectionism of Watt, the reflective critique of Brochard, etc.), *and then applied* to the object. No one suspected that in adopting a method he was at the same time fashioning the object [p. 77].

How could psychology for so long confuse perception and imagination?—because of prejudices, some of which are as old as Aristotle. Sartre demands an intuitive experience preceding experimentation: "We know now that we must start afresh, setting aside all the prephenomenological literature, and attempting above all to attain an intuitive vision of the intentional structure of the image" (p. 143).

He had done so himself at the outset and found a spontaneous and unfailing differentiation between perception and imagination through a description of what he observed in his mind when looking at an image—first reduction. He then reflected on its meaning—second reduction. Imagination is an act, not the passive observation of perception; a particular type of consciousness, the "intention" of something which is absent. Sartre will return to this subject first two and then four years later, in the two parts published as *The Psychology of Imagination,* with results pertinent to his aesthetics.

In 1937 Sartre took up again the story of Roquentin, then called *Melancholia,* after Dürer's woodcut. In all, he worked on it for four years, though far from exclusively. In the words of Simone de Beauvoir, he sought "the expression in literary form of metaphysical truths and feelings. . . . The plan was . . . deeply rooted in Sartre's mind, and . . . long established" (*Prime,* p. 227). When Paulhan and Ponge, as Gallimard's readers, accepted the manuscript for publication, Sartre also submitted to them his short stories. For the most part they deal with extreme situations.

In *The Wall,* life is disintegrating physically and mentally; it is seen from the point of view of impending death which leaves the victim without any project. A doctor has been introduced into the cell of the condemned Spanish loyalist civil war prisoners so as to leave no doubt in the reader's mind about the purpose of this story. At the end one of them, Ibbieta, freed after having unwittingly betrayed a friend through an inexplicable misunderstanding, breaks into laughter; Ibbieta is at a distance from himself as from everything else.

The piece of creative writing which was and has remained most enlightening about Sartre's over-all position is of that same early period. *Nausea* encompasses so much philosophy "in literary form," that one has perhaps come to understand particular aspects of this work of 1938 only in the light of *The Words* of 1964. The major tendencies, however, appear in the systematic *Being and Nothingness* published five years after *Nausea.* The phenomenological method anticipated in part by a number of French authors, found in Husserl, pursued to the end in *The Transcendence of the Ego* and in the *Imagination,* was now permitting Sartre—who admonishes himself: "I must beware of literature" [9]—to write a novel wherein he relates a primitive experience of life.

Consciousness is empty.[10] Nausea is nausea of something: of things, their proliferation and contingency; of people, their escape into the "spirit of seriousness"; of abstract humanism; of everyday comedy. Anny's art for art's sake proves equally futile; futile also the wish to find a *raison d'être* in anyone or in anything. But would it be meaningful to communicate this experience and its results? Perhaps. To make people aware of their contingency and their solitude might lead them to the conclusion the author reaches. After the dreadful ecstasy provoked by the realization of the facticity and the contingency of the root of the chestnut tree in the public garden, "the park smiled at me" [11] (p. 193). Roquentin, too, has reached a *dual*

[9] *Nausea,* p. 85.

[10] See *ibid.,* pp. 95–97.

[11] It is obviously an emotion which is expressed here. Sartre defines emotion as "a form of existence of consciousness," when one "intends"—comprehends—a magic world rather than the one of utensils; it is the immediate intuition of a totality (in fear, joy, etc.) rather than the recognition of its various components. "But there is a reciprocal action: this world itself sometimes reveals itself to consciousness as magical instead of determined, as was expected of it. Indeed, we need not believe that the magical is an ephemeral quality which we impose upon the world as our moods dictate. Here is an existential structure of the world which is magical. . . . The magical, as Alain says, is 'the mind dragging among things,' that is, an irrational synthesis of spontaneity and passivity. It is an inert activity, a consciousness rendered passive." (*The Emotions,* pp. 83–84.) One is reminded, when least expected, of Hugo, of Dürer and others. In a passage of Sartre's critique of Giraudoux we will find an explanation of this baffling experience. See pp. 31–32 below.

truth about himself: he is "alone and free" (p. 223). And while he remains hopelessly "alone" one can hear the motif of commitment through a good part of the book. The ragtime never fails as an antidote to Roquentin's nausea. The composer and the singer are not "bastards," they know and express their forlornness.[12]

It is in writing *Nausea* that Sartre has worked out the existentialist implications of his radical phenomenological observations of life, its contingency and its freedom, and the very problems this raises in literature.[13]

[12] On the meaning given to the ragtime by Sartre, Simone de Beauvoir has this to say: "Like most young people at the time, we were passionately devoted to Negro spirituals, and working songs, and the blues. Our indiscriminate affections embraced . . . "Some of these days" . . . ; men's lamentations, their withered joys and shattered hopes, had found a characteristic voice—a voice which challenged the polite assumptions of conventional art, which broke harshly from the very heart of darkness and rebellion" (*Prime,* p. 115).

Critics have often chosen to see in *Nausea* an attempt at "salvation through art," while minimizing the aspect of commitment. Maurice Cranston feels justified in his position when he recalls: "It is only when the little girl turns to run away that Roquentin lets the old man know that he is being watched. There is another incident in the Bouville Public Library. One of Roquentin's acquaintances, the 'Self-Taught Man' as he calls him, begins absent-mindedly to fondle a boy scout with whom he is sharing a book; another reader, 'The Corsican,' notices and, scandalised, creates a scene. In the commotion that ensues Roquentin first seizes 'The Corsican,' then weakly releases him. Afterwards Roquentin wonders why he let him go. He asks himself: 'Have these lazy years in Bouville rotted me?' " (*Jean-Paul Sartre,* p. 19).

Cranston does not take into account Roquentin's dreadful crisis (in stream of consciousness, the only sustained one in the book) which follows his failure to save the girl. As for the *Autodidacte,* Roquentin had indeed protected him against "The Corsican," actually an official of the library. Roquentin's subsequent complaint about himself only heightens his need to commit himself. Furthermore, since the effectiveness of the melody of the ragtime is contrasted with Anny's useless play-acting, one cannot speak of "salvation through art" (*ibid.,* p. 21) as the purpose of writing *Nausea.*

Before Cranston, Iris Murdoch wrote that "in *La Nausée* Roquentin receives the idea of the perfection he craves from an indifferent piece of music" (*Sartre, Romantic Rationalist,* p. 64). A different reading of the book, upheld by the above quotation from Simone de Beauvoir, considers this melody far from "indifferent." A "craving for perfection"—probably—but not in music; rather, by analogy with music, in a necessary accomplishment, in this case through commitment. It is the musically respected *Sixth Symphony* by Beethoven which is cited in *The Psychology of Imagination* as an example of art as analogon which is indifferent to the problem of the meaning of existence raised in *Nausea.*

[13] Robert D. Cumming explains in *The Philosophy of Jean-Paul Sartre,* p. 15:

Intimacy, Erostratus and *The Childhood of a Leader* complete the early prose writings. They show an intellectual author paying great attention to the visceral sensations since they are prereflective and as such impervious to conceptualization.[14] The last story represents another step in Sartre's system as a philosopher and a literary critic. Freud's views on erotic motivations are treated with irony and are shown reducible to a deeper human need, that of finding a *raison d'être.*

The specific contributions made by two additional monographs—on the emotions and on the imagination—written concurrently with the novel and the short stories, should be recalled before one can discuss the early articles of literary criticism intelligently from Sartre's own point of view.

The Emotions of 1939 starts out by rejecting the scientific

"The structure of the story *Nausea* reproduces the reflexive aspiration of consciousness in Sartre's philosophy: *Nausea* is a novel (at the higher reflexive level) about the pre-reflective experiences that led up to the writing of the novel. Proust's novel has a comparable structure. But in Proust (as in Husserl) experience is recaptured in its necessary structure by the reflective movement which transcends experience. Thus Proust's *recherche* is successfully completed in his terminal volume, *Le Temps retrouvé.* But Sartre has his ostensible protagonist in *Nausea,* Roquentin, tell the story to show that one cannot in fact 'catch time by the tail.' Furthermore, the true protagonist, nausea itself, is (in one of its manifestations) the reflexive experience of the discrepancy between the necessary structure of the story as told (as a work of art) and the sense of contingency—of the indeterminacy of the future—which is the experience of the sloppiness of living one's life that one seeks to alleviate by telling the story about it. This discrepancy, which self-consciousness (as well as Proust and the literary tradition) obscures by its loquacity, is preserved in *Nausea.* The novel is not completed within the novel, which ends with Roquentin's aspiration to regain his past experience by writing the novel, but with his actual future left dangling."

[14] Sartre is fully aware of this since he writes in *The Emotions* that "in order to understand clearly the emotional process with consciousness as the point of departure, it is necessary to bear in mind the twofold character of the body, which is, on the one hand, an object in the world and, on the other, something directly *lived* by consciousness" (p. 75).

Merleau-Ponty, whose point of departure is Heidegger's *Dasein* rather than Sartre's two-level consciousness, accentuates the description of this role of the body in consciousness on which Sartre relies in his short stories. Merleau-Ponty in his *Phénoménologie de la perception* (p. 274) refers to "the body . . . this strange object which uses its own parts as a general symbolism of the world and through which we can therefore 'visit' this world, 'understand' it and give it a meaning."

method of collecting unrelated data without regard for mean ings: the emotions are a type of consciousness within human reality, and thus when studying the emotions it is rather a matter of research on ourselves, and of phenomena which have meaning. Sartre partly accepts the findings of William James and Janet, those of Freud and some later psychologists, and in part he goes beyond them. In so doing he rejects psychological causality. Fear, for example, is fear of something indeed fearful: "The affected subject and the affective object are bound by an indissoluble synthesis" (p. 52). Again Sartre will not confine himself to either a materialist or idealist presupposition. Emotions are one of the ways of "apprehending" the world, at first nonreflective, an attempt to change a particular reality magically, by changing ourselves in fright, feinting or joy; sometimes in bad faith, as in the sour-grapes attitude or in "breaking-down" to avoid explaining coherently. This monograph, which Sartre calls an example of "a phenomenological psychology" as yet to be constituted (p. 92), shows that each aspect of emotional behavior is to be integrated into a total consciousness, because it is that totality as it creates itself:

> The emotion signifies, *in its own way,* the whole of consciousness or, if we put ourselves on the existential level, of human reality. It is not an accident because human reality is not an accumulation of facts. It expresses from a definite point of view the human synthetic totality in its entirety. And we need not understand by that that it is the *effect* of human reality. It is the human reality itself in the form of "emotion" [p. 17].

An emotion, then, is not the intentionality of the perception of utensils, of the existence of a world of means and ways, but the intentionality of one's being-in-the-world "degraded" by belief, by wishes and by fears. It is the emotional perception of objects by the subject, an incantation. We are here reminded of a sentence in one of Sartre's first articles:[15] "Husserl has

[15] "Une Idée fondamentale de la phénoménologie de Husserl: L'Intentionnalité," *Situations* I, 34.

brought back into things horror and charm. He has restituted to us the world of artists and of prophets." The "restitution" seems for Sartre to lie indirectly in the recognition of the role of the artist as creator of an imaginary object who proceeds to embody his emotion in this artifact. Incantation is above all a wish to go beyond the prevailing framework. (It is also perhaps in this sense that Camus felt that "all literature is contestation," and that Sartre, whom a German critic has called "the intellectual provocateur with the most genius since Voltaire," [16] will say that literature is by definition subversive.) The emotion is in the work of art—again, Alain's "the magical is the mind dragging among things"—and our mind, by its imagining intention, seizes this spirit, this emotion, through this "magic" object.

In *The Psychology of Imagination* (subtitled *Psychologie phénoménologique de l'imagination*) of 1940, the author reaches the limits of phenomenology as a primarily preexistential study of the structures of the mind. We also find a clear delineation of its method (Part One: The Certain) and examples of recourse to experimental psychology (Part Two: The Probable). While perception is observation of a real thing (three faces of a cube) and while conception gives us at once the knowledge of the object (the cube has six faces), imagination gives us only a profile, an *Abschattung,* which cannot be investigated further. Imagination—and it is now fully described and used to explain communication through the fine arts—is always an act intending a nothingness. One imagines something as either nonexisting (the centaur) or absent (Peter not in the café where expected) or existing elsewhere (Peter in Berlin) or intended as an object of the suspension of belief (the centaur). In imagination photographs, caricatures, impersonations as well as mental images serve as analoga of the real object to be "presentified" (rendered present). We know all this for certain through the reflective description of our own

[16] E. Vietta, *Versuch,* as quoted by Schlötke-Schraer, p. 20.

imagination when directed to and observed in various experiences. We also perceive perfectly well the nature of the physical analoga—the "analogical representatives"—of the paper and the dots, the canvas and the colors, the persons on stage: things and people all representing something other beyond themselves.

But what are the "analogical representatives" of a mental image? In the answer to this question we reach the limits of phenomenological description. Any attempt at reflection on our own mental analoga dissipates them: "We must, therefore, leave the sure ground of phenomenological description and turn to experimental psychology" (p. 70). However, such observations of others are not "eidetic" in Husserl's sense. Their findings remain without essential necessity; they are in the domain of probability.

Sartre denies the existence of "affective states" (*The Psychology of Imagination,* p. 88) because affective consciousness follows the law of all consciousness: it is consciousness of something, it is a way of transcending itself. He accuses nineteenth-century literature and Proust of having arrived at some sort of solipsism of affectivity (quite contrary to Pascal's theory of "love-esteem"). Classical psychology (and already La Rochefoucauld) has, he claims, confused reflective consciousness with prereflective consciousness. Feelings of something (Paul who is hateful) become in reflection a feeling (hate), but they are provoked by a hate-deserving person. For certain writers "feelings have no objects. For Proust and his disciples the tie between my love and the beloved person is at bottom but a tie of contiguity" (p. 88). It is true, however—Sartre being neither idealist nor materialist—that the meaning of the object perceived and imagined—absent and presentified or present and "absentified" (rendered absent)—is a new dimension conferred on the object by the observer. D. H. Lawrence excels, according to Sartre, in suggesting affective meanings while describing the forms and colors of physical objects. The charged description of such objects, as when in a certain context he speaks of "the long, white and delicate hands," elicits a response from some sympathetic chord, as it were, by its evocation of "these subdued affective structures which constitute their deepest reality" (p. 89). We have here an instance of an affective consciousness of hands.

The image in its very structure is a symbol for something which is absent or for a concept which appears on the prereflective level; it is an act of quasi-observation, an expression of quasi-hate, quasi-love, and the like; a magic incantation that causes the object of one's thoughts to appear, "an imaginary possession." The image is directed by a feeling—never a necessary cause, but only a willful motivation—which produces the imaginary object. In its unreality it negates and transcends reality from a particular point of view, thereby constituting a structure of the freedom of consciousness.[17]

[17] The following quotations, also from *The Psychology of Imagination,* may clarify some of the above summary:

"Association occurs as a causal linkage between two contents. But there can be no causal linkage between two consciousnesses: one consciousness cannot be aroused *from the outside* by another consciousness; but it arises by itself by its own intentionality, and the only tie that can connect it with the previous consciousness is that of *motivation.* Consequently we must no longer speak of automatisms and stereotypes" (p. 137).

"Synesthesia never occurs as the product of a pure association. The color occurs as the *sense* of the vowel" (p. 138).

"We must distinguish between two sorts of layers in a complete imaginative attitude: the primary, or constituent, layer and the secondary layer, the one that is commonly called the reaction to the image. . . . There are thus intentions, movements, a knowledge, sentiments that combine to form the image, and intentions, movements, sentiments, knowledges which represent our reaction, more or less spontaneous, to the unreal. The former are not *free:* they obey a directing form, a first intention, and are absorbed into the constitution of the unreal object. . . . The other factors of the psychic synthesis are more independent, they exist for themselves and develop freely" (p. 175).

"The unreal object happens in the consciousness of vomitings as the real cause of the real vomitings. By this very fact it loses its unreality and we fall into the illusion of immanence: memory thus confers upon it a quality which actual consciousness could not have given it, namely, as the *real cause* of the organic phenomena" (p. 177).

"We shall give the name of 'situations' to the different immediate ways of

Reading is imagination provoked by words which serve as analoga. Every reader can reflect on the experience he himself had when he was unreflectively fascinated while reading some pages, and check whether Sartre's descriptions hold true. The novelist, the poet, as well as the dramatist, create unreal objects. All art is unreal—precisely to the extent that it is art—and is as such in the domain of imagination. A consciousness which reflects reality, that is, pure perception, sees a square canvas, a distribution of paint, a frame: in short, a real object. The aesthetic object can only appear when consciousness operates a radical conversion, negating this reality as it calls forth an imaginary consciousness of the real analogon.[18] The artist does not produce his mental image, but only an analogon, a physical object, through which everyone can constitute the image if he will transcend the physical object before him (p. 247).

It is this negation at the heart of the aesthetic attitude which is at the bottom of the generally recognized "aesthetic distance," of the more sweeping thesis of the disinterestedness of aesthetic experience, and, more specifically, of Schopenhauer's belief in the suspension of the will in contemplation, and of Kant's remarks on one's indifference towards the actual existence or nonexistence of the beautiful object (p. 249).

---

apprehending the real as a world. . . . It is the situation-in-the-world, grasped as a concrete and individual reality of consciousness, which is the motivation for the construction of any unreal object whatever and the nature of that unreal object is circumscribed by this motivation" (p. 241).

"Every apprehension of the real as a world tends of its own accord to end up with the production of unreal objects because it is always, in one sense, a free negation of the world and that always *from a particular point of view*" (p. 242).

"Imagination is not an empirical and superadded power of consciousness, it is the whole of consciousness as it realizes its freedom; every concrete and real situation of consciousness in the world is big with imagination in as much as it always presents itself as a withdrawing from the real" [Sartre's "dépassement du réel" (p. 236) represents rather "a going beyond the real"] (p. 243).

[18] After having accused both psychology and the novelist of presenting as real the "degraded" knowledge of imagination (which of necessity fades) and of the typical, "le sentiment passe-partout," Sartre notes that to the contrary "Proust has well shown this abyss that separates the imaginary from the real" (p. 187).

Sartre, still primarily a phenomenologist, is led to a conclusion on the relationship between aesthetics and ethics, which he will partly contradict in his next stage as exponent of ontological freedom in commitment. He also felt differently about it in *Nausea* where the beautiful (the ragtime) was also the good (capable of giving density to the reality around Roquentin). But in *The Psychology of Imagination* he now writes:

> The real is never beautiful. Beauty is a value applicable only to the imaginary and . . . means the negation of the world in its essential structure. This is why it is stupid to confuse the moral with the esthetic. The values of the Good presume being-in-the-world, they concern action in the real and are subject from the outset to the basic absurdity of existence. . . . The attitude of esthetic contemplation towards real events or objects [produces] . . . a sort of recoil in relation to the object contemplated which slips into nothingness. . . . It is no longer *perceived;* it functions as an *analogue* of itself, . . . an unreal image [pp. 252–53].

One may understand Sartre's difficulty in developing his promised ethics if one considers his thesis of an absurd or contingent existence. This is a problem to which we will have cause to return. In phenomenology the differences between aesthetics and ethics correspond to those of imagination and perception, which are, indeed, irreducible and mutually exclusive. Yet, Sartre often reminds us, they go to constitute a total consciousness. Roquentin invariably found the objects of his perception more meaningful after an imaginary yet all-bracing aesthetic experience. It would seem that the aesthetic distance from a perceived situation permits a fresh approach to this situation. Imagination, that is, the rendering unreal, has as an exercise of freedom modified the limited, obsessive aspect of the situation and has placed it in a different *Gestalt* to the extent that its meaning has been modified.

Sartre's literary criticism is part and parcel of his reflections as a philosopher and as a creative writer. Thus some acquaintance with Sartre the phenomenologist and the novelist ought now to permit an evaluation of the early critical essays with Sartre's own understanding of them in mind.

Sartre's earliest article, "William Faulkner's *Sartoris,*" deals with the American novelist, to whom he returned almost a year and a half later in "On *The Sound and the Fury:* Time in the Work of Faulkner." [19] Sartre found *Sartoris* of interest precisely because Faulkner's technique was as yet not fully developed (as it is in *Light in August* or *The Sound and the Fury*). The key to both articles is to be found in this passage from the later review: "A fictional technique always relates back to the novelist's metaphysics. The critic's task is to define the latter before evaluating the former" (pp. 84–85). And this is the key to Sartre's particular contribution as a literary critic: to analyze literature primarily as a philosopher. At the outset it is his breakthrough in the phenomenological method and its immediate implications which allow him to go a step beyond the past categories of critical response.

Faulkner's technique is one that mingles past and present in the absence of any future. Sartre considers willful illusion (la déloyauté") "the mainspring of [his] art" ("*Sartoris,*" p. 78), stemming from his desire for silence and obscurity at the heart of consciousness, an expression of an ultrastoic puritanism. "Faulkner's volubility, his lofty abstract, anthropomorphic, preacher's style are still other illusionist devices," as are the gestures on which he dwells to avoid speech (p. 79).

> [The] psychological existence [of his characters] . . . is fixed and immutable, like an evil spell. Faulkner's heroes bear it within them from the day of their birth. It is as obstinate as stone and rock; it is a *thing* [p. 82].

In the later article, "On *The Sound and the Fury,*" the "super-present" of *Sartoris* becomes for Sartre the denial of any future,

[19] *NRF,* February 1938, and June–July 1939; translated in *Literary and Philosophical Essays.* (Henceforth: *Essays.*)

a stunting lack of progression, which leads to "l'enlisement," the sinking into a present obsessed by the past. Nothing occurs, everything has happened. Everything appears in the past, as if one were looking out backwards from a moving car. There is—and this is not the case in Proust—the past as an ever-present obsession; for Faulkner, writes Sartre, "pursues his thought to its uttermost consequences" (p. 90).

One may find this statement difficult to reconcile with Sartre's earlier characterization of Faulkner's "willful illusion." It is for the latter that the critic actually upbraids him throughout, and most emphatically on the following page: "All this artistry and, to speak frankly, all this illusion are meant, then, merely as substitutions for the intuition of the future lacking in the author himself" (p. 91). While dealing with Faulkner's fundamental problem, Sartre encountered once again the Heideggerian concept of the "lack" and became aware of the "project" of his later ontology, mentioned here for the first time *avant la lettre:* "Man is not the sum of what he has, but the totality of what he does not yet have, of what he might have" (p. 92). That there is something appealing in this "déloyauté" Sartre seems to recognize when he writes: " 'This can't last.' And yet change is not even conceivable, except in the form of a cataclysm" (p. 93).

What can this extraordinary art be if it serves the dishonest attempt to blot out the future? It is perhaps that Faulkner is effective—and goes to the very end of his thought—within his limitations. There are, in fact, innumerable descriptions which are perfectly "loyal" and on which Sartre will draw as verification for his own philosophical demonstrations, as for example the "look" of Christmas at the end of *Light in August.*

"Dos Passos has invented only one thing, an art of story-telling. But that is enough to create a universe." [20] "I know of none

[20] "John Dos Passos and *1919*" (1938), *Essays,* p. 95.

—not even Faulkner's or Kafka's—in which the art is greater or better hidden." Sartre, who had been among the very first to "discover" both Faulkner and Dos Passos would hardly be as enthusiastic about the latter today—at the end of the review Sartre calls Dos Passos the greatest writer of our time. But in August of 1938 Sartre was overwhelmed to find a novel, literature first and always, which represents consistently the phenomenological point of view.

For [Dos Passos's characters] there is no break between inside and outside, between body and consciousness, but only between the stammerings of an individual's timid, intermittent, fumbling thinking and the messy world of collective representations.

The author's approach is embodied in a style free from tradition.

What a simple process this is, and how effective! All one need do is use the American journalistic technique in telling the story of a life, and . . . [it] crystallizes into the Social, and the problem of the transition to the typical—stumbling-block of the social novel—is thereby resolved. There is no further need to present a working man type. . . . Dos Passos, on the contrary, can give all his attention to rendering a single life's special character. Each of his characters is unique. . . . What does it matter . . . since *he is* Society? [p. 101].

"He is Society"! We are reminded of Sartre's recurrent example of the yellow color of a lemon being the lemon, because the object is what it appears to be.[21] There just is no deeper significance (essence) behind any appearance (in space), or before it (in time, a hidden, potential essence now actualized); significance (essence) is created in the series of appearances. Consequently Dos Passos's characters do not narrowly act or speak "in character" or "out of character" since there is neither

[21] *Cf. Being and Nothingness* (henceforth: *Being*), pp. 186–88, especially the explanations on the "total interpenetration" of qualities, so that "every quality of being is all of being."

ontological nor psychological causality. There is a certain "indeterminacy of detail," they are free, but within a broader "statistical determinism," their individual actions will not change the over-all situation. To paraphrase Malraux, whom Sartre here quotes, their lives are destinies *before* the point of death. It is the style of American journalism as used by Dos Passos—factual, matter-of-fact, with the innuendoes of understatement—which suggests this metaphysics.

Sartre, in keeping with the aesthetics of *The Psychology of Imagination,* writes in his article on Dos Passos that "the novel . . . unfolds in the present . . . *with aesthetic distance*" (p. 95). Sartre envisions Dos Passos as having us jump into a mirror (much like Jean Cocteau in *Orphée*) into the imaginary life of art, where the very reflection of life is also a reflection on life—that is, he has us "read a novel" (p. 94). The reflection on life is minimized in Dos Passos; still, when we return from behind his mirror to our real world, we see it with his eyes and share his indignation. It seems obvious that we have here another reason for Sartre's praise of Dos Passos, who also denied the future and gave to his present "this unrelieved stifling atmosphere" (p. 98), just as had Faulkner ("*Sartoris,*" p. 82). The difference is that Dos Passos's simmering revolt might open up a future whereas Faulkner remains obsessed with his past.

If today Faulkner is widely considered a great author while Dos Passos is held to be just a good one, it is largely because Faulkner has gone to the very end of his vision, be it limited in time. Sartre gives us an insight into the mainspring of their respective works, but in his evaluation he wishes to free himself from the stupendous spell exercised by the artist Faulkner because Sartre cannot accept his fundamental "illusion." [22]

[22] In an unsigned introductory article to a survey, "La France s'interroge devant le roman américain" (France before the American novel), in *Le Monde* (weekly-selection, April 6–12, 1967), the newspaper states—with the benefit of an over-all perspective gained in thirty years: "In 1938 Jean-Paul Sartre invents

To Paul Nizan, his roommate at "Normale," Sartre will devote a lengthy commentary, an introduction to *Aden, Arabie* at its republication in 1960. In the contemporary short review of *La Conspiration,* let us note briefly the elaboration of another of Sartre's existentialist concepts.

One finds in Nizan a phenomenology, that is, a fixation and description, from the point of view of social and historical conditions, of that essence in motion, youth; the falsified and fetishized age.[23]

Implicit in Nizan, this concept is fully developed by Sartre in an analysis of "the age of inauthenticity"; these young middle-class people believe their youth gives them particular "rights."

A problem raised by Sartre here for the first time, and later answered by him in the same, unchanging vein, is whether or not "a communist can . . . write a novel." "I am not convinced of it," he says, "he cannot become the accomplice of his characters" (p. 29). (Sartre means "the accomplice" of the freedom of his characters.) Side by side with a commentary on Marx's "admirable analyses of the fetishism of Merchandise," of which Sartre was reminded by Nizan's analysis of youth, and after an expression of satisfaction with Dos Passos's revolt against capitalist society, we find in this review (as also in *Nausea* with its ironic reference to communist humanism, promised after the second five-year plan) strong reservations towards party-line communism.

If a communist cannot write a novel, can a Catholic? Surprisingly enough, Sartre believes he could: "The religious man is free." [24] Yet there is a denial of freedom in the very vantage

---

the American novel in three articles which establish in France the work of John Dos Passos and especially that of William Faulkner. For the first time the American novel is considered worthy of the French intelligentsia. . . . As regards Faulkner, Sartre gives a definitive interpretation of his vision of time. . . . In Sartre's wake, ten years later, Claude-Edmonde Magny designated what is now commonly called the age of the American novel."

23 "*La Conspiration* de Paul Nizan," *Situations* I, 27.

24 "François Mauriac and Freedom," *Essays,* p. 8.

point adopted by the author in *La Fin de la nuit.* He uses the third person ambiguously; at times "she" reveals her own thoughts, at others "she" is judged and given a destiny by the author, here and there even in the same sentence. Mauriac "wishes to show Thérèse as a predestined character"; for Sartre this would require a particular fictional technique. Mauriac deprives his heroine of freedom, since Thérèse does not exercise any free will—and therefore, argues Sartre, he should have taken an external vantage point, because from within we are in the realm of possibility. In Sartre's phenomenology of consciousness Thérèse's past may constitute a locus of motivation, but it does not determine her course of action. By the same token, a reader, who deciphers a novel through its signs and images (the analoga of *The Psychology of Imagination*), must be able to invest the author's imaginary hero with his own real freedom.[25] But is not every novel written by an all-knowing author? Sartre cites examples from Dostoyevsky and Meredith to show that the outcome is made to appear in doubt to the end of their novels, and he mentions Hemingway's convincing effectiveness as an outside observer.[26] Conversely, let us recall that what is supposed to upset the reader of Dos Passos's *1919* is precisely the "statistical determinism" of a society which is seeking to deprive men of their freedom, threatening to make of their lives a destiny.

[25] One is reminded of the etymology of the word "interest": to be among.

[26] The basic flaw of the rebuttal by Nelly Cormeau (Appendice—"D'une opinion de M. Sartre," *L'Art de François Mauriac*) lies in her lack of appreciation that the book under review was written in 1935, that François Mauriac is essentially an author of the second quarter of the twentieth century—at which period the privileged point of view of the omniscient author had become an anachronism. Furthermore, to meet Miss Cormeau on her own terrain, it cannot be denied that even the Princesse de Clèves, Eugénie Grandet or Henriette de Mortsauf, and certainly Madame de Rênal and Emma Bovary are to the end less predictable than the Thérèse of *La Fin de la nuit.* In the latter novel the author's omnipotence deprives the heroine of any freedom.

As for Miss Cormeau's challenge in the form of the question: Did M. Sartre by any chance not know in advance what Antoine Roquentin or Mathieu were to become? (p. 370), see footnote 13, pp. 16–17 above.

Vladimir Nabokov seems primarily concerned with reflection in his novel *La Méprise.* It would appear that his actual experience is almost exclusively one of books—the author, like the hero of the novel, may very well have read "from the end of 1914 to the middle of 1919 . . . exactly eighteen hundred books. . . ." [27] "Where is the novel?", Sartre asks. Nabokov's posture, twice removed from involvement, reflecting on reflections, is indeed conducive to the kind of irony which came to fruition in his later best seller *Lolita.*

"To me the interest of this work," writes Sartre in praise of Denis de Rougemont's *L'Amour et l'Occident,* "lies first of all in the fact that it bears witness to the recent and profound refinement of historical methods under the triple influence of psychoanalysis, of Marxism and of sociology." [28] But, as implied in this very quotation, he retains doubts about Rougemont's affirmations. He raises questions about them without denying the relevance of the categories of historical criticism applied by the author to myth and literature.

Sartre's judgment of Rougemont is a good example of his creative criticism. Since transcendance is the existential structure of man, "the lover depends to the very core of his existence on the other. . . . To desire . . . is to seek to reach, through a body, on a body, a consciousness . . . to desire the other's freedom, which in principle eludes him" (p. 68). Therefore, ontologically, "every authentic passion must have a taste of ashes" (p. 69).[29] To us this would explain why in myth, folk-

[27] Nabokov as quoted by Sartre, in *Situations* I, 60 ("Vladimir Nabokov: *La Méprise*").

[28] "Denis de Rougemont: *L'Amour et l'Occident,*" *Situations* I, 63.

[29] In this passage of the Rougemont article Sartre alludes to Heidegger's *zum Tode sein* (being for death), as he is wont to cite his predecessors (among them Husserl) in his early work. But it is clear that Sartre has himself just given a much more cogent, because intrinsic, explanation for this "useless passion" (on this Sartrian concept, used here in a more specific sense, see below, pp. 52–54). He also cites Valéry's characterization of consciousness as that "divine absence." On another occasion Sartre praises Proust for certain similar developments in *The Captive* (see *Being,* p. 366).

lore, legend and literature, before *Tristan and Isolde* and after, the tragic outcome was felt to be "satisfying" in contrast to the superficial "happy end" variety. Rougemont's analyses remain relevant inasmuch as they apply to the specific historical forms of a fundamental ontological condition.

Unlike the previously reviewed authors, on whom, with the possible exception of Mauriac, little had been written at the time Sartre considered them, Jean Giraudoux was well known in 1940, when his *Choix des élues* appeared. As a rule, the key to the strange attraction of Giraudoux's work, in both novels and plays, was sought in its preciosity. In his article for the *Nouvelle Revue Française* on this novel Sartre notes that it was hardly Giraudoux's best and was therefore interesting to the critic: "just because many of his charming devices have developed, in this book, into mechanical tricks, I found it easier to grasp the turn of this curious mind." [30] He finds Giraudoux's characters free to achieve their essence, that is, one of archetypes. There is no present indicative, there is no evolution into a future. "The noisy and unshapely present of surprises and catastrophes has shrunk and faded; it goes by quickly and tactfully, excusing itself as it passes" (p. 50). Instead, with Giraudoux's predilection for beginnings, his time is universal, as also revealed by his choice of vocabulary.

As previously, Sartre dwells on the novelist's art—the particular semantic field, tenses used and avoided, peculiar stylistic devices, unusual plots, particular characterizations—only inasmuch as it leads him to the author's metaphysics. There follows a comparatively lengthy analysis of Giraudoux's work and especially of *Choix des élues,* designed to make plausible the conclusion that this is the novel of natural history, of which Aristotle is the philosopher, resurrecting "a world that has been buried for four hundred years." Needless to say, his rejection of Giraudoux's metaphysics is such that he has but to name it.

[30] "Jean Giraudoux and the Philosophy of Aristotle," *Essays,* p. 45.

However, in the concluding paragraph, Sartre expresses his belief that everyone at times goes through "Aristotelian" experiences.

This evening of all evenings is a "Paris evening." A certain little street, one of many that lead to the Sacré-Cœur, is a "Montmartre street." Time has stopped. We experience a moment of happiness, an eternity of happiness [p. 58].

Sartre goes on to explain this as a "revelation" seized on things, which one actually possessed as a concept long before, an intuition of Necessity without necessity, a "revelation" which does not reveal anything. This paragraph, especially in its mention of the "humble and tenacious smile of objects," reminds one of a sentence in *Nausea.* Once the ecstasy provoked by the revelation of contingency in the contemplation of the roots of the chestnut tree has passed, Roquentin, looking back, finds that "the garden has smiled." He is now able to name, to overcome the obsession with the contingency of the tree as something already familiar to him.

We now may ask whether the Aristotelian Giraudoux is precious. If seventeenth-century preciosity is to be considered an attempt at countering *la Cour et la Ville* (the Court and the City), then dominating, by accentuating the sensibility of the declining aristocracy, Aristotelian immutability would serve equally well to render unreal, or at least to reduce to something merely temporal, a situation fraught with catastrophe.[31] And it is, indeed, this art of a modern preciosity which lends conviction to this metaphysics, since the reader is reminded of an earlier literary tradition which has survived many a crisis and demands only a playful acceptance, and, here transposed, permits Giraudoux to toy with Aristotelian forms.

Considering only the more superficial literary devices in-

31 One is here reminded of Jean Hytier's appreciation of Giraudoux who he said has "at least escaped the power of gravity" (*Histoire de la littérature française illustrée,* II, 422).

volved, criticism had so far failed to see that the message of the preciosity had changed. What permitted Sartre to recognize Giraudoux's novelty was his conscious suspension of judgment in analyzing the book before him:

I realized, first of all, that I had been diverted from the true interpretation of his works by a prejudice. . . . I had always tried to *translate* his books. . . . This time . . . I therefore pretended that I knew nothing at all about . . . this world . . . in which things are always meeting, . . . in which events have a natural resistance to thought and language, in which individuals are accidents. . . . I was not wrong. In the America of Edmée . . . rest and order came first. They are the goal of change and its only justification [*"Giraudoux,"* pp. 45–46].[32]

"Camus's *The Outsider*" (1943) has become one of the classics of contemporary criticism.[33] Sartre was the first to devote a considerable review to this work (known in America as *The Stranger*), which he examined in the light of *The Myth of Sisyphus*. What strikes today's reader, cognizant of the history

[32] Is it possible thus to consider a work by a highly civilized author, as it were "at face value"? Or has Sartre failed to recognize the irony in the novel and thereby misconstrued its tendency? We doubt it. Following are divergent comments by two recent critics:

"The novel as used by Giraudoux, demands a good deal of his readers. Not only must they be able to grasp the meaning of the text, which is thick with literary allusions; they must also be able to hear the novelist's exact tone of voice, to know when he is smiling, when he is pretending and when he is really in earnest. This is often a perilous undertaking. Sartre, for example, once considered this problem and came up with a strictly literal interpretation: The result was his portrait of Giraudoux as a twentieth-century Aristotelian: a man who has managed to persuade himself that existing reality is actually shaped in the neat outlines of intellectual concepts and nicely ordered in the pigeonholes of intellectual categories. This is an interesting portrait, but it looks less like Giraudoux than like an upside-down portrait of Sartre himself" (Germaine Brée and Margaret Guiton, *The French Novel*, p. 151).

"The novelist [Giraudoux] chooses the elect who will inhabit a world of escape with a pristine innocence, purity and happiness: a festival world where at last everything is in its place, adheres to its definition and, perfectly justified, scintillates in its most beautiful light; a minutely ordered gala performance wherein essences shine devoid of imperfections and utilitarian subordination" (Gaëtan Picon, "La Littérature du XXe siècle," *Histoire des Littératures* III, 1329–1330).

[33] Germaine Brée does not hesitate to consider this contemporaneous review as "definitive" (*Camus, A Collection of Critical Essays,* p. 1).

of the relationship developing between the two authors, is this early remark, so close to the parting remonstrance which ended a decade of friendship: "M. Camus shows off a bit by quoting passages from Jaspers, Heidegger and Kierkegaard, whom, by the way, he does not always seem to have quite understood" (*"The Outsider,"* p. 28). Nor does Camus recognize phenomenology; but phenomenology will help explain *The Stranger* fully.

The feeling of absurdity is provoked in the reader on the one hand by a description of daily lived reality and on the other by such a retelling of it that one can hardly recognize this reality. In a more specific instance this discrepancy appears in the prosecutor's charge concerning the murder, so utterly different from the experience imparted to the reader earlier that the conviction of the absurdity of justice is forced upon him. But in both cases, in lived absurd reality and in rational retelling, the same words must be used. The resolution of this contradiction calls for the recourse to a new technique.

Consciousness gives significance to events. So does the prosecutor's speech of indictment. But where absurd experience is projected Camus makes use of literary devices which filter out the meaning from the various descriptions, and even from Meursault's speech, as if he is making the analytic assumption that all reality is reducible to a sum of elements. Camus feels compelled to adopt this metaphysics because to him, death, the utter absurdity, deprives life of any future and makes of it a mere succession of presents. So that we find "the isolation of each sentence unit" obtained by Camus's telling his story largely in the discontinuous present perfect tense (*le passé composé*); by using disjunctives, oppositions or at best simple additions rather than causal or temporal connectives;[34] by

[34] In "Camus's *L'Étranger* Reconsidered," Ignace Feuerlicht offers a rebuttal to Sartre's presentation of these stylistic devices. His statistics of comparative frequencies remain unconvincing. Suffice it to state here that Frenchmen just do not talk like Meursault. The strangeness of the style of his speech and of the

Meursault's reluctance to talk; by a series of beginnings and by descriptions which in still other ways depict merely external relationships. Camus has produced a sentence which "does not belong to the universe of discourse. It has neither ramifications nor prolongations nor internal structure" (*"The Outsider,"* pp. 40–43).

Some aspects of this style remind Sartre of Hemingway and, altogether, of the American technique of storytelling. But with keen foresight he also notes his doubt that Camus would resort to it in the future; it does not seem to be his personal style and is used here deliberately for a specific purpose.

In his conclusion Sartre compares *The Stranger* to a *conte* of Voltaire, in that both are an apprehension of absurdity from the point of view of reason. One might object that the latter has logically led to irony, while Camus's poignancy lies in his unraveling the meaning of life from Heidegger's *zum Tode sein.*

Through an analysis of the distortions of Meursault's structures of consciousness as seen in his speech, Sartre lays bare the device which made the world look absurd; a world of events and of things from which meaning and aims were missing. Another kind of artistic distortion is practiced by Maurice Blanchot. Without knowing Kafka, he actually followed a similar path and Sartre finds that "by having unwittingly imitated him, M. Blanchot delivers us from him. He brings his methods into the open." [35] It is not that Blanchot is so much more obvious in his ways than Kafka is, but simply that in a comparison the basic procedures they have in common stand out clearly.

In the normal world things are conceived as utensils toward

---

descriptions of his actions constitutes their substance. The prosecutor, however, makes "sense" when treating of the very same content.

It is then surprising when Feuerlicht writes: "The difference in style in the two parts remains unexplained" (p. 616). Sartre had done just that.

[35] *"Aminadab* or the Fantastic Considered as a Language," *Essays,* p. 77.

an end. In the upside-down world of fantasy (or nightmare) the means revolt against their ends (the message of Aminadab, in one of Blanchot's novels, changes its content on the way: a normal Josef K. seeks justice) ; or else the means lead nowhere (the messenger never reaches his destination: K. makes incomprehensible efforts to stay in the village and useless attempts to reach the castle) ; or again there are ends for which there are no means. Any object in nature not usually conceived of as a utensil, or any isolated individual who constitutes an end to himself, must be excluded, lest the oppressive nightmare vanish. The fantastic imperative inverts the Kantian: everyone must always be used as a means, must never be an end. In *Aminadab* others tell us what we were all along—always tools. "Thus, our last resource, that self-awareness in which stoicism sought refuge, escapes us and disintegrates. Its transparence is that of the void, and our being is outside, in the hands of others" (*"Aminadab,"* p. 71).

"Albert Camus brought to my attention that *L'Expérience intérieure* [by Georges Bataille] is the translation and exact commentary of *Thomas l'obscur* [by Maurice Blanchot]." [36] Bataille wishes to communicate an *Erlebnis,* an experience, but Sartre finds instead either an extended philosophical reasoning which he refutes or the relation of an experience so highly personal that the reader cannot hope to share it. As to Bataille's philosophy: one cannot deny transcendance and have a mystical experience, so that "his rigorous logic masks the incoherence of his thought" ("Un Nouveau Mystique," p. 187). For the reader who has little or no recollection of *L'Expérience intérieure* Sartre's review remains interesting because of his remarks on the style of the essay. "There is a crisis of the essay," Sartre writes at the beginning; for we are still using the language of Voltaire. But Bataille has made an attempt to create the style of the modern essay (and of modern criticism) just as

[36] "Un Nouveau Mystique," *Situations* I, 183.

American authors, and Kafka and Camus (in *The Stranger*) have found the style of the contemporary novel. Bataille's method reflects at times "this wish to be succinct" of a Pascal, while at other times his pages, with "their breathless disorder, their impassioned symbolism, their tenor of prophetic predication" (p. 144), seem to stem from Nietzsche, with the added element of a certain surrealist exhibitionism. This produces "the martyr-essay"—Bataille "wishes to exist in his entirety and now, instantly" (p. 147). It is like reading at one and the same time *The Counterfeiters,* "Edouard's Journal" and the *Journal of the Counterfeiters.*

> Everything is commendable in this manner of expression: it offers a model and a tradition to the essayist; it brings us close to the sources, to Pascal, to Montaigne, and, at the same time, it offers a language and a syntax more suitable for expressing the problems of our era [p. 152].

Sartre allows himself a similar freedom in his own critical writing, quite different from his exposition of philosophy. As always, when meaningful, style is content; both Bataille and Sartre wish to reveal the individual, whereas Voltaire sought the universal.

Sartre devotes a patient and sympathetic study to Brice Parain,[37] who preceded him at the Ecole Normale Supérieure by five years, within the so-called "promotion des mobilisés" (the graduating class of the draftees). He shows himself again perfectly willing to enter into and follow another's train of thought. Parain, at "Normale," like many a brilliant son of peasants, had become a formidable dialectician," to whom, however, discourse was an art of persuasion rather than one of living. His war experience was to add "a further rupture in terms of language," and his return to the rear after demobilization confronted him with a veritable problem in communication. In the *Essay on Human Wretchedness* Parain notes:

[37] "Departure and Return," *Essays,* pp. 133–79.

The image of an object . . . evoked by a word is just about identical in the case of two persons, but on condition that they speak the same language, that they belong to the same social class and to the same generation, that is, that it fall, at least, within the norm where differences between the two persons may be regarded as practically negligible [cited in "Departure and Return," pp. 141–42].

Moreover, talk about social experience, historical truth and the like is an intellectualization. It is behind reflection and negation expressed in language that one finds existence, the one which stubbornly perpetuates itself.

While largely accepting Parain's analyses of the limitation of language as a means of communication, Sartre rejects his metaphysics, for to speak is to think, to exist:

The effectiveness, the eternity, of the *cogito* lies in the fact that it reveals a type of existence defined as the state of being present to oneself without intermediary. The word is interpolated between my love and myself, between my courage or cowardice and myself, not between my understanding and my consciousness of understanding. I shall call this the silence of consciousness [p. 172].

This raises the problem of being in good faith in one's own reflections:

I know what it is that I want to express because I *am* it without intermediary. Language may resist and mislead me, but I shall never be taken in by it unless I want to, for I can always come back to what I am, to the emptiness and silence [consciousness] that I am, through which, nevertheless, there is a language and there is a world. The *cogito* escapes Parain's clutches . . . [p. 172].

So that it is only in relation to the "Other" that the problem of language is to be situated, for it is to be understood by a freedom which is not ours. Since to speak is to act "in front of the Other, the great problems of language may turn out to be only a regional specification of the great ontological problem of the existence of the Other" (p. 173).

Francis Ponge, like Parain, had chosen to define man by his language. But if language had seemed to Parain "an original vice,"[38] to Ponge it seemed vitiated by society. *"In our very own mind* speaks the same sordid order," Ponge writes—"all these ugly trucks which pass *through us,* these factories (cited, "Parti pris," pp. 250 and 257). For Ponge it is a matter of restoring "the infinite resources of the depth of things . . . by the resources of the semantic depth of words" (cited, pp. 253–54).

Sartre sees a threefold "parti pris" (a taking of sides) in the use Ponge wishes to make of the semantic depth of words: (1) he takes the point of view of things against that of man; (2) he accepts ("en prendre son parti") their existence against the position of idealism which, by and large, reduces the world to mental representations; and finally (3) he fashions of this "parti pris" his aesthetic point of view. In his poems Ponge tries to describe things devoid of human significance as things which are not utensils; he deals not with a *Zeug* but a *Ding* in Heidegger's terminology. So that even his "washing machine," for instance, seems to be employed without any usefulness. Moreover, he refuses human significance to man himself. His "gymnaste" (athlete) has a "chef du corps" rather than a head and he is shown "less agile than a monkey," (cited, p. 255) like one species among others. Even "the young mother" is made to look like a mammal of a higher order.

While shunning the human significance of both things and man, Ponge will often display a knowledge of science in the most unexpected places. Leaves are "discountenanced by slow oxydation," and plants "exhale carbonic acid through the chlorophyllic process like a sigh which could last for nights" (cited, p. 285). He has failed to include science in his "methodic doubt," and in his descriptions he has preserved a prejudice against human significance; and yet his method is largely phe-

[38] "A propos du *Parti pris des choses,*" *Situations* I, p. 249.

nomenological. He wishes to consider all things as unknown, but, rather than to observe them merely from the outside, he tries to insinuate himself into things, like a novelist into his characters, to give them a voice, their voice. Ponge knows all along that one cannot "leave the condition of man" (cited, p. 256), but he can and does give a human expression to the *being* of a thing—not to its *appearance* as does Colette or Virginia Woolf. He achieves this result not by an animism of things but by a mineralizing of man. He endows his feeling with the characteristics of things. Adopting his approach Sartre can then speak of sober and haughty dryness as the feeling we get from a pebble.[39] We have in Ponge a phenomenological mediation between mind and matter reminiscent of the materialist one in Diderot's *Entretien entre D'Alembert et Diderot.* Of course, Sartre does not follow Ponge to the very end; for Sartre the object does not precede the subject. Consciousness is entirely on the outside among things, but it is there in relation to a human project. We find in things only what we were all along, although, indeed, we may in the process see ourselves more clearly. Ponge's "refusal of any complicity" (p. 257) with our society and his dogmatic realism, his urge to express the thing, to name it, have led him to create a poem-thing. Its organic unit is the paragraph, its over-all structure the juxtaposition of paragraphs. Even within the paragraph, conjunctions are actually used as disjunctives. In his style Ponge creates discontinuity in keeping with his attempt to hold human synthesis and *Gestalt* at bay. Sartre remarks on the affinity of his poems with the paintings of a Braque or a Juan Gris which also ask the observer continually to integrate separate parts. As a matter of fact Ponge had—by his own account—earned the friendship of these and other painters with the publication of his *Parti pris des choses.* Sartre considers this "perpetual oscillation from

39 "If my very feeling is a thing . . . can I not keep within myself at least as an affective scheme a certain type of sober and haughty dryness, which would, for example, be indicated by a pebble?" (p. 269).

interiority to exteriority," in which Ponge, "unable *really* to fuse consciousness with the thing, . . . has us fluctuate from one to the other" (p. 288), as an unsuccessful endeavor to reach a synthesis between inorganic dispersion (things) and living unity (man). Thus, following a rule true for most poets, his art goes further than his thinking.

In his poems Ponge has not only freed us from society, but he has also realized his innermost passion for the solid, for living unperturbed like a thing, an "in-itself": Ponge "has made the most determined effort to deepen this theoretical knowledge into an intuition" (p. 288). In the process "the poet Ponge has laid the foundations of a phenomenology of nature" (p. 293).

To this day, *Le Parti pris des choses* has kept a somewhat strange charm and offers the reader a satisfaction at first difficult to explain. It is that Ponge's poem—a kind of Husserlian "return to things themselves"—is a gratification of a deep-seated wish, a moment of repose, of repose from consciousness and from temporality.

Surprisingly, the author to whom Sartre turned in the last of this early group of reviews is the *fin de siècle* Jules Renard. Renard had spent his childhood among farmers, as had Brice Parain, and he had Parain's early distrust of language. He harbored "a villager's misanthropy."[40] Renard sought a short sentence which might come close to silence, but Sartre points out that whereas Proust's is not lengthy, Renard's is wordy in five lines; he has nothing to say: "Renard's *Journal* is tersely talkative, . . . a rhetoric of . . . pointillism." Following Realism and Naturalism with their "vast survey of reality" ("L'Homme ligoté," p. 299), Renard and his contemporaries could only "refine" and adopt the Goncourts's pretentious artistic pose.

Renard was unable to penetrate the real as Ponge was to do. Typical for the former would be a description such as the

[40] "L'Homme ligoté, notes sur le *Journal* de Jules Renard," *Situations* I, 295.

following: "A spider glides on an invisible thread, as if it were swimming in the air" (cited, p. 307). After having expressed something so positive, so scientific, the image which follows cannot but fail to lead us any further. Sartre states flatly: "there is poetry only when one refuses any prerogative to the scientific interpretation of reality and when one posits the absolute equivalence of all interpretative systems" (p. 309).

The world of Renard "is confined within the philosophical and scientific armature" of Taine: "Reality is first of all something that is being observed. That was the wisdom of the period, a literary version of empiricism" (pp. 306–7). This empiricism is actually predicated upon the belief in a fixed human nature capable of observing objective facts with immutability, an approach which had been exhausted by Realism and Naturalism. Renard in spite of some feeble attempts to "lose himself," to set aside some of his neat prejudices, does not see afresh. "Empty periods are those which have chosen to see themselves with an old outlook." To an existentialist on the contrary, "it suffices to paint oneself in order to produce something new." And Sartre boldly states: "One must invent one's way of seeing; thereby one determines *a priori* and by a free choice that which one sees" (p. 299). Here phenomenology separates itself profoundly from empiricism, because the former now attains its existentialist dimension. After having suspended all previously held judgment in the observation of phenomena, one must now invent (or reinvent) one's own criteria. The generally observed receives its unique meaning from the observer: "Man is the being through whom meaning comes to the world" ("Un Nouveau Mystique," p. 186). Renard points clearly in his very weakness to what Sartre rejects in the tradition of Realism and of Naturalism, as also to some aspects of the art-for-art's-sake Flaubert, from which Sartre wished to sever himself.

There is another motive which induced Sartre in 1944 to turn to a minor *fin de siècle* figure. "Jules Renard has created the literature of silence" is the opening sentence of his review. And in his early article on Faulkner he had pointed to "this silence, . . . the futile dream of a puritan ultra-stoicism (*"Sartoris,"* p. 83). Then in a series of reviews preceding that of Jules Renard's *Journal* we read that "Meursault is an example of this virile silence, of this refusal to indulge in words" (*"The Outsider,"* p. 32); that for Bataille "to speak is to tear oneself apart," that it is to "hide the familiarity of reality," and that his problem was how "to express silence with words" ("Un Nouveau Mystique," pp. 146–47); that Brice Parain cried out during World War I against "words, words!"; that Ponge attempts to "dehumanize words" when speaking for things. This concern for authors who aimed at silence points to some major preoccupations of Sartre.

There is the perennial problem of expressing the new in an old language. But more radically now the need arose for these authors—and for Sartre—to reinvent a language just as they tried to reinvent man. It may well have been the extreme historical situation that demanded a reevaluation which made Sartre more than any other before him so keenly aware of the elusiveness of consciousness as its ontological characteristic. The unattainable silence of the authors under review would at last prevail if consciousness, this "hole in being," could ever perfectly coincide with what it reflects.

Since *The Transcendence of the Ego* Sartre had been trying to rise to the challenge presented by his recognition that consciousness has to invent itself incessantly. If not in silence or repose, coincidence, however, may be reached in some lightning instants. Writing of Bataille Sartre notes:

For these minds—one ought to include among them Descartes as well as Epicurus, Gide as well as Rousseau—discourse, foresight, utilitarian memory, rational reasoning and activity tear us away from ourselves. To these they oppose the instant: the intuitive instant of Cartesian reason, the ecstatic instant of mysticism, the anguished and eternal instant of Kierkegaardian freedom, the instant of Gidian joy, the instant of Proustian reminiscence ["Un Nouveau Mystique," p. 169].

Proust seized "instantaneously" by his involuntary memory lives a moment of consciousness fixed in his body. It is the instant of knowledge without language, without distance from himself. But there is also, within certain limits, in spite of the elusiveness of consciousness and the multiplicity of experience, the possibility of expressing truths in language, and of maintaining philosophical discourse. In "Departure and Return" Sartre claims that the *cogito*—which does need to be couched in language—escapes Parain's "clutches," as does the "synthesis of identification," the linking of a thing and a word in the synthetic act of nomination, which universalizes the experience of the speaker and permits communication.

When I say that "I'm hungry," the word universalizes. This is taken for granted. But in order to universalize, *I* must first universalize, that is, I must disengage the word "hungry" from the disorderly confusion of my present impression ["Departure and Return," p. 171].

The dilemma of language which so absorbed Sartre all along is thus lastly the one of expressing one's own unique experience in a language which can convey it to the Other.

Literature has almost always attacked its subject matter on the level where the individual experience becomes generally comprehensible; it is as little an enumeration of raw data as a matter of theoretical abstraction. This is precisely the level at which existentialist philosophy places itself. "The novelty of existentialism is to be sought rather in the way Kierkegaard and Sartre solve the problem of communication," writes Cumming, who speaks of "the ways in which they were forced, by their otherwise quite different philosophies, to adopt literary works as a means of communicating these philosophies." [41]

At one point in his early career as a literary critic Sartre was prompted to define his own position: "The function of the critic is to criticize, that is, to take a stand for or against and to situate himself by situating" ("Departure and Return," p. 168). There is obviously no pretense at objectivity. How then did Sartre situate himself as a literary critic?

Sartre started out with an overriding interest in phenomenology as a philosophy of what Husserl called the *Lebenswelt* (the lived world), which was to overcome the dichotomy between idealism and materialism as much as that between philosophy and experience. He developed a rigorous analysis of the structures of consciousness while feeling compelled at the same time to elucidate certain experiences in his own mind and to commu-

[41] Robert Cumming, "The Literature of Extreme Situations," p. 381.

While he was limiting himself to an analysis of the complementary and necessary relationship between literature and philosophical exposition in these two philosophers, Cumming observes: "The role the interpretation of Hölderlin assumes in the exposition of Heidegger's philosophy, of literary classics generally in Jasper's philosophy, of his own dramatic works in Marcel's philosophy, suggests I have located an expedient common to the major existentialists" (*ibid.*, p. 409).

On the same question, it is surprising to find two self-contradictory statements in an otherwise sympathetic treatment by Eugene Kaelin in *An Existentialist Aesthetic, The Theories of Sartre and Merleau-Ponty.* At one point the author goes so far as to speak of a "bastardization of the philosophical medium" in the hands of Nietzsche when he uses literature as a vehicle for an exposition of his philosophy—for Kaelin an unfortunate combination—which "will most universally result in a like consequence," thus leading philosophers "generally to eschew the literary enterprise altogether" (*ibid.*, p. 387). A few pages on (403-4), Kaelin has praise for *Nausea* (he gives an interesting appraisal of its various styles) and *The Stranger* as the work of authors "successful in embodying the basic existentialist hypotheses" in "what has come to be called 'existentialist literature.'"

Credit should also be given to Everett W. Knight, who had noted the phenomenological vision already in Valéry, Gide and later writers in his *Literature Considered as Philosophy, The French Example,* and to Hazel E. Barnes, a professional philosopher and Sartre's translator, who has also interpreted his creative writing, as well as that of Simone de Beauvoir and of Camus, in *The Literature of Possibility.*

nicate them in creative literature. A close examination of his literary criticism shows it to be a mediation between his phenomenology and the "lived world" of the author under review. However, Sartre's criticism is literary by any definition: its point of departure is—in actual fact, if not in its apparent structure—the particular author's style. Sartre's contribution consists precisely in locating the innermost motive force of a style, that is, the author's way of apprehending "le monde vécu," his metaphysics. He did not set aside any of the vast accumulation of criteria available to the critic in virtually every discipline. But he regrouped these criteria seemingly at will, though actually restructuring them according to his own philosophical position. This primarily phenomenological criticism—some of which is as late as 1944—gives us some astoundingly perceptive "first" reviews, which in many ways are still definitive. And already some of the major innovations of Sartre's later stages, when he moves systematically into ontology and anthropology, are at issue in this first group of literary reviews.

Chapter 2

ONTOLOGY, AESTHETICS, ETHICS AND LITERATURE: THE PROGRAMMATIC ARTICLES

Sartre was not to be found among those in France who were involved in public debates about the threat presented by Hitler's rise to power. However, once the military draft, the course of the war and the Nazi occupation of France brought him closer to the dreadful reality, he deliberately chose commitment.[1] Sartre's will manifested itself especially in his wartime plays and his postwar literary criticism consisting in the main of programmatic articles in which Sartre defines what he considers to be the role and the aims of literature. He also widened the scope of his own endeavor by founding and assuming the editorship of *Les Temps Modernes,* a literary monthly and a *journal d'opinion.*

At about the same time Sartre set out to elaborate his own philosophical system. This task became mandatory after his

[1] The previous chapter shows the nonpolitical character of his philosophical and literary pursuits during the Thirties, notwithstanding their radical implications. By the beginning of 1940, however, Sartre had expressed to Simone de Beauvoir his decision "to hold aloof from politics no longer" (*Prime,* p. 342). A first step was the writing and production in captivity of *Bariona* which under the guise of a traditional Christmas play was actually an appeal to resistance: the Romans were shown occupying Palestine just as the Nazis were subjugating France.

breakthrough beyond Husserl's phenomenology: How was the description of one's consciousness—now deprived by Sartre of the last shred of substantiality (Husserl's *hylé*)[2]—to give a coherent account of its experience of the "lived world"? And this task was all the more pressing because of the now acute political need—perhaps corresponding to a deep-seated personal need—to define freedom in an ontology and because of his wish to clarify the normative ethical aspect of commitment.

With the writing of *Being and Nothingness* Sartre became a systematic philosopher. It is certainly not my purpose to uphold or to disprove part or all of this body of thought, but the main themes of this work are presented at least briefly in order to make Sartre's literary criticism fully intelligible from his own point of view.[3]

Sartre called *Being and Nothingness* in its subtitle a *Phenomenological Ontology.* Indeed, after defining the structures of consciousness in his four early monographs, he now dealt with the meaning of being as obtained through a description of consciousness in the world. Sartre—unlike his predecessor Heidegger—had kept to Descartes's *cogito* for his point of depar-

[2] Husserl called it "eine sinngebende Schicht," a meaning-bestowing stratum (*Ideen,* p. 172 of the original edition). Husserl's contemporary Proust seems to describe it similarly: "And then my thoughts, did not they form a similar sort of hiding-hole, in the depths of which I felt that I could bury myself and remain invisible even when I was looking at what went on outside? When I saw any external object, my consciousness that I was seeing it would remain between me and it, enclosing it in *a slender, incorporeal outline* which prevented me from ever coming directly in contact with the material form" (*Swann's Way,* p. 111, emphasis mine). Actually, however, as will be shown in the following pages, Proust is describing as "thoughts" only their reflective aspect ("my consciousness that I was seeing it . . .") which he believes separated by this "slender, incorporeal outline" from their prereflective aspect (implicit in "coming directly in contact . . .").

[3] An extreme example of the opposite approach is an article by Sidney Mendel entitled "From Solitude to Salvation: A Study in Regeneration." One finds explanations of Sartre's *Nausea* and of some of his plays through references to Swedenborg (p. 45), to Hobbes (p. 50), to the *Bhagavad-Gita* (p. 53), to the *Inferno* (pp. 53–54), and to Carlyle (p. 55), while only passing and scant attention is paid to *Being and Nothingness.*

ture,[4] but contrary to the French tradition he adopted Hegel's dialectical method of reasoning. He turned away from the French classical dictum according to which "that which is true is expressed clearly" and from a superficial clarity which had been implicitly accepted by many a generation of readers as a concomitant of truth. Sartre seems to find adequate understanding only in a complex train of thought.[5]

However, the description of actual experience, or of vicarious experience found in literature, is as prevalent in *Being and Nothingness* as is reasoning.[6] Description is persuasive in both directions: the reader feels that experience, personal and transposed into literature, agrees with Sartre's complex definitions; and the reader may also realize that they in turn validate at least some literature as a mode of apprehending the world philosophically. *Being and Nothingness* thus contains, seemingly at random, much literary criticism; but more importantly, it leads up to an aesthetics and to criteria of literary criticism which are an integral part of Sartre's philosophical system.

Sartre's point of departure, as has been said, remains the celebrated first and incontrovertible evidence of Descartes's *cogito:* I think therefore I am. But he now uses Husserl's concept of intentionality (all consciousness is consciousness of something) and his method of phenomenological reduction[7]

[4] "It took two centuries of crisis—a crisis of Faith and a crisis of Science—for man to regain the creative freedom that Descartes placed in God, and for anyone finally to suspect the following truth, which is an essential basis of humanism: man is the being as a result of whose appearance a world exists" ("Cartesian Freedom," *Essays,* p. 196).

[5] It may be said in this respect that Sartre is foremost among those authors who in the postwar period have through their very style changed sensibility in France.

[6] By contrast, one is here reminded of Malraux's observation in *Les Noyers de l'Altenburg* (p. 114) that "the train of thought which had been pursued for an hour in the presence of my father was exclusively a dialogue with culture. An idea never grew out of a fact, but always out of another idea."

[7] "Reduction" consists in a "bracketing out" (a temporary elimination) of the broader contexts of an object under observation, a suspension, a withholding of

(the effort to set aside all preconceived notions when observing this "something") in order to reexamine this *cogito.* If consciousness is always consciousness of something, then the consciousness of our own ego is that of an object. Sartre says: I think therefore there is an I (object) in the world. And further: the I (object) which is in the world *is,* whereas the I (subject) which thinks *is not.* Put into specifically Sartrian terms, there is a fullness of being, being-in-itself (*l'être-en-soi*), which is the being of things; and a nothingness,[8] being-for-itself (*l'être-pour-soi*), which is the being of consciousness. Consciousness is the very awareness of not being whatever is its object, of not being whatever it reflects upon: the for-itself is thus the negation of the in-itself. This reasoning led Sartre to a new understanding of Descartes's *cogito.* He split its "I think" into a reflective and prereflective level: I think (reflectively) that I think (prereflectively where consciousness is an immediate experience of something, in this case, of the object "I am").

Prereflective consciousness is absorbed by its object (as when "engrossed" in what one is doing—when reading a book, for instance). On the reflective level, however, consciousness is consciousness of itself—the reflective reflects on the prereflective; it is operating at a distance from being (as when one becomes aware that one is reading; at which point one can interpret that prereflective act, endow it with meaning, and posit alternatives). Consciousness is thus forever a separation

---

judgment, in order to obtain a genuine experience—untampered with by accepted ideas—which permits a true and valid description of the "lived world."

Sartre "reduced" Husserl's concept of consciousness by dispensing with any *hylé,* and he then turned his back on the "problems" of epistemology: I am conscious of a thing as being what it is.

[8] In this concept of nothingness, Sartre follows Spinoza (and Hegel) for whom *omnis determinatio est negatio,* which Sartre inverts to read "every negation is determination" (*Being and Nothingness,* p. 16); and especially Descartes for whom in Sartre's reading "doubt is a breaking of contact with being" ("Cartesian Freedom," p. 190).

from being, a pure existence without essence (without a fixed particular nature). It is only a project of essence: it aims at assuming a fixed meaning; it lacks completeness and is filled with the possibilities envisioned for the future. As a phenomenologist, Sartre has eliminated the duality of appearance and essence (as also of the exterior and the interior), because it is the series of appearances of phenomena which reveals their essence. Thus existence (for Sartre, the consciousness of one's being in the world) precedes essence (the meaning which this being may acquire through acts in time).

Hence the term "existentialism" in Sartre's philosophy is in contradistinction to all kinds of deterministic—that is, essentialist—modes of thought. According to the latter, we become what we are because of a potential due to creation,[9] to heredity, history, society, family and other factors determining our "nature." Sartre does not discard these factors; they form the situation of the ego which reflective consciousness is forever questioning. Self-consciousness is the awareness of one's ego in a situation (in the world) which it has not created; but it is consciousness that interprets and gives meaning to this situation, and reacts to it at every moment. And when all the motivating influences on consciousness have been tracked down, there comes an ultimate moment of choice, irreducible to any single explanation: the moment of the exercise of freedom. Freedom can be understood only in terms of the ontologi-

[9] Sartre's atheism is not a proof of the nonexistence of God but rather a putting into parentheses (a "bracketing out") of a concept which cannot be described as existing in a consciousness which lacks interiority. "Even if God existed, that would not change anything. . . . Man must recover himself and convince himself that nothing can save him from himself, not even a valid proof of God's existence" (Sartre, *L'Existentialisme est un humanisme,* p. 95). To Sartre God does not appear as a cause of man, but as an imaginary ultimate aim, as an ideal value on the horizon of man. It is as such that the concept of God is part of this complex surging-forth of consciousness that gives meaning to and freedom from a given situation: "God, value and supreme end of transcendence, represents the permanent limit in terms of which man makes known to himself what he is" (*Being,* p. 566). To be God is man's project.

cal structure of reflective consciousness: since consciousness is a tearing away from the situation in which it finds its ego; [10] since it is constantly negating its ego by looking at the present from the point of view of the future; and since it is by definition a spontaneous surging forth without cause or necessity. Thus man is free in the formulation or revision of his aims. We do not become what we are: we become—to a greater or lesser degree—what we choose to make of our situation.[11]

Since consciousness, the for-itself has its being outside of itself and since it exists without necessity, it is restless and tortured, and wishes continuously to acquire the density of being of a thing which is what it is, an in-itself. It thus seeks coincidence with itself—often called repose or serenity—in a synthesis, in an ideal value: the being-in-itself-for-itself. Sartre sees in this attempt of the for-itself to escape its nothingness,

[10] Sartre finds that in irony, directed against others as against oneself, man "annihilates what he posits within one and the same act" (*Being*, p. 47).

[11] Herbert Marcuse has objected to Sartre's concept of freedom because of what he considers its irrelevance to most everyday lives and especially in extreme situations when "freedom" is the choice to die, that is, when it brings about the end of man together with his freedom. "The free choice between death and slavery is neither freedom nor choice, because both alternatives destroy 'man's reality,' which is said to be freedom" ("Existentialismus: Bemerkungen zu Jean-Paul Sartres *L'Etre et le Néant*," *Kultur und Gesellschaft 2*, p. 66).

As a Hegelian dialectician Marcuse would have to recognize that to postulate a world in which the victim lacks freedom is also to exonerate the oppressor as determined. There is certainly a huge difference between them, but it lies in their *respective* alternatives; it cannot obliterate their dialectical relationship possible only in the realm of freedom.

Furthermore, Sartre emphasizes strongly that it is a matter of freedom *from* a situation, which remains the very important foundation from which man can seek to wrench himself: "In connection with what exceptional *situation* have you experienced your freedom?" ("Cartesian Freedom," p. 180).

In an addition to the 1965 edition of his article, Marcuse notes with esteem, despite his earlier reservations, that Sartre has since 1949, when Marcuse first leveled his criticism, been engaged in "the road of radical contradiction" (*ibid.*, p. 83), and that if he has against his will become an "institution"—one need only recall, for instance, his reasons for refusing the Nobel prize in 1964—it is one "in which conscience and truth have found a refuge" (*ibid.*, p. 84). This is already implicit in the very position to which Marcuse objected: the freedom from a situation is "Widerspruch," contradiction to reality. (There will be reason to return to Marcuse's study in the discussion of the Other.)

and to find justification for its existence in density of being, both the ultimate and the initial project of man, arrived at by what Sartre calls his original choice.[12] This project is always the outline of a solution of the problem of being. But this is not first conceived and then realized; we *are* this solution. We make it exist by means of our very engagement (*Being*, p. 463).[13]

Our individual original choice, continuously renewed or to the contrary uprooted and replaced by a new choice, is our very own solution to this problem of being.[14] Yet it remains a problem without a solution. This "direct project to metamorphose its own for-itself into an in-itself-for-itself" in order to become

[12] "At each moment I apprehend this initial choice as contingent and unjustifiable; at each moment therefore I am on the site suddenly to consider it objectively and consequently to surpass it and to make-it-past by causing the liberating *instant* to arise. Hence my anguish, the fear which I have of being suddenly exorcized (*i.e.*, of becoming radically other); but hence also the frequent upsurge of 'conversions' which cause me totally to metamorphose my original project. These conversions which have not been studied by philosophers, have often inspired novelists. One may recall the instant at which Gide's Philoctetes casts off his hate, his fundamental project, his reason for being, his being. One may recall the *instant* when Raskolnikoff decides to give himself up. These extraordinary and marvelous instants when the prior project collapses into the past in the light of a new project which rises on its ruins and which as yet exists only in outline, in which humiliation, anguish, joy, hope are delicately blended, in which we let go in order to grasp and grasp in order to let go—these have often appeared to furnish the clearest and most moving image of our freedom. But they are only one among others of its many manifestations" (*Being*, pp. 475–76).

Sartre had shown earlier that some authors who tried to reach a moment of silence, an instant of knowledge without language (discussed on pp. 42–44 above) were thereby seeking the point of coincidence with oneself. Such an instant can now be seen also as the moment of utter freedom.

[13] Hence consciousness of oneself is not knowledge of oneself, since we lack the necessary distance from "what we *are*" to observe it.

[14] It is the existence of such an original choice, unique to the individual, which explains the fact that almost every author's output can be reduced to one fundamental theme or to a style, analogous to what the traditional *explication de texte* called *la composition de fond.* It is perhaps also the mainspring of the particular melodic material or the kind of harmonic progression which will make a composer identifiable within the first few bars of many a composition. Development within the same material is patently manifest among painters and sculptors: one need only recall the horsemen of Marino Marini, the bottles of Morandi and the people of Giacometti. No matter what may be the variety of expression of some artists, each one works and reworks a unique vision of being.

"the *Ens causa sui* [the being who is his own cause], which religions call God"[15] cannot be realized. "Man is a useless passion" (*Being*, p. 615).

Nonetheless, what does take place in the realm of consciousness is an attempt at coincidence of the for-itself with itself through reflection, through observation of its own thoughts, through their "recuperation" and a consequent reaching of agreement with oneself. This effort may well constitute one of the mainsprings of the intellectual effort. Yet "reflection is a recognition rather than knowledge. It implies as the original motivation of the recovery a prereflective comprehension of what it wishes to recover (p. 156). The effort at recuperation through reflection leads to awareness, not to any durable coincidence. But it constitutes as pure reflection (not as the impure alternative which is a product of self-deception, of bad faith) a part of the apodictic, incontrovertible evidence of the *cogito*. This process of recuperation seems to describe the process which some authors have called the self-dictation of creative writing.

In the domain of the imagination, the striving to secure "value" (or coincidence of the in-itself-for-itself), while also "useless" in the final analysis, as is shown at a later stage of Sartre's philosophy when he introduces the "other," does yield more tangible results. The yearning for permanence, usually as a hope of eternity, is then understood as the desire to reach a concrete existence "in flesh and blood" that would also be an essence, achieving at last in a work of art this perfect coincidence of form and content. This form which is content, this

[15] Montaigne may be considered to intimate such a concept when he quotes on the final page of his *Essays* an Athenian inscription: "You are as much a god as you will own/ That you are nothing but a man alone." Montaigne then links it to the well-known "It is an absolute perfection and virtually divine to know how to enjoy our being rightfully" (p. 857). Characteristically, if for Montaigne it is virtually divine to become man, for Goethe's Faust what prevails is the determination to outgrow "the measure of a man," as Montaigne had termed it, in order to reach divine knowledge.

expression of an ideal state of the world, this is what Sartre defines as beauty:

[Beauty] haunts the world as an unrealizable. To the extent that man *realizes* the beautiful in the world, he realizes it in the imaginary mode.[16] This means that in the aesthetic intuition, I apprehend an imaginary object across an imaginary realization of myself as a totality in-itself and for-itself. Ordinarily the beautiful, like value, . . . is implicitly apprehended on things as an absence; it is revealed implicitly across the *imperfection* of the world [*Being,* pp. 194–95].

This ontological definition of beauty is at the heart of Sartre's aesthetics, and colors every aspect of his literary criticism. He restates it in *What is Literature?* in the sentence: "We should, I believe, no longer define beauty by the form nor even by the matter, but by the density of being" (p. 223). Just as it is in the series of tangible in-itself phenomena that the elusive for-itself becomes essence, so form that embodies content has become beautiful. Beauty is a form that is essence; although beyond attainment in perceived reality it can be "realized" in a successful work of imagination.[17]

Man's anguish, to which Pascal had already given voice, in Sartre becomes awareness of the fundamental search for value, and awareness of freedom precisely because of the utter contingency that results from this denial of both teleological value

[16] In his last work, *Das Glasperlenspiel* (1943), Hermann Hesse, who had created something of an unfinished prototype of Roquentin and of Meursault in *Der Steppenwolf* (1926) after he had sought escape in the oriental *Siddhartha* (1922), treats at length of the unbounded success of the monastic "magister ludi" in his invention of a new musical counterpoint which (in Sartrian terms) "recuperates," that is, represents and integrates, all knowledge, and his immediate failure when he intervenes in the reality of society.

[17] Early in life Sartre had himself taken this fulfillment in art as something real. Simone de Beauvoir writes that, about 1930, "the creative act, in his view, meant assuming responsibility for the world" (*Prime,* p. 38). Sartre's radical change of opinion in this respect is at the heart of *The Words* (1964), in the pitiless interpretation of his childhood as predicated upon a pretense that was false to the core.

and necessary cause.[18] There is no justification for man; he is superfluous. And yet he cannot escape his "facticity": the very fact that he is and that he must "exist" some role.[19] Nor can he escape his contingency: he is not free not to be free; he cannot help but choose and interpret a role to play (see p. 486). Simply: we have to be something in the world (our facticity); yet no matter what we choose to be or how we interpret our choice, our existence will be meaningless and without justification (our contingency).

This anguish is hard to bear; therefore "we are this solution of the problem of being" (p. 463), mostly in impure reasoning, in self-deception (let us recall "les divertissements" in Pascal) and in bad faith. The most common form of escape from freedom is psychologism, which presupposes the belief in "drives," "complexes," states of mind, as a necessary determinant of the for-itself (see pp. 167–70). There is an infinity of ways to assume this posture.[20] Sartre shows that Proust's descriptions of a chronological succession of psychological states of mind do not lead to causal links between them. They point rather to the very limitation of such attempts at explanation as mechanical constructs, external to the structures of consciousness: one cannot reduce its freedom to the classifications of Proust's intellectualist analyses.[21] Psychologism is a flight from the fact that we are what we are not—that we have an indeter-

18 Let us recall the telling experience of Roquentin in *Nausea* and compare, in *Being* (pp. 464–65), the entire paragraph with its key sentence on "the gratuitous determination of the for-itself by itself."

19 Levinas remarked that existentialism is the transitive use of the verb "to be."

20 All characters of *The Roads to Freedom* have been fashioned so as to represent some particular kind of solution in bad faith to this problem of being. In spite of convincing passages, the three volumes are weak as literature because here—unlike in *Nausea* and in the short stories—a philosophical insight precedes the immediate experience of the author. To paraphrase a well-known dictum: one can write bad literature with a good philosophy.

21 As when jealousy is given as the "cause" of Swann's love for Odette. See *Being*, pp. 168–69.

minate existence—towards a state of being in which we are what we are—in which we have an existence with some necessary essence, poeticized as "an ever fixed mark." It is a flight toward a for-itself that pretends to have the being of an in-itself. But since psychologism is such a widespread form of self-deception, does it not have validity in some respects? We will see further on that it is indeed valid as the point of view of the "other" toward us, but one we falsely assume toward ourselves. Is there then an authentic way of living the problem of being? This question does continue to preoccupy Sartre and to reoccur at every stage.

Psychologism raises still another question: If the chronology it sets up is a false one because eternal and preestablished—as is the chronology of all science—which temporality is ontologically sound? Along with "tendencies," "forces," "appetites" and "complexes," given as "states" (though they are actually forms of in-itself existence from the point of view of the "other") and considered as a heritage from the past, a condition of the present and a determination of the future, Sartre discards the entire chronology of psychologism, including Bergson's theories of duration (see pp. 166–67) and scientific as well as everyday acceptance of time.

In order to understand Sartre's radically new concept of temporality, which further integrates his aesthetics to his ontology, it is necessary to consider in its barest outlines the manner in which consciousness creates time in the world: "Universal time comes into the world through the for-itself."[22] Time develops in a dialectical motion as the for-itself defines and there-

[22] "The For-itself rising into being as the nihilation of the In-itself constitutes itself simultaneously in all the possible dimensions of nihilation. . . . It is the being which by being causes all the possible dimensions of its nihilation to exist. . . . The mode of being of the For-itself . . . is diasporatic [cohesive in dispersion]. . . . When something simply is what it is, it has only one way of being its being. But the moment that something is no longer its being, then various ways of being it arise simultaneously" (*Being*, pp. 136–37).

fore negates the in-itself. This takes place in three basic "ecstasies" [23] of consciousness: (1) the for-itself is not what it is; (2) it is what it is not; and (3) in a perpetual movement to and fro, it is what it is not and is not what it is (see pp. 137 ff.).

The first negation (the for-itself is not what it is) expresses the relationship of one's consciousness to its past: the for-itself is an awareness of something that it has left behind, it is a for-itself present to a past in-itself. Sartre here recalls, in reference to consciousness, Hegel's "Wesen ist, was gewesen ist"—essence is what is past (which Sartre writes as *est été*). This first temporal dimension deals with a series of past phenomena of the for-itself which have solidified into essence. The in-itself always has essence (a tree is a tree), but the for-itself only acquires essence through a series of acts (Garcia: I was a coward) to which it is present as to its past. "The past is substance," remarks Sartre, who would formulate the *cogito* as "I think, therefore I was" (p. 119).

In fact that shame which I experienced yesterday and which was shame for itself is always shame in the present, and its essence can still be described as for-itself. But its being *is no longer* for itself since it no longer exists as reflection-reflecting.[24] Though capable of description as for-itself, it simply *is*. The past is given as a for-itself *become* in-itself. . . . [This shame] has the permanence and the constancy of the in-itself. . . . The past, which is at the same time for-itself and in-itself, *resembles* value or self [Being-in-itself-for-itself]. . . . Hence arises the fact that memory presents to us the being which we were, accompanied by a plentitude of being which confers on it a sort of poetry. That grief which we *had*—although fixed in the past—does not cease to present the meaning of a for-itself, and yet it exists in itself with the silent fixity of the grief of another, of the grief of a statue [*Being*, p. 119].

It is through the past that the for-itself belongs to a universal temporality. And when at the point of death a certain human

23 Sartre uses Heidegger's term *"ek-stase"* to express the distance of the for-itself from itself in its multiple dimensions.

24 This point is taken up again in the discussion below of the third negation.

existence becomes entirely in-itself, for others to observe and to judge, and all its possibilities ended, a man's life has in the words of Malraux become a destiny: this is the tragedy of death. It is in the other two negations of consciousness that we "exist" a perpetual escape from this universal temporality into the future and in the present.

In its second movement of negation (the for-itself is what it is not) reflective consciousness recognizes itself as a lack of being. It is directed in the main towards "totalizing" itself, that is, acquiring the part of being it lacks by means of a project thrust into the future. This motion towards the future has forever been represented as a longing for eternity. But "the eternity which man is seeking is not the infinity of duration, of that vain pursuit after the self for which I am myself responsible; man seeks a repose in self, the atemporality of the absolute coincidence with himself" (*Being,* pp. 141–42). One might then say that the illusory coincidence of the for-itself absorbing an in-itself in contemplation (of a "serene" landscape or, still more imaginary, of a painting or of some extremely slow musical progression as that of a Bach Chorale-Prelude or of a still-life poem by Ponge) is "fulfilling" because it is, indeed, a moment of repose, of escape from the flight of consciousness in time. This momentary coincidence would then be, as it were, the temporal aspect of the ontological coincidence for-itself-in-itself, which is in fact, as will be recalled, what Sartre defined as beauty; [25] and this ideal value is equated to what men have called "God." [26] This pursuit of coincidence in the future is as futile as it is unending: every future will only become another present.

The third negation (in a perpetual movement to and fro the for-itself is what it is not and is not what it is) defines the present. It is the presence of the for-itself to an in-itself "in the

[25] See pp. 54–55 above.
[26] See pp. 53–54 above.

form of flight" (p. 123). This escape from the reflected (the object) to the reflecting (the subject) and vice versa is the presence of the for-itself to a being which it reflects through negation. It is "a perpetual flight away from the 'in-itself' which threatens it" (p. 147) and which is sealed at the point of death.[27]

Through consciousness, then, temporality exists as a single structure; because consciousness is "diasporic," it conserves cohesion in its very dispersion. Temporality would vanish if it were not a synthesis of the for-itself; for the past is no more, the future is not as yet, and the present is the future becoming the past in an elusive instant.[28]

Einstein, who once said that there were trees before there were men to contemplate them, also remarked (somewhat facetiously) that he tried to place himself in the position of the Creator of the universe as a way of finding worthwhile hypotheses of a unified theory of its laws. Sartre has resolutely given up playing God. He remains thoroughly Cartesian and

[27] Marie-Denise Boros has successfully demonstrated that the image of the crab which occurs so frequently in Sartre's life in the Thirties and appears consistently in his creative work from *Nausea* to *The Condemned of Altona* represents this fear of the "engulfing of the for-itself into the in-itself." (See her article "La Métaphore du crabe dans l'oeuvre littéraire de Jean-Paul Sartre.") It is necessary, however, to proceed one step further, so as to show also the fascination the image of the "crab" may have for man: it can represent the resolution of man's problem of being in an antivalue, in a total reification of consciousness.

Robert Cumming links this particular image to other Sartrian analogues for hands, which "are often soiled by contact with things." Sartre wished thereby to move from (to "reduce") conceptual visualization—the higher aesthetic sense of past philosophy—to tactile (and gustatory) experience, in order to "discredit the visual illusion of esthetic distance" (see Cumming, *The Philosophy of Jean-Paul Sartre,* pp. 18–20).

[28] One can now show that the instant is not the moment of immobility but one of movement. Zeno's understanding of temporality had limitations, which he obviously realized in the formulation of his four paradoxes, but could not overcome (see J. Burnet, *Early Greek Philosophy,* pp. 318–20). Sartre points out by way of a solution that movement means to be in one place and in another at the same time. This dialectical reasoning—as well as recent mathematical theories in which the continuous replaces the notions of discreteness and of infinite divisibility—has solved Zeno's paradoxes. (See *Being,* pp. 208–14.)

Husserlian in his point of departure and his method. He would not deny that there were trees prior to man; but if "trees" are to be so designated and related to one another as "forests," and to be integrated into an infinite number of discoveries and meanings, this is done by man, who temporalizes himself while establishing relationships and meanings in a human universe, the only one Sartre claims to know. Man is "the being through whom meanings come to the world." [29]

This existential concept of temporality runs counter to the absolute and causal chronology of science and psychologism, which has come to be the accepted one and which is that of the run of conventional (essentialist) novels in their narration of past events.[30] Philosophic and literary schools which embody a deterministic point of view have consistently chosen the past, the being-in-itself of man, as their temporal expression. "The meaning of Realism, of Naturalism, and of materialism lies in the past . . . as if it were present" (*Being*, p. 202).[31] The existentialist novel, on the other hand, is one of becoming; it

[29] "Un Nouveau Mystique," p. 186. The consciousness which notes the presence of trees, however, also becomes aware that it is nonessential to their being (see *What is Literature?*, pp. 32–33).

[30] In a penetrating analysis of the *mémoire involontaire* (in a lecture of November 21, 1966, at Columbia University), M. Georges Poulet remarked, contrary to the usual reading of Proust, that Proust aimed not at restoring "a past frozen in a time which has elapsed," which is that of the traditional nineteenth-century novelists such as Balzac or Gautier, but rather "a past where one still desires a future, . . . a past to which adheres the affective tonality of the moment. . . . Time retrieved will then be a kind of reliving the feeling for the future." In Sartrian terms: a value (the in-itself-for-itself of the past) is being saved from dead solidification by a presentification also of the future it once had.

[31] There is a detailed and telling analysis of Realism and Naturalism in *What is Literature?* and especially of Maupassant's technique of storytelling, which will be best understood once the entire philosophical background for the literary criticism has been established at least in its major outlines. Yet one might here remark that even authors of those literary schools have had to acknowledge in the fashioning of their plots that suspense and unpredictability are among the ingredients of an interesting novel; an acknowledgment by author and reader of the ontological openendedness of life. At the same time, however, it was "satisfying" to be spared the anguish of facing up to the freedom of the protagonists by being kept at a comfortable distance from it in time.

squarely faces the open-ended future; and therefore its narration is in the present tense. On the whole, the postexistential anti-novel, too, uses the present tense, because it also denies determinism; but it is without a future since it chooses to remain within an inexplicable present.

Consciousness, while temporalizing itself in its existence, meets the "other":

What we discover within ourselves is the other; not as specific knowledge, nor as a constituent element of knowledge in general, but inasmuch as he involves our being concretely and onticly,[32] within the empirical circumstances of our facticity.[33]

Sartre shows that it is the prereflective, self-evident *cogito* which leads both to the basic character of consciousness and to the existence of the "other" and that the "being-for-the-other" (*l'être-pour-autrui*) is not an external relationship but a structure of consciousness:

The Other by rising up confers on the for-itself a being-in-itself-in-the-midst-of-the-world as a thing among things. This petrifaction in in-itself by the Other's look is the profound meaning of the myth of Medusa [*Being,* p. 430].

Just as we experience in vertigo the freedom of our consciousness, so do we become aware of the "other" through the feeling of shame or of pride under his gaze. It leads to the "unitary apprehension with three dimensions: '*I* am ashamed of *myself* before the *Other*'" (p. 289). That is: the *I* subject (for-itself) sees the *I* object (in-itself) as it is seen by the other, who reveals to me my "being-for-others." For to the other we are a body and under the other's gaze we realize what static characteristics we possess for him.[34]

32 The "ontic" is the merely empirical experience of anguish in life; ontologically, this experience is considered as a revelation of being. Many authors, notably Malraux and Camus, remain ontic; Sartre becomes ontological.

33 Sartre, "Conscience de soi et Connaissance de soi," *Bulletin de la Société Française de Philosophie,* p. 51.

34 According to Herbert Marcuse (in *Kultur und Gesellschaft 2,* pp. 58 and

Sartre illustrates the two radically different points of view of one's for-itself toward one's ego as against that of the other toward one's ego in the following extreme case: an assassin cannot understand that his past act sticks to him in the eyes of others, that his act should stamp him as a person of a definite character; in short, that he could only be an in-itself. To himself he remains a for-itself, free from his past act; that is—in existentialist syntax wherein the verbs *to be* and *to act* are transitive—he knows himself free to act different meanings. In like manner, we fail when, to the contrary, we would very much like to personify, as it were, a certain feeling, to be its essence:

All novelists have noted the maudlin aspect of any suffering,[35] because one brings it about and yet is incapable of sustaining it. In

62), Sartre has ably disproven the ontological existence of the other as it appears in Husserl, Heidegger and Hegel, without being able to posit it himself in pure ontology, but only in the ontic-empirical domain. True enough, Sartre does write as cited by Marcuse that "the Other's existence has the nature of a contingent and irreducible fact. We *encounter* the other, we do not constitute him" (*Being*, p. 250); but Sartre goes on to speak of a "contingent necessity," a "factual necessity" no less imperative than that of the *cogito* itself and no less apodictic. Simply: there is an ontological truth in the ontic revelation of the other in shame or pride, just as anguish discloses the prereflective structure of consciousness in freedom and just as acts of either self-deception or awareness point to either impure or pure reflective consciousness. Sartre will leave the ontological for the ontic when he enters into the arena of commitment, though even then without entirely severing his ties to the former, as is shown in the discussion of his *What is Literature?*

The difficulty here is that which nonexistential philosophy—so very well represented by Marcuse himself—always has in recognizing the philosophical value of experience and thus of literature. Of this, more in the conclusion.

[35] To cite some examples from *Les Faux-Monnayeurs* (*The Counterfeiters*): Profitendieu notices with dismay that his physical ailment has more weight than the moral pain he is supposed to feel; that he has "liver pain" (p. 27). Gontran de Passavent finds himself unable to rise to the pathos his father's death requires (pp. 58–60). Lady Griffith is at a cynical distance from the grief over "the sinking of the Bourgogne" as Robert de Passavent from that over his father's death, since they as society people have understood and accepted the reality of living at a distance from their emotions. Altogether, *The Counterfeiters* concerns us here. In its counterpoint it is the most accomplished of Gide's works, since it represents the perfect structure for a novel dealing so prominently with the being-for-others of its characters. Perhaps also Gide's own immense curiosity towards others can be understood as a concern with what he is to others, with his being-for-others.

all suffering there is the suffering of the others, which we see only in the form given to it by their bodies, which at that moment appears to us like a being. Even the dream of a suffering is a suffering which is, and not a consciousness of it.[36]

To the other we are what we are, a being-in-itself, an essence which we cannot achieve for ourselves except in imaginary ways.

The upsurge of the Other touches the for-itself in its very heart. By the Other and for the Other the pursuing flight [the freedom of the for-itself] is fixed in in-itself. . . . This fixed flight is never the flight which I am for myself; it is fixed *outside*. The objectivity of my flight I experience as an alienation . . . [*Being*, p. 362].

For the other, I have a fixed nature over which I have no power; my original fall, says Sartre, is due to the existence of the other (p. 263).

Hence, I can decide to reject the other as a subject, as my judge; I can treat him in turn as an object under my gaze: this is an expression of my internal negation of the other as a subject. Or, to the contrary, I can attempt to "recuperate," to retrieve my ego, by voluntarily becoming an object of fascination for the other, that is, by obtaining recognition of myself: this is an expression of my acceptance of the other as a subject who has, however, been charmed by me into this role:

In so far as the Other as freedom is the foundation of my being-in-itself, I can seek to recover that freedom and to possess it without removing from it its character as freedom. In fact if I could identify myself with that freedom which is the foundation of my being-in-itself, I should be to myself my own foundation [p. 363].

Language is such an appeal to the other's liberty, an attempt to fascinate the other's subjectivity, and to assimilate through the other my own possibilities. A case in point might be, indeed, the writer (as well as the actor, the artist or the composer) who tries, as an object, to reclaim his being-for-others

[36] "Conscience de soi et Connaissance de soi," p. 71.

(the image of himself that he has created through his art) in the eyes of his (subject) audience. His fame is akin to justification of himself by the others; and especially by the critics, who in the exercise of their freedom tell him who he is, yet at the same time depend on him for their existence. The infinite variety of human conduct towards the other lies in this "original fact" that all men's interactions are a "project of assimilating and making an object of the Other" (p. 363). This relationship is therefore in either case one of conflict, which cannot but perpetuate itself in failure.[37]

Love is a special way to reach out towards one of the two fundamental solutions to our being-for-others, the attempt at assimilation of the other through self-objectification. It is so desirable because in love our existence is "taken up and willed

[37] There is a distinction between the ontological being-for-others and the sociological fact of being with others. The latter is an objectification of a larger group in the face of a common subject, or vice versa. For Sartre, this relationship is not the harmony of belonging of Heidegger's *Mitsein,* but rather Hegel's struggle between master and slave. Characteristically, Sartre notes that "here as everywhere we ought to oppose to Hegel Kierkegaard, who represents the claims of the individual as such." Since what matters for Sartre is "the recognition of his concrete being and *not* the objective specification of a universal structure" (*Being,* p. 239; *Etre,* p. 295, for my insertion in italics), which latter is Hegel's aim. Sartre, therefore, describes at length the individual's conscious experience of his being-for-others, and his attempt, as unceasing as it is useless, to regain mastery of this being which he is creating for others.

A special case of being with others which is precisely not one of *Mitsein* has been treated by Sartre in his *Portrait of the Anti-Semite.* It is one of several convincing demonstrations—others of which, in the literary field, will be treated at length—of the integral comprehension offered by Sartre's ontological categories, of his full espousal of "le monde vécu," and of the humanistic aspect of his philosophy of negation. The "being with others" becomes the being-for-others, which integrates the other's view of oneself into one's own consciousness of oneself, when the Jew whose "physical and hereditary characteristics" which are only "one factor among others of his situation, and not a determining condition of his nature" (p. 53) becomes a man whom "other men look upon as a Jew" (p. 57). As a matter of fact, as a Jew "he is irrevocably fixed," since the Jew's being-for-others is a "duplication of the fundamental relationship with others" (p. 66). Anti-Semitism, a special case of the "spirit of seriousness," is a "poor man's snobbery" (p. 21); it is "in opposition to the Jew . . . that [the anti-Semite] realizes the right of his own existence" (p. 22). "He is a man who is afraid . . . of himself, of his conscience, of his freedom, of his instincts, of his responsibilities, of solitude, of change, of society and of the world—of everything except the Jews" (pp. 43–44).

even in its tiniest details by an absolute freedom which at the same time our existence conditions" (*Being,* p. 371). Love is a wish to be loved,

> Thus love relations are a system of indefinite reference—analagous to the pure "reflection-reflected" of consciousness—under the ideal standard of the value "love," that is, in a fusion of consciousnesses in which each of them would preserve his otherness in order to found the other [*Being,* p. 376].

But when I "succeed" and the other loves me, he is disappointing because he then in turn wants to be loved: this would make me an object for an object; and where I sought justification, I now must justify. "He is swallowed up in his objectivity" (p. 376). The admiring Estelle who tries so desperately to attract Garcin (hence, to become his object) is of no use to Garcin, and we know that if Inès interests him, it is because as a subject she possesses Garcin's being-for-others. Garcin refuses to leave the *No Exit* chamber because the freedom of his being-for-others is alienated to Inès, since she possesses its image. "Hell is the others," and the others cannot but be hell in a cyclical relationship.

Love as the ideal value of the being-for-others is triply destructible: (1) since it is a hopeless attempt mutually to justify each other's existence as subjects (hence the perpetual dissatisfaction of the lover); (2) since one becomes an indifferent object when the other ceases to love (therefore the ever-present sense of insecurity); and (3) since there is a reevaluation of the bilateral relation which takes place under the gaze of third parties (wherefore the distance felt as shame or pride by one or both of the lovers). All three possibilities and their innumerable variants force one back to one's unjustifiable subjectivity. It is through love, language and masochism that one tries to assimilate the freedom of the other. And it is in indifference, desire, hate and sadism that one objectifies the other in order to have him recognize one's own freedom. Since these two basic attitudes inevitably fall short of their aim, one tends to try first one and then the other in repeated succession; and often to reach in masochism and sadism their exacerbated form.

Our body is the center of reference for our consciousness, a means of recognition of the world, the instrument which we are; but not the justified foundation for our existence since it is merely contingent. However, our body as an object in the world, as our in-itself which our for-itself has to negate, manifests what we are to the other. In the body we find the revelation of desire, which is "an attitude of enchantment" (p. 394) towards the other. Of this fundamental desire of the other (aspects of which are maternal love, pity, generosity, and so on) which lasts throughout life, sexuality is only a particular manifestation (pp. 406–7).

The freedom of the other limits our freedom:

> The for-itself arises in a world which is a world for other for-itselfs[,] . . . thereby . . . alien[,] . . . already looked at, . . . a world whose temporal meaning is already defined by other temporalizations. . . . It is *in this world* that the for-itself . . . must choose itself. . . . For it is by a choice that he will apprehend the Other as The-Other-as-subject or as The-Other-as-object" [p. 520].

God is the Other as an absolute (as when Cain is forever marked by his deed and pursued by the gaze of the Other). The other is a major factor of our situation, and our individual significance lies in our adherence or our chosen distinction from him. We shall find in the less ontological and more sociological and historical *Critique de la raison dialectique* still more stringent limitations on the individual's freedom by the other, when in organized society. Even in that confining situation, however, it is the for-itself which gives meaning.

Our reflection obviously does not give us meaning in the eyes of the other; reflection alone is not even sufficient to obtain lucidity for ourselves. "Since the problem of self-identity cannot be resolved by reflection it becomes explicitly a problem of action in . . . *Being and Nothingness.*" And in *The Flies* "Orestes advances beyond the inconclusive experience of reflection (comparable to Roquentin's experience in *Nausea*) and arrives at an irreparable action with which he must identify himself." [38] Sartre himself in his thinking followed the evolution that he worked out in his literature: [39] action now becomes for him a necessary complement to reflection. He is severe toward the earlier stage of his thought, previous to *Being and Nothingness* (a stage which to us would seem unavoidable and certainly useful). Some twenty-five years after the publication of *Nausea,* he condemns his early, and still major, work (where nonetheless he had achieved consciousness of the world) in *The Words* (where he has at last gained self-knowledge):

> At the age of thirty, I executed the masterstroke of writing in *Nausea*—quite sincerely, believe me—about the bitter unjustified existence of my fellowmen and of exonerating my own. I *was* Roquentin; I used him to show, without complacency, the texture of my life. At the same time, I was *I,* the elect, chronicler of Hell [pp. 157–58].

Only the other (as Sartre had stated already in *Being and Nothingness*) can obtain the objective view of the "elect" on us. We can become aware of what we are for the other not through reflection but only through the effect of our acts on the other. Furthermore, our acts represent a disclosure for ourselves.[40]

[38] Cumming, *The Philosophy of Jean-Paul Sartre,* pp. 26 and 27.

[39] *The Roads to Freedom* culminates in Mathieu's realization that freedom as freedom is meaningless; that he has to commit himself to action.

[40] Sartre (who denies the validity of Freud's theories on the existence of the subconscious) has repeatedly made the point that consciousness is not knowledge of ourselves (especially in the chapters called "Transcendence" and "Having, Doing and Being" in *Being,* and in his "Conscience de soi et Connaissance de soi"). This position poses a problem of self-knowledge which has remained unresolved, but cannot be discussed here; it should be the object of a special study. However, if not fully understood in philosophy, it is "solved" empirically, that is, acted out in life and explicated in literature. What consciousness cannot communicate in knowledge, action reveals. Sartre is too harsh in his criticism of his Roquentin, for the latter has an intuition (already in his pure reflection) of

" 'Having,' 'doing,' and 'being' are the cardinal categories of human reality" (*Being,* p. 431). And doing and having can themselves be reduced to being. The for-itself acts in order to be (for the other as for itself); it acts in order to have, as a means to attain being. The act is an expression of the freedom of the for-itself, and it is only a series of acts which will constitute its essence: existence, as has been said, precedes essence. If Sartre was among those who early thought highly of Malraux and Saint-Exupéry, as well as Dos Passos, Faulkner and others, it is because their heroes move primarily in the realm of action: for "the for-itself is the being which is defined by action" (p. 431). In his descriptions of "doing" Sartre for some pages leaves the purely phenomenological and ontological domain and situates the for-itself in the arena of history.[41] Yet nowhere does he set forth stronger arguments for the freedom of consciousness:

> (1) No factual state whatever it may be (the political and economic structure of society, the psychological "state," etc.) is capable by itself of motivating any act whatsoever. For an act is a projection of the for-itself toward what is not, and what is can in no way determine by itself what is not. (2) No factual state can determine consciousness to apprehend it as a *négatité* [as something that is to be opposed] or as a lack [as a situation lacking in certain desirable features]. Better yet no factual state can determine consciousness to define it and to circumscribe it [*Being,* pp. 435–36].

The Lyons worker who rioted in 1830 had simply lived his situation as "natural" until the emergence of new factors on the horizon as future possibilities led him to "negate" it in his

his limitation and of a possible solution (in his reaction to the melody of commitment), which is realized in the active commitment of Orestes. It is only when Orestes actively defies Jupiter, and not when he speculates about the situation, that he comes to know that Jupiter is merely claiming omnipotence. Altogether, the crucial difference between Orestes and Roquentin lies in the fact that Orestes acts to change the city and himself, while Roquentin simply tries to escape.

[41] See *Being,* pp. 433–35. He deals with such different events as Constantine's motivation for establishing Byzantium and the motives of the Lyons workers' revolt in 1830. Adherents of *Being,* later bitter opponents of the *Critique,* have paid too little attention to these and other such pages in the earlier work.

mind as "intolerable." Yet nothing could have obliged him to entertain these hopes of a better future in comparison to which he now interpreted his present condition as plight. The act and its motivation and ends are one and inseparable once they have coalesced in a "pure temporalizing nihilation of the in-itself" (p. 438), a tearing away from a given situation. They form a totality which is not reducible to any one of its factors, notably not to a motivation determined by a past condition. The past exists only as knowledge. Sartre's position is reinforced by the consideration of the uniqueness of each and every "situation." Just as in the apologue by Kafka a man waits anxiously outside a door which was built to serve only himself, so each person finds only uniquely individual situations, which for Sartre—unlike for Kafka—each person has also fashioned for himself. Even the adversity of a situation is relative to the individual's aims and outlook. In extreme cases, it is in desertion or suicide that one will decide whether, for instance, such an overwhelming historical fact as warfare is of one's own choosing.[42] In any case, to be aware of a motive and to reflect on it is already to objectify and to transcend it: "I am condemned to be free" (*Being*, p. 439).

"Doing" is reducible to "having." One creates in order to be the cause of a concrete existence. It is a symbolic appropriation of the world. Such is the motive for scientific research; or for sports—especially satisfying, for example, is skiing where one gains possession of the snow field in speedy gliding, without having the for-itself sink into an in-itself matter.

[42] There is a considerable body of evidence by eyewitnesses from Nazi extermination camps. They agree in reporting that there were a small number of inmates ready to carry out the killing of fellow immates (the "Kapos"), and an indeterminate number (much more difficult to establish but perhaps smaller if one limits oneself to clear-cut cases) of inmates choosing immediate death; and that the large majority of people took the passive position which is best characterized by the phrase Malraux overheard in a Chartres camp: "As for me, I'm waiting for it to blow over" (*Les Noyers de l'Altenburg*, p. 25).

To have is first to create. . . . What I create is still me—if by creating we mean to bring matter and form to existence. . . . The totality of my possessions reflects the totality of my being. I *am* what I *have*" [pp. 590–91].

This aim of appropriation through creation is still more relevant in a highly personal creation as is a work of art. In any event, it can only be a matter of symbolic satisfaction. The elusiveness of the for-itself, unable to coincide with its in-itself for any length of time, and the knowledge of death, undermine all such attempts at being. This realization can lead to an antivalue (the in-itself absorbing the for-itself) in destructive actions (an example from everyday life: smoking). To do, to have, is to desire—because of the void of the for-itself—to possess the world through a particular object. Pascal, Stendhal and Proust all understood, regardless of their respective theoretical concepts, that desires transcend themselves—"les divertissements," or "la cristallisation" and jealousy in love, all lead beyond their immediate objects of desire to this underlying basic relationship of man to the world.[43] Love, for instance, is not the desire of a particular woman but an attempt to seize the whole world through this woman. This, for Denis de Rougemont, is the explanation of Don Juan: "he *is* not enough to *have*." [44]

We do (and we appropriate so as to have) in order to be in relation to a fundamental project which, as has been seen, is our unique individual variation of the ideal value: for-itself-in-itself, or perfect coincidence with ourselves. Sartre presents the outline of a method of phenomenological psychoanalysis designed to permit a description of each original choice. This existential psychoanalysis ought also to develop and make use of the phenomenological psychoanalysis of things (as practiced

[43] See *Being*, p. 562.
[44] *L'Amour et l'Occident*, p. 178.

poetically by Francis Ponge and more consciously by Gaston Bachelard) in order to establish objective correlatives for individual preferences.[45] Sartre himself developed his psychoanalytic method fully when he applied it in his *Baudelaire* and in his most considerable critical opus to date, the *Saint Genet.*

Freedom is the being of the for-itself which is defined by its actions because it thereby manifests itself and becomes essence.[46] One is consequently free only in one's choice of a particular course of action (or of inaction, that is, passive action: acceptance of the acts of the other).[47] The ethical problem raised by an act, absurd and gratuitous in its very freedom, is only treated negatively in *Being and Nothingness* (particularly in the pages on evasive conduct in bad faith): for what positive, meaningful commitment can there be in an existence aiming at a "useless passion"?

Sartre's phenomenology leads to reflective consciousness as contestation and his ontology to an awareness of impure reflection as bad faith. "Ontology itself can not formulate ethical precepts. It is concerned solely with what is, and we can not possibly derive imperatives from ontology's indicatives" (*Being,* p. 625). Yet it leads to considerations on the actions in bad faith by which man avoids facing up to his ontologically unjustifiable existence and his uselessness; actions which represent a false claim to morality and a pretense in their "spirit of

[45] Sartre tells us that he had wished to establish the significance of the bestiary of Lautréamont and the lapidary of Rimbaud, a study which he has not as yet undertaken (see *Being,* p. 601).

[46] Breton: "liberté, couleur d'homme" (freedom, man's color).

[47] One is surprised to read in Henri Peyre's otherwise sympathetic survey of Sartre's work, that "for Sartre, however, freedom is total" (p. 18), since Peyre himself quotes Sartre as saying: "I take the situation, and a freedom chained in situation . . ." (p. 35).

Once again, Mathieu's final step can serve as an elucidation: he realizes the fact of being "embarqué" whether he wishes to or not only after a long stretch of living "freely"—that is, in fear of entanglement—at the very end of *The Roads to Freedom,* in a burst of gunfire, a release of pent-up frustrations. Sartre told Christian Grisoli (*Paru,* No. 13, p. 8) that "the conditions of a real liberation will finally be defined in *La Dernière Chance.*" This last volume, however, has been left hanging.

seriousness." "Ontology and existential psychoanalysis . . . must reveal to the moral agent that he is *the being by whom values exist*" (p. 627). Man gratuitously invents his values, there is no cause for moral conduct; but there is the knowledge of what is immoral, given in pure reflection: "Since every structure of consciousness is free, it represents the way of a freedom which is reflective and moral." [48] Nothing but our own reflective consciousness could oblige us to face up to our anguish, to be authentic. It is close to doing just that since it is by its very nature perpetual contestation. Thus, for Francis Jeanson, one must postulate in existentialist morality that "what had been a spontaneous contestation becomes an obligation to contest." [49] But Sartre denies "the necessity of [pure] reflective acts. We could conceive of a society where reflection would forever represent a world of lies. This society can be conceived of rather readily since it is ours." [50]

It is therefore perhaps utopian to envisage Kant's Kingdom of Ends, "wherein one would practice pure reflection," which Sartre equates to morality.[51] This means to Sartre, to Simone de Beauvoir [52] and to Francis Jeanson,[53] that morality signifies to

48 "Conscience de soi et Connaissance de soi," p. 77. Sartre's concept of the immoral "spirit of seriousness" reminds one somewhat of the German Romantics' disdain for the "philistines," but now the term is grounded in ontology. One remembers also Yeats' lines: "The best lack all conviction, while the worst/ Are full of passionate intensity" ("The Second Coming").

49 Francis Jeanson, *Le Problème moral de la pensée de Sartre*, p. 351.

50 "Conscience de soi et Connaissance de soi," p. 82.

51 *Ibid.*, p. 90. In *Being*, Sartre had ruled it out as practically impossible to meet the other on a plane of equality: "Even if I should want to act according to the precepts of Kantian morality and take the Other's freedom as an unconditioned end, still this freedom would become a transcendence-transcended [therefore a means] by the mere fact that I make it my goal" (p. 408).

52 See *Pour une morale de l'ambiguité*, especially p. 186 ("To declare that existence is absurd, is to deny that it can give itself any meaning; to say that it is ambiguous, is to posit that its meaning is never fixed, that it must be conquered incessantly"); and p. 19 ("The existentialist conversion is to be compared rather to the Husserlian reduction: man should 'put within brackets' his wish to be, and thus return to the consciousness of his true condition").

53 "Even the decision to adopt a moral attitude would not permit man to take himself seriously. . . . (It) is not founded on any absolute sign, no guarantee

renounce any evasion of the anguish of freedom, to refuse any reliance on authority, to abandon any hope of attaining coincidence, to perpetually question one's ends: in short, it is to "live one's dualism," to "refuse being, since being is refused to us." [54] Sartre explained in an interview:

Being and Nothingness leads to the necessity and the promise of an ethics. I am working on this ethics of existentialism at the same time as on *La Dernière Chance*.[55]

But this projected fourth volume to *The Roads to Freedom* has not gone beyond two chapters, and the ethical treatise has not been written. We have only a footnote which maintains that an existential ethics is conceivable despite the fact that because of his being-for-others, in final analysis, man makes means of others or is so used:

These considerations do not exclude the possibility of an ethics of deliverance and salvation. But this can be achieved only after a radical conversion which we cannot discuss here [*Being*, p. 412].

Sartre, who had surmounted the dichotomy of idealism and of materialism in his prereflective *cogito* (consciousness-in-the-world) came close to isolating man from the lived world in some idealistic fashion through his postulation of the freedom of reflective consciousness and its incapacity to perform mean-

---

justifies it from the outside. In [this decision] resides the radical invention of man by man" (Jeanson, *Le Problème moral*, p. 351).

[54] "Conscience de soi et Connaissance de soi," p. 79. This means also that authenticity is of short duration. As Valéry remarked on Stendhal, there always lurks the prospect of the convention of the nonconventional: "What strikes, amuses and even charms me, in this wish of the natural on the part of the Egotist, is that it requires and comprises necessarily a *convention*. To distinguish the natural from the conventional, a convention is indispensable" (Paul Valéry, "Au sujet de Stendhal, Préface pour Lucien Leuwen," *Œuvres complètes de Stendhal*, VI, xix). It all leads to this "taste of ashes" which for Sartre accompanies even success. And to the feeling expressed by Simone de Beauvoir at the end of a large and active portion of her life: "I realize with stupor how much I was gypped" (*Force of Circumstance*, p. 686).

[55] Grisoli, p. 10.

ingfully. At one time, in a sociological description, Sartre remarked that "there is [in impure reflection] the outline of a nature because there is, after all, a greater consistency in the relation from the immediate [perception] to complicity [in impure reflection] than from the immediate to the pure [reflection]."[56] Sartre does not develop this consideration on the prevalence of conduct which seeks meaning in bad faith. It remains a statistical fact which as such does not contradict what to him is the apodictic truth of the uselessness of human endeavor revealed by pure reflection. It is rather in the structure of the being-for-others, and in the effort to attain being through doing and having, that Sartre will account for the social fact of human involvement, and that not exclusively as a consequence of impure reflection.

Whereas—at least still in *Being and Nothingness*—authentic behavior cannot be sustained, in the aesthetic pursuit we may succeed, though only in a symbolic manner. We have seen that beauty was for Sartre the ideal value for-itself-in-itself, perfect coincidence of the for-itself with the in-itself in a form that is what it is while it is a form which is essence. The obscene is ugly, for its movement is contrary to the purpose of the body and shows constraint into something unnatural; but in graceful movement the body exists in harmony with its purpose and manifests its freedom.[57] Anguish can be expressed in a statue where as an in-itself it will be what it is. One might say that in literature such a reification of sentiment is obtained when death transfigures the for-itself into an in-itself, as in the fate of Aude (*The Song of Roland*), of Eurydice (*Suréna*) and of Madame de Rênal (*The Red and the Black*), among many others. They die with an expression of grief on their lips; they are so movingly "beautiful" because of the depth of their

[56] "Conscience de soi et Connaissance de soi," p. 90.
[57] See *Being*, p. 400.

feeling, which suggests coincidence, and especially because of the permanence of their feeling which we lack so sorely: theirs is fixed forever.

Furthermore, since doing is reducible to having, "if I create a picture, a drama, a melody, it is in order that I may be at the origin of a concrete existence." It exists through me, "I stand to it then in the double relation of the consciousness which *conceives* it and the consciousness which *encounters* it" (pp. 576–77). This is as close as man can come to being his own foundation, to justifying his existence in an *ens causa sui.* And this achievement—which would be only imaginary—is impossible even as such: one cannot have the distance from one's own work or act to see it as others do. One cannot at the same time "conceive" and "encounter." One's work or deed is alienated from oneself to the other.

Pure reflection led Sartre to postulate the ontological uselessness of man, an ethics normative in negative injunctions, and a concept of beauty as the symbol of unattainable coincidence. But acts add to our knowledge about ourselves and about others, project our ever-renewed awareness, give us meaning and relate us to the "lived world." Apparently, Sartre's own "radical conversion" which was to lead to "an ethics of deliverance and salvation" [58] is embodied—though not presented in a treatise on ethics—in his "praxis" of social commitment. This "praxis" cannot change the ontological subject-object relationship among men, but it may tend to minimize the use of man as a means in the social arena. Not only Sartre's plays but also his literary criticism after *Being and Nothingness* are to be understood as a part of his *praxis:* it is precisely in the programmatic articles of *Les Temps Modernes* that Sartre embraces "le monde vécu" by developing the criteria of a literature which would face up to the condition of man and exhort him to commit his freedom.

[58] See above, p. 74.

With the liberation of France and the emergence of the Resistance movement from the underground began Sartre's active involvement in the public arena. His "Présentation des *Temps Modernes*" [59] was a clear declaration of intention, of an intention to intervene in the political fortunes of his country by promoting a change in its habits of thinking. He set forth the aim of the magazine as nothing less than the formulation of a synthetic anthropology (an anthropology of the individual as part of a collective group), and that not only as a pure science but as a means of furthering an actual liberation.[60] The philosopher and creative writer was to enter the realm of *praxis* as an editor and literary critic, as well as a participant in politics. "The war," Simone de Beauvoir tells us, "had effected a decisive conversion." Before the war,

> as a thinker, a writer, his primary concern had always been to grasp meanings. But after Heidegger and Saint-Exupéry, whom he read in 1940, had convinced him that meanings came into the world only by the activity of man, practice superseded contemplation.

Could *praxis* disclose an ethics, to which ontology had denied any ultimate justification and even any sustained reality?

> Although he adhered to the idea of *praxis,* he had not given up his old, persisting project of writing an *ethics.* He still aspired to *being:* to live morally was, according to him, to attain an absolutely meaningful mode of existence.[61]

These lines, written by Madame de Beauvoir before 1963, reminisce on Sartre's privately expressed thoughts at about 1945–46. It will be recalled, however, that Sartre stated publicly not much later that one has to "refuse being, since being is refused to us." [62] Actually, Sartre was to seek in *praxis* a way of

[59] *Les Temps Modernes,* October 1945.
[60] See "Présentation," p. 23.
[61] Beauvoir, *Force of Circumstance,* pp. 5 and 7.
[62] See above, p. 74.

being meaningful within given limitations: those of social concern, this side of metaphysics.

The aim of *Les Temps Modernes* was the constitution of a synthetic anthropology because Sartre condemned the bourgeoisie for its analytical bent of thought. Against the doctrine of caste privilege of the *ancien régime,* the bourgeoisie had postulated equality in human nature and denied the existence of social difference by divine right. And so today it claims to see individuals and not classes.[63] The existentialist Sartre is far from denying the uniqueness of man, but he sees him as unique in his way of reflecting on his situation—hence his freedom and his personal responsibility—and in his acts to influence society.[64] Sartre opposes the art-for-art's-sake attitude as one of irresponsibility: even the mere silence of Flaubert and of the Goncourts in the face of the repression of the Commune makes these authors responsible for these events. Was it their task to intervene? Voltaire, Zola and Gide have at similar moments in their lifetimes accounted for their responsibilities as authors: "The author is *in situation* in his times: each word is consequential. And so is his silence" ("Présentation," p. 13). We act because our very existence is an act influencing our time; we cannot help acting. And we must try to act morally, even despite the knowledge that the categorical imperative cannot be realized.

In the context of a synthetic anthropology,

> each period discovers an aspect of the human condition, in each period man chooses himself before the other, before love, before death, before the world; and when political parties clash over the disarmament of the Free French forces or over the aid to be given to the Spanish Republicans, this metaphysical choice, this singular

[63] One should perhaps point out that under the *ancien régime* the bourgeoisie claimed to speak for the entire Third Estate, which it did. However, it was equality before the law and political freedom which it achieved for all, not economic equality. The latter condition made for marked differences between collective entities that, indeed, are minimized in bourgeois thinking, which stresses the existence of individual vertical mobility.

[64] See "Présentation," p. 23.

and absolute project comes into play. Thus, by taking part in the singularity of our period, we ultimately reach the eternal, and it is our task as authors to suggest the eternal values which are implicit in these social and political debates [p. 15].

It is thus in our everyday interventions that we will find metaphysical value, and hence action replaces ethical theorizing for Sartre.

No matter how total the social conditioning of man, each person remains a center of irreducible indetermination.[65] This is in keeping with the "facticity"[66] of his existence as propounded in *Being and Nothingness:* that is, he must take a point of view on his situation, interpret it at a distance from himself, and act—or refuse to act—in accordance with his awareness of his situation. "It is to the defense of the autonomy and the rights of the individual that our magazine shall devote its efforts" (p. 28).[67] And it should not surprise the reader of Sartre's earlier criticism that this largely political manifesto,

[65] See *ibid.*, p. 26.

[66] "*Facticité*" is a neologism in French which has been transposed as such into English philosophical terminology.

[67] In "Materialism and Revolution" (*Les Temps Modernes,* 1946; translated in *Essays*) Sartre renews the position of ontological freedom now in the arena of *praxis* and political intervention. In this polemic against the French Communist party theorists aimed at a wide audience, Sartre explains that "freedom is a structure of human action and appears only in commitment; determinism is the law of the world. . . . [Man's] freedom is like the illumination of the situation into which he is cast. But other people's freedoms can render his situation unbearable, drive him to rebellion or to death" (pp. 244–45). It would thus seem that we are leaving the realm of freedom; but it must be remembered that Sartre insists that even though "oppression leaves them no choice other than resignation or revolution . . . in both cases they manifest their freedom to choose" (p. 245). The key to this article—the first in which Sartre faces up to the synthetic total reality of man which will be fully developed in the *Critique*—is the following sentence: "Both idealism and materialism cause the real to disappear in like manner, the one because it eliminates the object, the other because it eliminates subjectivity. In order for reality to be revealed, it is necessary for a man to struggle against it" (p. 247). Materialism cannot account for man's "possibility of *rising above* a situation" (p. 235). A distinction which has become current in our time was probably formulated here for the first time by Sartre when he remarks that the young Marx had insisted on the correlation between subjectivity and the world (see pp. 247–48); whereas, broadly speaking, Engels likened (free) man to (determined) nature (see pp. 205–8). Now, for Stalinist Neo-Marxism, "the stakes are down in advance; there exists a science of history and the interlinking of facts is rigorous" (p. 248).

which extols literature as a social vehicle—"a social function" (p. 16)—concludes by emphasizing that the magazine will try to develop literary techniques best suited to its stated aims, while warning that in committed literature the commitment should not make anyone forget about literature.

Historicity preoccupied Sartre as it did almost everyone in those days when people were confronted in their everyday lives with extreme situations, the peripheral and concrete manifestations of events of huge proportions. Sartre expresses the belief in "La Nationalisation de la littérature" that history characterizes our century as did Cartesian mathematics the seventeenth, Newtonian physics the eighteenth, and Lamarck's and Claude Bernard's biology the nineteenth.[68] But Sartre takes a position against the tendency then prevalent in criticism to consecrate contemporary works as national monuments for all time. By a system of extrapolation each new work was evaluated on a balance sheet as if it stood at the end of history and of literature.[69] Thus someone wrote "a final estimate of the contemporary theater" in 1945, and it seems that Lalou spoke of *Nausea* as Sartre's "literary testament." Altogether, there was talk of "the crisis of the novel" as if critics had already acquired the distance which allowed Hazard, for instance, to speak of "the intellectual crisis of 1715." "Critics no longer care to appraise . . . works, but seek to assay their national importance" (p. 50).

In this article, Sartre's main concern was the elaboration of a point made summarily in the "Présentation": he wished to lead

[68] Francis Ponge, who assigns the focal role of history rather to the nineteenth century, points to linguistics as the polarizing discipline in our century. This may prove to be correct for some of its middle decades as an expression of epistemological despair. It should be pointed out that Sartre himself was concerned with the problem of language in his early reviews (see pp. 42–44 above). Up to the Second World War, however, it would seem that the thought of the period was organized around Marxian sociology and Freudian psychoanalysis.

[69] See "La Nationalisation de la littérature," *Situations*, II, 38.

the critic to an awareness of the contemporary scene and to involvement in it, here and now, with (as he put it elsewhere) "the means at hand," since the future (that is, "historic") evaluations of books and their critics necessarily become "the devil's share." [70]

Michel Butor has recently buttressed Sartre's argument for contemporaneousness by adding to it another dimension.

> The most certain criterion of a work's novelty is the power it exerts to transform previous literary criticism. When we notice that a book leads us to change the way we read old ones, we can be sure that it is itself of importance.[71]

And in its very innovation the new work can also imply a critique of the older work ("its inadequacy") and, in its wake, that of an entire society.[72]

Whether as a critic one wishes to anticipate future evaluation or to reappraise the past,

> one cannot leave subjectivity—not the individual's subjectivity but that of the period; the critic must avoid making absolute judgments and share instead the lot of the authors.[73]

There is not only the subjectivity of the individual but also the uniqueness of each historical period. "Let us wager, that is all we can do" (p. 45). Because we are men. Sartre's wager is one of social commitment. Involvement and awareness—that is, acceptance in good faith of the unavoidable facticity of existence—are linked to social commitment in an as yet purely voluntary equation:

[70] The history of criticism illustrates this as a fact; it is the continuous, ever-equal appraisal of a work which is nonexistent. On each author and on each work, one ought to write an "X. and the critics" and to bring it up to date at particular stages throughout their history, as was done by J. Robert Loy for *Jacques le fataliste* in his first chapter of *Diderot's Determined Fatalist.*

[71] "Toute invention est critique," p. 24.

[72] See *ibid.*, p. 25.

[73] "La Nationalisation de la littérature," p. 43.

[The author] is responsible for everything: wars lost or won, revolts and repressions; . . . [he is an] accomplice of the oppressors . . . [if not] the natural ally of the oppressed. . . . To live and to write ought to be one [p. 51].

The critic, a subject in his own period, cannot but become an object for the following one. And if he attempts to speak for generations to come, rather than for his own, he is liable to fail to represent anyone or anything at all in the future.[74] It is Sartre's "firm resolve to be instrumental in deflating literature" (p. 53) by replacing empty consecration of literary works in pretentious, artificial distance with an at least limited comprehension in contemporaneousness.

More than comprehension is at stake in contemporaneousness. If we are not to remain aloof, how are we to become involved? In an earlier article in reference to Brice Parain and Camus,[75] Sartre declared:

Man's response to the absurdity of his condition does not lie in a great romantic rebellion, but in daily effort. Our *true* revolt lies in seeing things clearly, keeping our word and doing our job. For there is no reason for me to be faithful, sincere and courageous. And *that is precisely why* I must show myself to be such.[76]

[74] Today we know for certain that in the case of Voltaire, for whom perhaps more than for anyone it was indeed "one to live and to write" as Sartre demands, the theater represented his most influential vehicle of communication. His plays were certainly as contemporary in content as censorship would allow, but in form an imitation of the classical theater. And on account of their anachronistic pathos and rigidity, they live only as part of the history of the Enlightenment. (See Madeleine Fields, "Voltaire et le *Mercure de France*," for the importance of Voltaire's theater in his lifetime when he was "for all of France the great poet of tragedies whose enormous output dominated the stage and the salons of Europe" [p. 212].) However, the sprightly, ironic and polemical *contes*, written at first for the entertainment of his enlightened aristocratic hosts, continue to educate and to delight us. (Philippe Van Tieghem tends to believe that, among others, *Micromégas* and *Zadig* had been written by Voltaire for one of the "games" at the château de Sceaux as the guest of the Duchesse du Maine. (See pp. viii–ix of his Introduction to *Voltaire, Contes et Romans*.)

[75] "Departure and Return," p. 178.

[76] "[Jean Lacroix] has himself told how as a militant young student he took all the commands of his faith very seriously. When he was accepted at the École Normale Supérieure he objected violently to the bawdy songs which were traditional. On the day of hazing they wanted to humiliate him, but an older student

This moral attitude, coupled with the demand for a social anthropology and for contemporaneousness in criticism will become the literary commitment of *What is Literature?* What is the direction of this social commitment? Is Sartre's wager the atheist version of the religious leap into belief? Cumming sees a continuity in Sartre's successive stages of development, a continuity in the unfolding of his phenomenological analysis.[77] From consciousness of something (in perception, imagination and emotion) Sartre moved to consciousness of the other which leads him on to action. Action is also consciousness of making something and appropriating it as one's own. The latter, true for the artist, cannot be maintained for most of the participants in modern production, notably its workers. At this point (in the *Critique de la raison dialectique*) consciousness of something becomes "the consciousness of the use to which it is put." [78] It is this point of view, this "intentionality," which is already at work in the programmatic articles. Sartre was now responding to his very early desire to grasp concrete reality, which had attracted him to Husserl in the first place.[79] Furthermore, he faced up to the brute encounter with an extreme historical situation by an expansion of his field of endeavor. Throughout, he continued, indeed, to hold on to his point of departure and his method of investigation. But it is Sartre's existentialist moral attitude and ontology which guide him in his involvement in the contemporary scene. And it is in this context that Sartre now raises the question of the meaning of writing, of the author's (and the critic's) reasons for writing, of his choice of a public and of his situation on the contemporary scene, in one of his major critical works: *What is Literature?*

---

admiring his courage stepped in and took him under his wing: that was Jean-Paul Sartre" (Colette Audry, "La Vie d'un philosophe," p. 34).

[77] See *Sartre,* especially pp. 39–41.

[78] *Ibid.,* p. 41. Sartre now fully develops this, Heidegger's version of intentionality, of which he had already made use in the *The Emotions,* to show that this intentionality vanishes in the magic world of the emotions (see p. 62).

[79] See above, pp. 10–11.

In his introductory remarks to this work Sartre summarily ridicules some objections raised against his theories concerning committed literature. Indeed, as the literary expression of ontological committed freedom, it is the axis around which his critical program will turn. At the outset, in the 1930s, Sartre had reflected on his phenomenological and literary experiences which were to lead him to a systematic philosophy and aesthetics, which are now, in turn, to permit him to analyze literature and to establish criteria of literary criticism. However, unlike his Neo-Marxist opponents, who force particular works of literature to fit the pattern of ready-made theories,[80] Sartre posits his theories only after his painstaking and exhaustive descriptions in *Being and Nothingness* and, furthermore, he does consider works, authors, literary genres and periods on their own terms and in their own context before explicating them in the light of his own system of criticism.[81]

Challenged to explain why poetry is as little committed as painting or music, Sartre gives his definition of poetry: [82] in poetry, words are not "used" as means, they are not merely

[80] An example of such an aprioristic attitude is furnished by George Lukacs in his writings, notably in *Existentialisme ou Marxisme?* To cite at random: in chapter two, "The Myth of Nothingness," we read on page 90: "The flight towards interiority leads to a tragi-comic dead-end." Thus does one of the best philosophers among those who call themselves Marxists understand Sartre's modification of Husserl as a "flight toward interiority"; whereas Sartre's original contribution in his descriptions of consciousness had been precisely to eliminate any and all vestiges of interiority. (See above, pp. 5, 10–12, 47–51.) Even at its best, Lukacs's reading of Sartre is limited, because for Lukacs there is no problem of metaphysics but only that of social man. The entire ontology of *Being* is then flattened out to mean a demand for an "abstract freedom" arising from the leveling off of class differences under the Nazi occupation (pp. 103–4). Needless to add, that in the hands of someone like Roger Garaudy the criticism of Sartre descended to the level of name calling.

[81] As will be shown, it is entirely gratuitous for Philip Thody to declare: "Pompous, tendentious, superficial and inaccurate, *What is Literature?* is very far from being one of Sartre's better works" (*Jean-Paul Sartre, A Literary and Political Study*, p. 168). I shall return to Thody's book where it is more specific in its discussion of Sartre as a literary critic, which—it must be recalled to excuse somewhat such a summary statement by the author—is not, however, his subject.

[82] See *What is Literature?* pp. 5–13.

signs to signify a reality which lies beyond; they form the thing which we are to consider: a poem is a substance and its own signification. "Its sonority, its length, its masculine or feminine endings, its visual aspect, compose . . . a face of flesh which *represents* rather than expresses signification" (*What is Literature?* p. 8). One might say, then, to use Sartrian terms, that in a poem a certain transformation of the world has taken place already through the "imagining intention" [83] on the part of the poet, who has couched it in the characteristic nonprosaic form. The purpose of poetry is not to exhort the reader to change life (to commit himself) but to lead him, if only for a moment, to what we might call an experience of transfiguration.

Prose, however, is for Sartre utilitarian by definition; [84] words serve, prose constitutes a particular moment of action, the prose author has chosen "a certain method of secondary action which we may call action by disclosure." He cannot but disclose a certain aspect of the world, a disclosure which the author in his partiality has selected; and disclosure is invitation to change. Moreover, metaphysically, he must choose as man, for even "God, if He existed, would be, as certain mystics have seen Him, in a *situation* in relationship to man" (p. 17). It can be readily seen that for Sartre *les belles lettres* are not useless art-for-art's-sake entertainment. He assigns to prose authors the role of disclosing knowledge, so that the reader cannot plead ignorance. And for the reader, Sartre implies, such knowledge is an obligation to act on the level of such awareness:

> The writer has chosen to reveal the world and particularly to reveal man to other men so that the latter may assume full responsibility before the object which has been thus laid bare. It is assumed that

[83] See above, pp. 18–22.

[84] "Prose is, in essence, utilitarian" (*What is Literature?* p. 13). Sartre reminds us of the famous "if the word Love comes up between them, I am lost," uttered by Count Mosca as he sees Fabrice and Sanseverina leave in a coach. He also quotes the sally by Brice Parain that words are "loaded pistols" (*ibid.*, p. 18).

no one is ignorant of the law because there is a code and because the law is written down. . . . The function of the writer is to act in such a way that nobody may say that he is innocent of what it's all about [p. 18].

And just as inaction was acquiescence in the other's action,[85] so even silence is a moment of language, an act of refusal to speak.

Style does make for the value of prose, but since in prose words are to signify (rather than to constitute in themselves the signification as in poetry), since words are here to be transparent, "it would be absurd to slip in among them some panes of rough glass" (p. 19). In prose, therefore, aesthetic pleasure is pure only when it does not interfere with communication, when it exists as though "thrown into the bargain," when its beauty unobtrusively predisposes the reader towards its content.[86] Usually, to choose one's subject and one's style are one; the good author's choice of style does not precede that of a subject. Commitment, Sartre claims, does not undermine style. To the contrary, just as physics proposes ever new problems to mathematics and spurs it on, so social and metaphysical exigencies demand of the author a new language and new techniques.

Since to Sartre literature is action through disclosure, since authors have struggled in order "to destroy, to edify, to demonstrate (p. 24) in their own day, he concludes his chapter, "What is writing?" with an attack on a certain kind of critic whom he calls "cemetery watchmen" (p. 22). For, enjoying "the well-known superiority of live dogs to dead lions" (p. 25), this sort of critic reduces the author to harmlessness in a "melancholy cuisine," a process of leveling off, according to which

[85] See above, pp. 69–71, for Sartre's cardinal categories of having, doing and being.

[86] Sartre will be in a position to define this beauty which provides "aesthetic joy" for the reader in its various structures in the next chapter of his essay. It is taken up below.

man is neither good nor bad, "genius is only great patience," there is a lot of suffering in a man's life; all of which is to reassure the reader that the author's vital and arduous preoccupation was "only" literature and that living authors are just as inoffensive as the dead ones.

"Why write?" The many different descriptions which can be given of the aims of authors can be reduced to a profound choice common to all human activity. In a quest of being we wish to become essential in respect to the world, and we feel so disposed towards our creation. However, after having written a book, the author meets in its pages only his own subjective efforts at producing them; he cannot look at his book as an objective creation. (The artisan shoemaker can wear his shoes, but the author can only relive his creative efforts.) After years have passed an author may meet his own book as an object, that is, at a time when he would probably no longer be able to author it. It is for the reader that a book reveals unsuspected possibilities, raises expectations, and a future, which give it its objectivity:

> The operation of writing implies that of reading as its dialectical correlative. . . . It is the conjoint effort of author and reader which brings upon the scene that concrete and imaginary object which is the work of the mind. There is no art except for and by others [p. 37].

The author only directs the reader's creative imagination and the work exists only at the level of the reader's capacities. Since the reader, unlike the author ignorant about the work, must make something of the words through his imagining intention, he can progress in the knowledge of the book and he can multiply the imaginary creations it elicits, and so the book can seem to become inexhaustible and opaque in its many interpretative possibilities just like a thing.[87] It is thus only

[87] Perhaps we have here an explanation for one of the criteria of a good book: Will it reveal new facets at a rereading? Moreover: how often and at what

through the consciousness of the reader that the author is creator of an object: "To write is to make appeal to the reader that he lead into objective existence the revelation which I have undertaken by means of language" (p. 40).

The author appeals to the reader's freedom: in a book there can only be suggestions on the part of the author for the aesthetic pleasure of the reader, there are only solicitations by the author to participation by the reader in producing the object, and the work is an event which cannot be explained by a past but is a new beginning.[88] This appeal to a freedom cannot be an attempt to appropriate the reader as he remains passive, that is, to have him simply accept the author's passions, whereby his freedom would be alienated: "Hence the character of pure presentation which appears essential to the work of art. The reader must be able to make a certain aesthetic withdrawal." [89] Both credulity and the knowledge of one's freedom go into the aesthetic consciousness which is one of "belief by means of engagement" (p. 44). It is the reader who endows the character of a book with his own emotions while knowing that he can put the book aside. Sartre defines as "generous a feeling which has its origin and its end in freedom. . . . Reading is an exercise in generosity" (p. 45).

In the contemplation of a landscape our pleasure lies in a certain order we are "given" to observe, but before long we realize that the various relationships which we felt to be "final" can be reorganized by different ways of looking at it. We

---

intervals can one pleasurably read it again? It goes without saying that the answers reveal mainly a subjective predilection for a given work, but the rereadings, establish this predilection more surely than a single reading.

[88] Empirically, it is well known that a fair amount of "good will" and effort is required in aesthetic enjoyment. What is this "good will" but our willingness in freedom to extend ourselves towards the "appeal" exercised by the work of art, to respond with our life to a dead canvas, to a grouped series of tones, to the printed words, in order to meet it in an imagining intention?

[89] It is this moment in the author-reader elaboration of literature, which, Sartre points out, Gautier has mistaken for "art for art's sake" and the *Parnasse* for the impassibility of the artist.

remain free to the point where the aesthetic sensation will vanish completely, since we can cease to consider the landscape as an aesthetic object. It is the painter who makes of this "finality without end" of the spectacle of nature, and of its illusory order, a human intention. Cézanne's tree has "a deep finality" which the painter has fixed in the total and purely aesthetic relationship prevailing on his canvas. Similarly, the reader meets words which have been "expressly willed," so that "reading is induction, interpolation, extrapolation" on the part of an alert reader, a free agent; but "the creator has preceded him along the way." To this extent the reader's experience is also one of pleasurable security. The author by his decision to write places himself at a distance from his passions, his emotions have become free emotions; [90] and at the same time the author places himself "in an attitude of generosity" towards the reader: "thus my freedom, by revealing itself, reveals the freedom of the other." There exists, then, a dialectical relationship between reader and author in their creation and recreation, in their respective freedom, in their dual generosity.

Regardless of how limited the subject matter, it appears "against the background of the universe" and aims at a "total recovery of the world" (see pp. 45–51), since this is the aim of artistic activity as such. Each picture, each book, writes Sartre, is a recuperation of total being by producing a spectacle of the world not only as it is but as if it had its foundation in the author's freedom. We have here a specific case of the general, ontological structures of doing in order to have (here an artistic object) and of having in order to be, that is, of one's being in the eyes of the other (in this case, the reader) from whom this now objective being (the book) seems retrievable.

A work of art is successful when it produces aesthetic joy. Sartre gives an involved description of the aesthetic consciousness (in this case, of the reader), which is, indeed, a highly

[90] We know that the act of writing by itself can be considered a catharsis.

complex one (pp. 52–54). Three major elements can be isolated: (1) the work appears as an end, in a world of means to ends and ends to means; (2) through the artistic object, seen as offering a task to be fulfilled, man's project is modified; and (3) the work, predicated upon a certain trust among author and readers, leads to an imaginary consciousness of the world as "the harmonious totality of human freedoms."

It is necessary to enter more fully into Sartre's analysis of the structures of aesthetic consciousness. The aesthetic object represents, in the first place, then, an appeal to leave the utilitarian domain of reality, an appeal to an absolute end, which is an ideal value (beauty: the form which is essence). The positional consciousness (explicit, reflective consciousness) of this value is accompanied by the nonpositional (underlying, prereflective) one of one's freedom. And with the nonpositional, implicit recognition in joy of one's freedom goes that of one's creative participation as constitutive of the object. (That is, we willingly abandon ourselves to an imaginary pursuit of an ideal, to an artistic creation in which we participate.)

This leads into the second aspect which Sartre terms "the essential structure of aesthetic joy," when a book appears to the reader as an object depending on him for its creation.[91] Now, the positional, reflective consciousness of one's pleasure in co-creation ("jouissance") has as its corollary the nonpositional, prereflective one of being essential to an object considered essential.[92] For the reader, this means attainment of what Sartre terms "the feeling of security" (in contradistinction to the anguish arising from the realization of the contingency of one's existence). It has as its source the knowledge of a rigorous harmony of subjectivity and objectivity (the harmony in the collaboration of writer and reader in the making of a book).

[91] This is also the moment where for once the creation appears *as an object* to the artist as well.

[92] See above, pp. 54–55.

Furthermore, since the aesthetic object is actually the world as one imagines it, aesthetic joy is part of the consciousness of the world as value, and as a task offered to human freedom. (Let us recall that beauty is revealed as an absence, as lacking—"un manque"—in the world, therefore beckoning us—"le manquant"—as an appeal to change and to fulfillment.[93]) Therefore, the aesthetic consciousness becomes a moral imperative. "I shall call this the aesthetic modification of the human project." Since in aesthetic joy the given becomes an imperative and reality a value, this aesthetic level of consciousness is one of recuperation and interiorization of what I am not, and hence a fulfillment of aspirations in imagination. Usually the world is the horizon of our situation, a synthetic totality of what is given to us as obstacles and tools, but now it becomes "a demand addressed to our freedom." [94]

Finally, the structures of aesthetic consciousness described above imply, as a third corollary, a pact in freedom among the many readers of a book and its author (the "generosity" discussed earlier).[95] Aesthetic joy is, then, a positional consciousness which imagines the world both as being (in its reality) and as having to be (in the artistic re-creation of it), as entirely

[93] See *Being,* pp. 195–96.

[94] A few years ago, in an article—"On Style"—Susan Sontag also argues that "art is connected with morality," since "art may yield moral pleasure; but the moral pleasure peculiar to art is not the pleasure of approving of acts or disapproving of them. The moral pleasure in art, as well as the moral service that art performs, consists in the intelligent gratification of consciousness" (pp. 550–51). One wonders what this "moral pleasure" and this "intelligent gratification" consist of, and later passages such as the one describing art as being "moral in so far as it is, precisely, the enlivening of our sensibility and consciousness" (p. 555) do not bring us closer to a grasping of the connection between art and morality, even though this critique stems from a valid intuition. The thrust—and the flaw if one follows Sartre's thinking—of Miss Sontag's reasoning is precisely her denial that art is an implicit "approving of acts or disapproving of them."

[95] This particular aspect of the aesthetic consciousness had been somewhat approximated by the Unanimist author when he wrote in his postscript "L'Auteur au lecteur," that he wished to offer "a meeting ground" to his readers and friends, "a spiritual family," to which, indeed, he had appealed in his novel. (Jules Romains, *Les Hommes de bonne volonté,* XXVIII, 329).

ours (as co-creators) and as entirely foreign (as readers of the author's creation). Subtending this dual awareness accompanied by an outgoing generosity, "nonpositional consciousness *really* envelops the harmonious totality of human freedoms insofar as it makes the object of a universal confidence and exigency" (p. 54). It is Kant's "city of ends" that Sartre here posits, even though he considers it unrealizable, as the ultimate aim of the literary pursuit.

To write is an attempt to become essential by disclosing the world and proposing it as a task to the reader. However, the real world is revealed only in action, when one tries to change it. Similarly, in the world of the novelist, density is obtained by involving the reader in an imaginary commitment, in an imaginary action aiming at change. Realism, in its striving for noninvolvement, was in error: even if the author discloses a universe of injustice, his must be an appeal to generosity in the "going beyond" this state of injustice which the work suggests. It ought not to appear as a natural fact, but as a demand for change, a becoming leading towards the kingdom of ends.[96] Sartre maintains that there has never been any good book "whose express purpose was to serve oppression" (p. 58). One does not write for slaves: "Writing is a certain way of wanting freedom" (p. 59).

The "other," to whose freedom the author addresses himself, is, of course, an individual living in a particular situation. And so is the author, who by his choice of a subject, selects his potential readers (or by a choice of readers selects his subjects).

[96] It can be argued that on the whole Flaubert, for one, has not actually applied his preconceived theories in his novels. In *Madame Bovary* utter triviality becomes poignant tragedy; in *L'Education sentimentale* the author willfully downgrades the Revolution and, one is tempted to say, "calculates" the portrayal of the anti-hero's banality: in both cases the reader is severely shocked, not resigned. Perhaps Flaubert could not do otherwise but violate his aesthetics of objectivity once he was writing for a reading public to whom he had to reach out. Sartre will make Flaubert, whom he criticizes already in *Being,* the subject of a special study. It is taken up below; see also p. 102 *n* 111.

Accordingly, Sartre presents us in his chapter "For whom does one write?" with a summary history of the author-reader relationship through the centuries, including a more detailed appraisal of Realism and the mid-twentieth-century movements, in order to account for its concrete manifestations at each stage of an ever changing process.

The author endows his society with an unhappy consciousness, for to name is to show, and to show is to invite to change (if the reaction to the author is one of shame) or to maintain (a reaction of cynicism, for Sartre). Yet the ruling circles have generally commissioned the writer so as to obtain from him a portrait, an image of themselves which they could assume. The author, therefore, is working against the interests of those who support him: such is the original conflict Sartre ascribes to the writer, a conflict which usually gives him a bad conscience. The objective aspect of this conflict is the antagonism between "the conservative forces, or the real public of the writer, and the progressive forces, or the virtual public." It is a distinction between the privileged few who commission the author, and the many—among them the voiceless, who are not even part of the reading public—for whom the good author cannot fail to speak in what has been defined as an exercise in generosity (see pp. 74–76).

In the absence of a potentially larger reading public this conflict vanishes. In the twelfth century "the clerk wrote exclusively for clerks" (p. 77). This "specialized body" (p. 79) had as its role the contemplation of the Eternal; the contestation bore on details in the name of incontrovertible principles, which it was to reaffirm. In this particular case, literature identifies with the ruling ideology, and the writer, for once, has a good conscience. "The barons counted on the clerks to produce and watch over spirituality":

> In this sense, [the clerk] realized, in effect, the ideal of Benda, but one can see under what conditions: spirituality and literature had

to be alienated, a particular ideology had to triumph, a feudal pluralism had to make the isolation of the clerks possible, virtually the whole population had to be illiterate, and the only public of the writer could be the college of other writers. It is inconceivable that one can practice freedom of thought, write for a public which coincides with the restricted collectivity of specialists, and restrict oneself to describing the content of eternal values and *a priori* ideas. The good conscience of the medieval clerk flowered on the death of literature [p. 80].[97]

Sartre gives here an interesting example—at the other end from what he himself generally calls literature (that is, contestation)—of the specific conditions that had to prevail in order to produce literature which fell in line with ideology and maintenance of faith and yet remained literature (without descending into propaganda and the pulp magazine output). However, even in or about the twelfth century, it would seem that this phenomenon was limited to the Latin texts of the monastic clergy.[98] The Old French literature of the troubadours, of Chrétien's *Lancelot,* and especially of the different versions of *Tristan et Yseult,* read and spoken of in the ladies' chambers (*la chambre des dames*), was likely both to attract and perplex part of the nobility, even though, no doubt, "the barons counted on the clerks to produce and watch over spirituality."

Again, in the seventeenth century, on a broader scale, Sartre claims, the real and the potential reading public coincide. This reading public is "the society,"[99] wherein the gentleman ("l'honnête homme") exercises the censorship of good taste, for he is upper class and himself a specialist: "the public of

[97] Since there are writers addressing a "college of other writers," there is literature. "The death of literature" refers to the narrow limitation of the writing which took place, which is its lack of contestation.

[98] One might consider that even among them the contestation of a Roscellin or an Abélard had wider ramifications than Sartre here implicitly recognizes.

[99] Sartre refrains from calling it *la Cour et la Ville,* even though he so defines its various constituents: portions of the Court, of the clergy, of the "magistrature" and of the wealthy bourgeoisie. See p. 81.

Corneille, of Pascal, of Descartes, was Madame de Sévigné, the chevalier de Méré, Madame de Grignan, Madame de Rambouillet, Saint-Evremond." Besides the clergy and the official historiographers, court poets, jurists and philosophers who uphold the Throne and the Church, there are men of letters symbolically grouped in the French Academy. The values of all are fixed by tradition; a belief in immutability refers them to antiquity, whose models cannot be surpassed, and no singularity breaches their concept of a human nature. Strongly integrated in contemporary society, their critique is directed at the marginal nonconformist: their literary activity is "a ceremony of recognition," and for them "style is the supreme courtesy of the author toward his reader." They are classical. Yet the literature of this period, Sartre points out, "is a perpetual *cogito*" (p. 90), in that it represents a constant effort to see oneself clearly and to gain a perspective on one's actions. Hence it is literature of only psychological dimensions, and as such limited to moral considerations aiming, in the studied avoidance of religious, metaphysical and social problems, simply to liberate man from his passions.

In naming Madame de Rambouillet among the classic readers of classic authors, Sartre seems to place the aristocratic opponents of the court, the *Précieux* and *Précieuses,* among those whom he has just described as the ill-adjusted stragglers on the sidelines, though still part of the prevailing establishment. However, the inclusion of Saint-Evremond, also mentioned as belonging to this group of readers and authors, raises more serious objections. Saint-Evremond, and with him Gassendi, Cyrano, possibly the Molière of *Dom Juan,* pursued by the zealots (*la cabale des dévôts*), were more or less libertine. Moreover, Sartre does not consider Sorel, Scarron and Furetière, the last possessing the rare distinction of having been expelled from the French Academy, who were writing novels sharply removed from the "noble style." More striking still is the case of the Pascal of *The Thoughts,* whom one has some difficulty placing in his time because of his extreme metaphysical concern. The seventeenth century, then, did produce a considerable body of literature of contestation. The unusual aspect of Classicism—in Sartrian terms—lies in the fact that for once great literature appears in support of a ruling ideology; its real public is even then, however, far from coinciding with its potential public.

"The eighteenth century was the palmy time, unique in history, and the soon-to-be-lost paradise, of French writers" (p. 91). In that century, literature, as Sartre conceives of it, appears in its full bloom. For the first time a real public, the rising, politically oppressed bourgeoisie which forms an increasingly active reading public, seeks from the author enlightenment on its role. The author is, at the same time, still solicited by the aristocracy whose belief in its own values is receding along with the general movement of thought from revealed truth to pragmatic concepts. Thus, the author now enjoys a measure of independence from court, clergy and *la ville,* he is beyond the fray, his is the autonomy of the true *writer.*

> Spirituality,[100] literature,[101] and truth: these notions were bound up in that abstract and negative moment of becoming self-conscious. Their instrument was analysis, a negative and critical method which perpetually dissolves concrete data into abstract elements and the products of history into combinations of universal concepts [p. 98].[102]

100 Now: "this abstract movement which cut through all ideologies. . . . The power of continually surpassing the given" (p. 97).

101 That is: "négativité" due to the writer's refusal to become aristocrat or to remain bourgeois (see p. 98).

102 This is especially true for one of the major works of the century, the *contes* of Voltaire. Every concrete detail is a biting criticism of the contemporary scene, and its purpose is to reveal some universal truth, which cries out for an immediate rectification of the present. In a lecture given to the Modern Language Association in December 1966, Aram Vartanian addressed himself in much the same manner to the *Lettres persanes* and convincingly demonstrated that even the letters from the exotic Harem allude to Paris and to Versailles.

In his very effort to achieve free expression for himself, the eighteenth-century author speaks for the needs of the bourgeoisie, which is actually powerful but still deprived of political freedom or equality before the law and in all spheres of life. Thus, it is now no longer a question of freeing *l'honnête homme* from his passions but of giving political freedom to all: [103]

> The appeal which the writer addressed to his bourgeois public was, whether he meant it or not, an incitement to revolt; the one which he directed to the ruling class was an invitation to lucidity, to critical self-examination, to the giving up of its privileges [p. 101].

These authors, Sartre affirms, were preparing at long range not only the taking of the Bastille but also the night of August the fourth.[104] For the first time since the Reformation, authors as authors intervene prominently in public affairs; and, if not in theory then undeniably in fact, they consider literature as a permanent exercise in generosity, as a free appeal to the freedom of their readers. Sartre's definition of committed literature, literature wherein the author "tries to achieve the most lucid and the most complete consciousness of being embarked" (p. 70), is the only one applicable to that eighteenth-century literature which in its "spirituality" and its "truth" moves into anthropology, education, constitutional law, sociology, history, ethics, encyclopedism, philosophy, science and politics; the authors remaining *hommes de lettres* throughout.

Once the bourgeoisie had gained its objectives, the writer felt bereft of much of his *raison d'être* and lost his privileged position. Nineteenth-century bourgeois thinking, no longer based on an ethics of Providence, and not too sure of the basis

103 The eighteenth-century author shares the bourgeois aspiration to speak for all humanity and for all time, in "universal concepts."

104 Perhaps, indeed, praise ought to be apportioned in the reverse order: the *philosophes* certainly did all they could to prepare the night of August the fourth, whereas the taking of the Bastille may have been only an indirect outcome of their endeavor, an event for which the unenlightened court and its clerical and aristocratic allies must be given most of the credit.

of its values, is utilitarian; and, furthermore, it sees need, oppression and wars not as evil but as part of a pluralistic universe, all the elements of which are reducible, however, to some system of ideas. Whereas the writer

> radically distinguishes things from thought. His freedom and the thing are homogeneous only in that both are unfathomable, and if he wishes to readapt the desert or the virgin forest to the Mind, he does not do so by transforming them into ideas of desert and forest, but by having Being sparkle as Being, with its opacity and its coefficient of adversity, by the indefinite spontaneity of Existence.[105] That is why the work of art is not reducible to an idea; first, bcause it is a production or a reproduction of a *being,* that is of something which never quite allows itself to be *thought;* then, because this being is totally penetrated by an *existence,* that is, by a freedom which decides on the very fate and value of thought. That is also why the artist has always had a special understanding of Evil, which is not the temporary and remediable isolation of an idea, but the irreducibility of man and the world *to* Thought [p. 108, for my emphasis see *Situations,* II, 159].

Authentic literature cannot but refuse the utilitarian demand for "the bourgeois breviary," for an "Art of Making Good" or an "Art of Commanding," for a literature whose psychology is founded on self-interest, that is, a literature of psychologism, of idealism, of determinism, of utilitarianism—in short, one might say, of "the spirit of seriousness" in its crassest form. Some accepted to serve, but the best refused, a refusal which led literature into an unprecedented situation: from 1848 to 1914 the author writes in principle against his public. In the century of Classicism there was a perfect accord between writer and reader at least within certain boundaries which were considerable. The author of the Age of Enlightenment found two equally "real" classes of readers. Romanticism, in its beginnings, had been an unsuccessful attempt to restore this favorable situation. But writers, with the sole exceptions of

[105] We have here an explanation for Diderot's superiority over Condillac or D'Holbach, not to mention La Mettrie.

Michelet and Hugo, refused what Sartre calls "the unclassing from below" (p. 113), the closing of ranks with the proletariat:

> The formal liberties which the essayist, the novelist, and the poet were to defend had nothing in common with the deeper needs of the proletariat . . . [which] wanted the material improvement of its lot [p. 114].

One must raise the question whether the proletariat ever was, as Sartre assumes, a "potential public," for it has never become a "real public." It has, in fact, in more than a century of its history—and no matter what explanation is to be offered—been unable to relate consistently its own demands to those "formal liberties" without which it could not hope to attain or to maintain them.[106] At present, when their specifically proletarian demands are being met in the so-called welfare state, the lower classes are notorious as the "the real public"—with some fluctuations depending on time and place—of the picture tabloids of the large cities of the world and of the other mass media, or of the output of Socialist Realism.[107]

[106] Yet J.-J. Rousseau had already warned that even though democracy can function only if what prevails is "a good deal of equality in rank and fortune," it must also avoid the situation in which "the least numerous sooner or later attain the greatest authority" (*The Social Contract,* Book III, Chapter IV). Economic equality and political democracy are interdependent for this farsighted *philosophe,* who had no experience of either.

[107] For the philosopher-sociologist Herbert Marcuse the two-dimensional culture (more or less the one described by Sartre in his sociology of the history of French literature discussed above) has been flattened out in today's society. So immensely successful in its technology, it is able to satisfy the basic needs of man and to adopt and to incorporate cultural values (originally of contestation) "into the established order, through their reproduction and display on a massive scale." (See p. 57 and the chapter "The Conquest of the Unhappy Consciousness: Repressive Desublimation," in *One-Dimensional Man.*) "Higher culture becomes part of the material culture. In this transformation it loses the greater part of its truth." To Marcuse the higher culture is of a largely "feudal" character in its "conscious, methodical alienation from the entire sphere of business and industry" (*ibid.,* p. 58)—yet it is the only authentic culture. Therefore, in contrast to Sartre, who expects to transform a potential reading public (the proletariat) into a real public, Marcuse does not entertain such hope. Hence he continues to value highly not only the eighteenth-century French literature but also the nineteenth-century "decadents" and Surrealism, and precisely in areas where Sartre has reservations about them.

Sartre views the author of the second part of the nineteenth century as a study in self-deception: his break with the bourgeoisie is only symbolic. Just as the bourgeoisie refuses to recognize social classes (in contradistinction to the aristocrat who bases his privileges on his belonging to a particular caste), so the author refrains from asking himself for whom he exercises his pen and likes to believe that in his solitude he is writing for himself or for God. Actually, however, to a certain degree a reading public of specialists has again come into being in the literary clubs (*les cénacles*); and as for the past, the author feels a mystical communion with its great authors, just as for the future he hopes to live on in "glory"—attitudes which are meant to recall the autonomy enjoyed under the *ancien régime*. The author tries to imitate the aristocrat's nonutilitarianism, his life of pure consumption. That is what art ought to be for Realism and the Parnasse; the art-for-art's-sake adept

taught nothing, reflected no ideology, and above all, refrained from moralizing. . . . The logical conclusion of all this was the hope of an absolute creation, a quintessence of luxury and prodigality, not utilizable in this world[,] . . . the heightened artificialism of Des Esseintes, the systematic deranging of all the senses. . . . There was also silence: that icy silence, the work of Mallarmé—or the silence of M. Teste for whom all communication was impure. [*What is Literature?*, pp. 122–24].[108]

Whatever the cause ascribed to the movement, Sartre continues with his harsh criticism:

The extreme point of this brilliant and mortal literature was nothingness. . . . Flaubert wrote to disentangle himself from men and things. His sentence surrounds the object, seizes it, immobilizes

[108] It was probably not only a fear of a "déclassement" into the proletariat (for this possibility recall the fate Flaubert reserved for Berthe in *Madame Bovary*), which led these exceptionally gifted artists to estrangement from society. Their extreme refinement, which is, indeed, also a historical phenomenon, is plausible precisely as a way to resist absorption by the new masters, so productive, so rapacious and so sordid. Dandyism is an attempt at evasion from bourgeois norms, an evasion which, of course, could not lead anywhere.

it and breaks its back, changes into stone and petrifies the object as well [p. 124].

Even committed Naturalism is unacceptable to Sartre because its "determinism . . . crushed out life and replaced human actions by one-way mechanisms" (p. 125). These one-way mechanisms always depict the slow disintegration of an enterprise, a man, a family, a society.

Are we confronting here an *a priori* opinion on the nineteenth-century author, whom Sartre calls "a shame-faced bourgeois, writing for bourgeois without admitting it to himself"? The answer is in the negative, because Sartre does not rest his case on his historical hypothesis but on an analysis of the stylistic procedures of the author of this period:

> His technique betrayed him because he did not watch over it with the same zeal [with which he projected his "maddest ideas"]. It expressed a deeper and truer choice, an obscure metaphysic, a genuine relationship with contemporary society [p. 130].

Sartre finds a common technique in the writing of authors he considers widely divergent, say, Barbey d'Aurevilly, Fromentin, Maupassant, Daudet. In *Dominique* just as in most of Maupassant, there is what might be called the internal narrator: "one finds a primary subjectivity which manipulates the levels of a secondary subjectivity and it is the latter which makes the tale" (p. 133). In Maupassant, almost invariably, this storyteller looks back at a past episode of disorder from a secure present vantage point in polite society which cultivates respectful agreement with an order where any disquieting diversity or novelty has been reduced to a reassuring monotony.[109] Even when the device of the character-narrator has been abandoned, he remains present implicitly in the novelist's subjectivity

109 Furthermore, it can be pointed out, this storyteller is not always held to the objective technique advanced by Maupassant in his theories. Ernest Simon shows that in *Pierre et Jean* "the analytical clearly dominates the objective technique" ("Descriptive and Analytical Techniques in Maupassant's *Pierre et Jean*," *The Romanic Review*, p. 52).

through which the event has been filtered. In Daudet also, who, in his gracious manner, addresses his readers as Maupassant's *conteur* speaks to the guests in the salon ("Ah! . . . And do you know why? You won't guess in a million years!"), we find the same ceremonial evocation of the past. This author-narrator interposes himself between the event and his public, and thus creates a subjective past, that of his own memory, which is part, not of whatever is going on in the drawing room, but of a distant, closed period of time. In these narrations even the future is reduced to a past ("They did not think at the time that . . ."). Additional comfort is offered the reading listener by the literary device that attributes a wide experience to the raconteur which supposedly permits him to make universally valid statements ("Daniel, like all young people . . . ," or "Eve was quite feminine in that she . . . ," or "Mercier had the nasty habit, common among civil-service clerks . . . ," etc.). When Symbolism discovered the close relationship of beauty and death it made explicit the theme of mid-century literature, that of the beauty of the past.[110]

"Will anyone doubt," Sartre asks, "that I am aware how incomplete and debatable these analyses are?" (p. 144).[111] Yet, Sartre continues, it cannot be denied that in the last analysis,

> each particular work surpasses, in a certain way, all conceptions which one can have of art, because it is always, in a certain sense, unconditioned, because it comes out of nothingness and holds the world in suspense in nothingness [p. 146].

[110] For Sartre's concept of aesthetics as related to temporality, see above, pp. 57–62.

[111] Furthermore, Sartre had just stated: "The authors [of the latter nineteenth century] are not to be blamed; they did what they could; among them are some of our greatest and purest writers. And besides, as every kind of human behavior discloses to us an aspect of the universe, their attitude has enriched us despite themselves by revealing gratuity as one of the infinite dimensions of the world and as a possible goal of human activity. And as they were artists, their work covered up a desperate appeal to the freedom of the reader they pretended to despise" (p. 140).

To illustrate: Jansenist ideology, the rule of the three unities and those of French prosody do not constitute art. Racine's art is a reinvention of classic rules, achieved

> by conferring a new and peculiarly Racinian function upon the division into acts, the cesura, rhyme, and the ethics of Port Royal. . . . To understand what *Phèdre* could not be, it is necessary to appeal to all anthropology. To understand what it *is*, it is necessary only to read or listen [p. 145].

We know that for Sartre to read and to listen mean not simply to adopt the work's manifest content—within the limits prescribed by anthropology—but to correlate it to its style so as to reach its metaphysical core and make it explicit.

It is, then, with a keen awareness of the limitations inherent in all generalizations, which in this case permit only an approximation of the dialectical movement between author and reading public in different periods, that Sartre leads us to his concluding definitions aiming to discover, "be it as an ideal, the pure essence of the literary work" (p. 146).

Sartre calls "alienated" that literature which has no explicit awareness of its autonomy. In this category are works which in their singularity go beyond ideology, but only implicitly. "Abstract" literature, indifferent to its subject matter, poses only formally the principle of its autonomy. In "concrete" literature, on the other hand, formal aspects and subject matter crystallize. The aspiration for literary glory is a hope to attain universality, to find again and again—in a Nietzschean eternal return—the forum the author had in his lifetime, since he cannot reach out beyond a small reading public. In "concrete and freed" literature, at an ideal stage of "concrete universality," when all men in a given society would be readers and the object of an author's work, literature would be truly "anthropological." [112] Since no means for its realization are at hand, this is a utopia:

[112] See *What is Literature?*, pp. 146–51.

Thus, in a society without classes, without dictatorship, and without stability,[113] literature would end by becoming conscious of itself; it would understand that form and content, public and subject, are identical, that the formal freedom of saying and the material freedom of doing complete each other, and that one should be used to demand the other, that it best manifests the subjectivity of the person when it translates most deeply collective needs and, reciprocally, that its function is to express the concrete universal to the concrete universal and that its end is to appeal to the freedom of men so that they may realize and maintain the reign of human freedom [p. 154].

The tasks which literature can and should accomplish are set forth in the conclusion of the fourth chapter of *What is Literature?* Entitled "Situation of the Writer in 1947," that chapter leaves behind the willfully limited appraisal of past literary history, which considered primarily the author-reader relationship along with the author's role as a contestant or as an ideologist of the ruling circles. Now Sartre focuses on the currents prevailing in his own time and on delineating still more clearly his own role. He distinguishes three living generations of writers. The oldest, for the most part, made themselves known before 1914; some of them were still active in 1947. Representatives of the second generation made their entry on the scene after 1918, either as Surrealists or as individuals representing humanistic values (Jean Prévost, Pierre Bost, André Chamson, Claude Aveline, André Beucler, and others). The third generation, writing just before World War II and after, Sartre terms "ours."

Sartre sees the author of the first generation divided between his productive efforts at Cuverville (Gide), Frontenac (Mauriac), Elboeuf (Maurois), at the university (Romains) or at the embassy (Claudel), and a lingering belief, dating from Symbolism, in the absolute gratuity of art. He is divided be-

[113] Sartre had previously stated: "literature is, in essence, the subjectivity of a society in permanent revolution" (p. 153).

tween the spirit of seriousness and the spirit of contestation. His kind of literature seeks alibis in a morality which is summed up for Sartre in the remark of a young acquaintance that "one should do what everyone else does, and be like no one else." Whether we encounter the Gidian restlessness or the Mauriacian sin, "it is always a matter of proving that man is worth more than his life [an *a priori* essentialist concept], that love is much more than love [existence is more than as revealed in phenomena], and the bourgeois much more than the bourgeois [in an exercise of the spirit of seriousness]" (p. 168). According to some we have here an example of "the narrow-minded judgments" of Sartre, which are supposed to have led him "to the condemnation of almost all the writers whom [he] mentions, with the notable exception of the *philosophes* of the eighteenth century and the American novelists of the nineteen-thirties." [114] Yet, it is rather the generalization on Sartre as a critic which is both uninformed and pointless, not Sartre's own kind of generalization on certain literary movements, which he repeatedly qualified [115] because of his understanding of the unique and open-ended character of the great works in any literary school. Sartre himself is the first to point out:

> In the greater writers there is, of course, something else. In Gide, in Claudel, in Proust, one finds the real experience of a man, a thousand directions. But I have not wanted to draw a picture of a period but rather to show a climate and isolate a myth [p. 168].

As a reaction to the absurdity of World War I, the earlier generation's attempt at reconciliation came to be replaced by an attitude of resounding negativity. Surrealism wished to discredit the world of reality. Yet, according to Sartre, the Surrealist actually wanted to escape "consciousness of self and consequently of one's situation in the world." Surrealism is not Hegel's negativity, but

[114] Philip Thody, "Sartre as a Literary Critic," p. 62.
[115] See for instance above pp. 98 and 102.

The *Impossible* . . . the imaginary point where dream and waking . . . merge. Confusion and not synthesis, for synthesis would appear as an articulated existence, dominating and governing its internal contradictions. But surrealism does not desire the appearance of this novelty which it would again have to contest. It wants to maintain itself in the enervating tension which is produced by an unrealizable intuition [pp. 172–73].

Surrealism reconstructs only in order to destroy, in an attempt to leave behind the human condition. Still, Sartre pays tribute to its poetic achievement, its contribution to the liberation of man, which, however, is that not of total man but only of his imagination.

Somewhat eclipsed by the brilliance of the Surrealist fireworks but unperturbed by its display, a number of gifted authors concurrently treated of the everyday people in a laborious society. Prévost, Bost, Chamson, Aveline and Beucler adhered to a certain "discrete humanism" (p. 192). It is, they thought, possible to remain a man even in adversity. Will power, patience and effort replaced determinism in their understanding of their characters' modest existence in some profession, some friendship, some social solidarity or some sport. Because of the social origin, outlook and reading public of these authors, Sartre writes that "they made literature Radical Socialist" (p. 197). Their literature, as capable and attractive as it was unpretentious, did not rise to the level of tragedy in a period of tragic dimensions:

They limited themselves, in all honesty, to stories of lives which were ordinary and without greatness, while circumstances were forging careers which were exceptional in Evil as well as in Good. . . . Their lucidity dispelled within them that bad faith which is one of the sources of poetry; their morality . . . was revealed as inadequate for great catastrophes [p. 198].

Their influence in fact vanished just as did that of the Radical Socialist party.[116]

116 *Cf.* Thody's claim that for Sartre the literature of extreme situations is the only one, to the point "that he is unable even to consider the possibility of a

The third generation, "ours," rises up against the traditions of the reconciled "ralliés," who made up the first generation, and leaves behind "les radicaux" of the second, who share with the Surrealists a lack of concern for history. Malraux—in stark contrast to the quietism and subjectivism of his "radical" predecessors—"had the immense merit of recognizing as early as his first work that we were at war and of producing a war literature." As for Saint-Exupéry, who sketched "the chief features of a literature of work and tool," he pioneered "a literature of construction," as against the Surrealists' "literature of consumption" (p. 205).[117]

During the Nazi occupation, when torture and death were an everyday event, and in the period of the Resistance movement, man was more than ever steeped in history; he had no alternative but to choose his place in it. At that time only a literature of extreme situations, of metaphysical limits, was conceivable:

> What are Camus, Malraux, Koestler, etc. now producing if not a literature of extreme situations? Their characters are at the height of power or in prison cells, on the eve of death or of being tortured or of killing. There you have their everyday life. On every page, in every line, it is always the whole man who is in question [p. 217].

For Sartre, "metaphysics is not a sterile discussion about abstract notions which have nothing to do with experience. It is a living effort to embrace from within the human condition in its totality." So that he defines the task of what is actually existentialist literature as one "which unites and reconciles the

---

novel which describes fairly peaceful everyday events" (*Sartre, A Literary and a Political Study*, p. 68).

[117] "Surrealism ties in with the destructive tradition of the writer-consumer," writes Sartre (p. 169)—that is, one who imitates "the lighthearted squandering of an aristocracy of birth," and its nonproductive consumption. After 1918 one writes "in order to consume literature: one squandered literary traditions, hashed together words, threw them against each other to make them shatter" (pp. 126–27). One does not have to agree with Sartre's critique of Surrealism to appreciate his distinction in favor of Saint-Exupéry's "literature of work and tool."

metaphysical absolute and the relativity of the historical fact, . . . the literature of great circumstances" (pp. 216–17).

Having, doing and being are the three cardinal categories of existence as described in *Being and Nothingness.*[118] But it is in *praxis,* through an action in history to change its course, that we gain knowledge of being,[119] to which the other categories are reducible. And it is in *praxis* that we can obtain that synthesis of historical relativity and moral and metaphysical absolutes which is "our subject" (p. 233). For any *praxis* in a historical moment reveals also a general metaphysical truth.[120] As for this *praxis:* "What is the relationship between morality and politics?"

> We can, *if need be,* attack these problems in the abstract by philosophical reflection. But if we want to live them, to support our thoughts by those fictive and concrete experiences which are what novels are, we had *originally* at our disposal the technique which I have already analyzed here and whose ends are rigorously opposed to our designs [p. 217].[121]

Indeed, Sartre's major purpose and the conclusion of *What is Literature?* amounted to a self-evaluation as an author and critic, after *Being and Nothingness* had provided him with a definition of being and of beauty. What, then, are the stylistic techniques which Sartre proposes to existentialist committed

118 See pp. 433 ff., and above pp. 69–71.

119 "Things have as many aspects as there are ways of using them. . . . One knows the hammer best, says Heidegger, when one uses it to hammer. And the nail, when one drives it into the wall, and the wall when one drives the nail into it. . . . Saint-Exupéry has opened the way for us. He has shown that, for the pilot, the airplane is an organ of perception" (p. 232).

120 "I admit without difficulty the Marxist description of 'existentialist' anguish as a historical and class phenomenon. Existentialism, in its contemporary form, appears with the decomposition of the bourgeoisie, and its origin is bourgeois. But that this decomposition can *disclose* certain aspects of the human condition and make possible certain metaphysical intuitions does not mean that these intuitions and this disclosure are illusions of the bourgeois consciousness or mythical representations of the situation" (p. 244).

121 Sartre's critique is here directed at the various techniques of the traditional, "essentialist" novel of the nineteenth and twentieth centuries. (Words in italics above are my own translation—*cf. Qu'est-ce que la littérature?* p. 251.)

literature? They can be summarized briefly, since they have been elaborated in the course of this critique of preceding literary currents, especially those of the nineteenth century, which have already been considered here.

Since the author himself is "situated," he cannot claim objectivity; he can only write the novel of situations. He must "make the technique of the novel shift from Newtonian mechanics to generalized relativity" (p. 218) through the exclusion of an internal narrator or an omniscient witness. In the absence of "inner life," [122] no incursions into that domain nor explanations resulting from any knowledge about it can be valid. The privileged position of the author should, altogether, be limited through the presentation of his characters in the third person, through their actions and their speech. Furthermore, the use of the present tense is recommended as being nondeterminist; for it does not offer the past as an explanation, but rather duplicates the exact chronology of the consciousness of the character who also always faces the future in the present. "The multidimensionality of the event" (p. 222) can be approximated through the subjectivities of the various characters, through something similar to Joyce's "raw realism of subjectivity without mediation or distance," and, finally, through a temporality which does not permit the reader to survey the whole of the character's situation.[123] Things do not come to life in sheer description:

> We must plunge things into action. Their density of being will be measured for the reader by the multiplicity of practical relations which they maintain with the characters [p. 233].

[122] The metaphysical basis of Sartre's rejection of any "inner life" is discussed above, pp. 11–12. In its place, there is the fundamental project of the character, which the critic, rather than the author, should discover in its metamorphoses or entirely new departures. This thesis will be developed by Sartre especially in his *Saint Genet.*

[123] One sees clearly the filiation between these ideas of Sartre and some of the subsequent criteria of the anti-novel.

The stylistic procedures proposed by Sartre are intended to involve the reader, without any distance, in the character's consciousness, and this character is so fashioned as to approximate the living reader's structures of consciousness.

Such existentialist prose works, "if our results turn out successful, . . . will not be diversions, but rather obsessions. They will not give a world 'to see' but to change" (p. 231). The author's facticity will not give him any other option if he wants to remain lucid and in good faith. "We had to do our job as men in the face of the incomprehensible and the untenable, to wager, to conjecture without evidence, to undertake in uncertainty and persevere without hope" (p. 219).[124] The work of art is an "absolute end," opposed to bourgeois utilitarianism as well as to "the infernal circle of means" (p. 258) of the Communist party.

Art is gratuitous and offers itself to its reader as a categorical imperative (p. 229). Sartre claims no less than that "it is . . . up to us to convert the city of ends into a concrete and open society—and this by the very content of our work" (p. 268). However, the kingdom of ends has remained an empty abstraction because man has not been able to change his society into a socialist one, which for Sartre would constitute "the last means before the end" (p. 272). Sartre himself has pointed to the utopian character of this aim (see p. 154) as well as to the paradox inherent in any other approach to the kingdom of ends, since man would have to become a means even to this end.

"Meanwhile, let us cultivate our garden. We have our work cut out for us" (p. 234). Sartre's garden, like that of the equally untiring, irascible, forever provocative Voltaire, is that of wide commitment in the here and now: "for good will is not possible in this age, or rather it is and can be only the intention of making good will possible" (p. 270).

124 The responsibility of the author is discussed above, pp. 81–82.

Chapter 3

OCCASIONAL ARTICLES

Sartre, who was one of the first readers of Dos Passos and of Faulkner, of Camus and of Ponge—among others—was also the critic to coin the term "anti-novel" for the kind of novel which is a contestation of itself. In his preface [1947] to Nathalie Sarraute's second book, *Portrait of a Man Unknown*, Sartre bestows high praise on an author who was eventually to become one of the exponents of the anti-novel school of literature that would displace existentialist literature from its dominant position. Madame Sarraute has subsequently stated herself what she meant and means to do as an author: "Not only does the novelist no longer hardly believe in his characters, but the reader, on his part, can no longer bring himself to believe in them." [1] Madame Sarraute tells us [2] that already as a child she was struck by her elders' change in attitude depending on the person to whom they were talking. She met what she calls "imitative feelings" for the first time in literature when reading *Madame Bovary*. Yet Nathalie Sarraute feels that the greatest

[1] *L'Ere du soupçon*, p. 56.

[2] I refer to lectures of hers at the Harkness Theatre, Columbia University, on February 3, 1964, and again on April 12, 1966.

literary influence on her is that of Dostoyevsky. She notes, for example,[3] the gesturing, the inflection of voice, the ungainly choreography, the clowning speech, in which Dostoyevsky reveals "the underlying movements" for which everyday speech is the accepted deception. Nathalie Sarraute wanted to be and has become the author of the "subconversation."

It is interesting to note that, in a very few pages, Sartre shows a keener understanding of the first two books of Madame Sarraute than the novelist, a subtle critic in her own right, has gained of her own work. Sartre is far from contradicting Nathalie Sarraute, but already simply as the "other" he possesses the better vantage point.

In the effort to avoid the reader's and one's own suspicion that characters are fashioned according to some time-honored prescription, the modern novelist generally reflects more acutely than ever on his technique, "the novel is reflecting on its own problems."[4] Madame Sarraute tries to preserve "her sincerity as a storyteller" (p. 137) by presenting her characters from the outside in such a manner that their underlying tendencies—their "tropisms"—can be guessed from that surface appearance. Sartre finds Nathalie Sarraute's theme in *Portrait of a Man Unknown* to be Heidegger's "das Man" and "das Gerede"—the "one" and the "talk"—by which he designates everyday trivial conversation. Beyond this protective curtain of inauthenticity lies the ontological truth which sometimes rises to threaten a character's poise, and usually betrays itself in precipitous speech, unseemly gesturing, an "unnatural" tone of voice, a barely noticeable "irrational" response and so on.

[3] *L'Ere du soupçon,* pp. 24–28.

[4] Preface to *Portrait, Situations,* p. 136. This trend, which Sartre sensed as early as 1947, is today more dominant than ever. Nathalie Sarraute was to write *The Golden Fruits,* which, with literary criticism as its theme, is in a way her most modern novel. Does not the contemporary painter or composer tell us before anything else and very bluntly: this is my technical innovation? It is as such that his work depends on the critic for its success, and it is as such that it is experimental and most often ephemeral.

There is, then, an intuitive apprehension of such signals as threats to the reassuring understanding which it is everyone's aim to maintain. Again, for Sartre the critic, all of this becomes apparent in the author's style:

> The best thing about Nathalie Sarraute is her stumbling, groping style, with its honesty and numerous misgivings, a style that approaches the object with reverent precautions, withdraws from it suddenly out of a sort of modesty, or through timidity before its complexity, then, when all is said and done, suddenly presents us with the drooling monster, almost without having touched it, through the magic of an image. . . . She has achieved a technique which makes it possible to attain, over and beyond the psychological, human reality in its very *existence* [pp. 140–41].[5]

Sartre believes that for Nathalie Sarraute man is not a character, not a story nor a set of habits but "a continual coming and going between the particular and the general" (p. 140). This particular, "an intangible authenticity" (p. 141), would seem to have to be something highly individual, yet Madame Sarraute has repeatedly told us of her conviction that in their tropisms all people are alike. Not only does this fine and perceptive author go beyond psychology, as she maintains, she actually bypasses also the moment of existential choice to probe still more deeply into a mineral and vegetal magma, the primeval source of man's motions and emotions.

> It suffices to read in *L'Humanité*—"A corpse has just died"—to realize how heavily this man of eighty-four, who scarcely wrote any more, weighed upon today's writing.[6]

But, at his death, Gide was also displeasing to many in different quarters. As a matter of fact he united against himself "the

[5] In her New York lectures Madame Sarraute explained that the two levels she portrays—that of the banal surface appearance of the traditional "character" and that of his inner movement, the tropism, underlying it—appeared in her novels instinctively at first. Only later did she realize this difference in style and meaning.

[6] "The Living Gide," *Situations*, p. 50.

righteous" of the right and of the left.[7] In the face of this conjunction Sartre wishes to treat not of what separated him from Gide but rather of "the priceless gifts he bestowed upon us" (p. 50).

Gide's life was "a rigorously conducted experiment" (p. 52), through which, Sartre says, he has enlightened us more fully than by a hundred demonstrations. In the process he freed literature from the fetters of second-generation symbolism.[8] After careful deliberation and with great caution, which show in his concern with writing well, Gide has with equally great courage ventured to say all in his *Corydon,* the *Journey to the Congo* and the *Retour de l'U.R.S.S.* His "wary audacity" provides the internal tension of his work, "this play of counterbalances," which parallels that of his puritan constraint and his hedonistic nonconformism.

> Every truth, says Hegel, has become so. We forget this too often, we see the final destination, not the itinerary, we take the idea as a finished product, without realizing that it is only its slow maturation, a necessary sequence of errors correcting themselves, of partial views which are completed and enlarged. Gide is an irreplaceable example because he chose, on the contrary, *to become his truth.* Chosen in the abstract, at twenty, his atheism would have been false. Slowly earned, crowning the quest of half a century, this atheism becomes his concrete truth and our own. Starting from there, men of today are capable of becoming new truths ("The Living Gide," p. 53.)

This literary experience, conducted in the French tradition of lucidity and rationalism, prompts Sartre to consider Gide

[7] The single most striking consequence of this widespread attitude towards Gide was the fact that neither the French government nor any combination of private groups had prevented the dispersal by auction sale of the contents of the house at Cuverville and the sale of the house itself.

[8] Sartre, in his earlier article on Nathalie Sarraute, expressed the opinion that, in some respects, *The Counterfeiters* is an Anti-Novel. Indeed, even if we do not at all consider *The Journal of the Counterfeiters,* we have here a highly self-conscious novel. One should also note that, in part, Nathalie Sarraute's style is reminiscent of Gide's in its classical understatement and its use of innuendo.

beside Hegel, Marx and Kierkegaard, as one of the points of reference for French thought of the last thirty years.

When Léopold Sédar Senghor was about to publish an *Anthologie de la nouvelle poésie nègre et malgache,* he asked Jean-Paul Sartre to furnish him with an introduction. Sartre entitled his sizable contribution "Orphée noir," because he sees a descent by the Black poet into his past in order to understand his present situation by probing into the meaning of his "negritude." Like Eurydice, however, it vanishes in the process of definition and becomes a universal value.

Sartre, thanks to his existentialist field of reference, can describe the broad history of the Black peoples so as to intersect and connect this history with the innumerable individual destinies which are involved. For three thousand years the Negro has lived under the gaze of the white man and the Negro's color obliges him to assume his condition in authenticity. It is now on the level of reflection that he attempts to take stock of his condition, that he interiorizes the objective history of his race in order to seek within himself what these poets have termed negritude. Thus reappears subjectivity, the relationship one has with oneself, the source of all poetry." [9] Another cause for poetic expression is a problem of language, the need to negate the white's French prose.

Unlike the hundred different topics encountered in an anthology of white poets, here we find only one major theme: the manifestation of the Black soul. The memory of slavery continues to haunt the Negro.[10] Later colonial and quasi-colonial developments have deepened the belief in a manicheistic division into black and white, in which the values that the white's language has conferred on the colors have been inverted. At the

[9] "Orphée noir," *Situations,* III, 239.

[10] "My todays open each on to my past/wide eyes that roll with rancor with/shame" ("Mes aujourd'hui ont chacun sur mes jadis/de gros yeux qui roulent de rancoeur de/honte" [Damas, poet from Guayana, *ibid.,* p. 273]).

same time, the non-African meditates on his exile[11] and his hope for a return to the African continent, which is a return to its past as much as to its future.[12] The Black poet turns his back on European technology,[13] and unlike the French poet he has not been severed from folklore by ten centuries of learned poetry. He remains or places himself under the spell of native rhythms, so that it seems to Sartre that the tom-tom is leading to a poetic genre like the sonnet or the ode of the Western past. To the white man and his knowledge of tools the black man opposes his intuition of the land[14] and, altogether his understanding through sympathy—in Bergsonian terms, through intuition rather than intelligence. As a laborer in the field, he is an agent of the fertility of nature, and in the poetry of Senghor, of Rabéarivelo and of Laleau there appear images of erotic pantheism.

The Negro's agricultural passivity and patience are counterpoised as wisdom to the white engineer's frenetic and absurd activity. The Black stresses his ability to endure and last through untold hardship, but he is anti-Christian in his rejection of dolorism; he refuses to suffer, he is aggrieved and injured, but he is not guilty. Still, Sartre terms negritude a Passion. The Negro's Fall[15] was the onset of slavery and colonialism; his Redemption will be his freedom; and in the process he has assumed the human condition of all, even of the white man. There is a Black epic, with its golden age, that of tribal Africa, an era of dispersion and of captivity, a time of awaken-

11 The "eternal boulevards of cops" ("éternels boulevards à flics" [*ibid.*, p. 241]).

12 "A new myself of what yesterday I was/yesterday/without complications/yesterday/when arrived the hour of uprooting" ("Nouveau moi-même de ce qu'hier j'étais/hier/sans complexité/hier/quand est venue l'heure du déracinement" [*ibid.*, p. 242]).

13 "Those who have invented neither gunpowder nor the compass" ("Ceux qui n'ont inventé ni la poudre ni la boussole" [Césaire, *ibid.*, p. 264]).

14 "Porous to all the winds of the world" ("Poreux à tous les souffles du monde" [*ibid.*, p. 264]).

15 *Cf. Being*, p. 263: "My original fall is the existence of the Other."

ing, periods of heroic revolts and, then, the upsurge towards total liberation.

Sartre claims that to Mallarmé poetry was "an incantatory attempt to suggest being in and through the vibratory disappearance of the word" ("Orphée Noir," p. 246). He cites Mallarmé's "to evoke, in a deliberate obscurity, never directly, the object left unspoken by allusive words, which reduce to an equal silence, calls for an endeavor close to creation." [16] Sartre believes that this silence is reached by clashes of words which obliterate language and he returns to his conviction, already developed in *What is Literature?*,[17] that from Mallarmé to Surrealism the aim of French poetry had been the destruction of language. The Negro poet also seeks to destroy a language that is white, while bursting out with rhythms and aspirations which he nonetheless has to express in its words. "The black herald is going to degallicize them; he will pound them, break their usual associations, couple them by violence" (p. 247).[18] For David Diop, the Negro is still "black as misery," but for Césaire he is not deprived of light, he exists as refusal.[19] Freedom takes on the color of the night, and freedom is the point of departure and the ultimate aim of negritude. And if Sartre detects in Lero a certain impassibility and impersonality,[20] in Césaire's poems an explosive projection carries us forward in a "perpetual surpassing." For once, Sartre writes, pure poetry is committed as "committed automatic writing" (p. 258, see also

[16] ". . . évoquer, dans une ombre exprès, l'objet tu par des mots allusifs, jàmais directs, se réduisant à du silence égal, comporte tentative proche de créer . . ." ("Magie," Pléiade, p. 400).

[17] See above, p. 107*n*.

[18] "With little steps like roller-bearings/with little steps like a seismic tremor" ("A petits pas de roulements à billes/à petits pas de secousse sismique" [Césaire, *ibid.*, p. 247]).

[19] "Our faces beautiful as the real operative power of negation" ("Nos faces belles comme le vrai pouvoir opératoire de la négation" [Césaire, *ibid.*, p. 251]).

[20] "Where Spring does its nails/The propeller of your smile thrown afar" ("Où le printemps se fait les ongles/L'hélice de ton sourire jeté au loin" [Lero, *ibid.*, p. 256]).

p. 285). And this is not a contradiction in terms, so overriding is the unique obsession, even when it is prereflective and no matter how variously it is expressed.

Negritude is not an aim, it is the antithesis to the white civilization, a conflict to be resolved in nonracism. "Like all anthropological notions, negritude is a shimmering of being and having to be, negritude makes you and you make it: at once oath and passion" (p. 279).[21] The Negro poet assumes what the others have made of him, and in his rhythms and his "Geste noire," in his passion and in his refusal, we reach "that nudity without color" (p. 282) which speaks for us all.

In a "lettre au directeur des *Temps Modernes*," Albert Camus took exception to a critique of *The Rebel* by Francis Jeanson which had been published in Sartre's magazine in 1952. In his "Reply to Albert Camus," Sartre starts out by upbraiding Camus for his third-person approach to Jeanson, which—worse still—suddenly leads to an amalgam of Jeanson and Sartre when Camus treats of "your article," writes that "*you* had no right" and the like. The acrimonious tone at the outset of the reply and its bitterly polemical development, which take up more than half the "Reply," astonish as much as Camus's device of supposedly answering Jeanson in a lengthy and accusatory letter in which he actually confronts Sartre, his comrade-in-arms for a decade. The explanation for their mutual irascibility is to be found in the fact that both had come to feel that a break was as inevitable as it was painful. Indeed, Sartre has never written so enthusiastically about any person or author as about Camus in this very letter of "rupture."

Already towards the end of 1946 a sharp political dispute had divided Camus (and Koestler, then in Paris) from Sartre who, incredibly enough, supported Merleau-Ponty's position in

21 "The seas lousy with islands cracking flame-throwing roses between their fingers and my lightning-struck body intact" ("Les mers pouilleuses d'îles craquant aux doigts des roses lance-flamme et mon corps intact de foudroyé" [Césaire, *ibid.*, p. 259]).

defense of the Moscow trials.[22] As Simone de Beauvoir notes: "Two things marked the beginning of that summer [1952]: Sartre quarreled with Camus and effected a reconciliation with the communists." [23] Their respective political evolutions are well known; they can best be summed up by recalling that Sartre later spoke out against the Soviet repression of the Hungarian uprising, whereas Camus, indeed, tried to stand aside from history with respect to his native Algeria.[24]

In the latter part of his "Reply" Sartre—with the spontaneity in point of view and in formulation that characterizes most of his literary criticism—sums up what Camus had been to him: an almost exemplary man in an "admirable conjunction

[22] At that time, Merleau-Ponty, who was to change his outlook radically, argued that, since what matters is the objective reality of one's acts not one's intention, Boukharine was subjectively only in opposition, but objectively a traitor to the Soviet Union (see Simone de Beauvoir, *Force of Circumstance,* p. 106). Madame de Beauvoir also tells us that "this quarrel was to last until March 1947," and goes on to explain—in 1963—that this "outburst" had taken place for the simple reason that "Camus was going through a crisis caused by the feeling that his golden age was drawing to a close" (*ibid.,* p. 111).

[23] *Ibid.,* p. 259.

[24] This was precisely the core of the debate between Jeanson and Camus referred to above. Condensing into one sentence his earlier criticism of *The Rebel,* Jeanson wrote: "I had reproached you for placing Evil in history and Good outside of it" ("Pour tout vous dire," *Les Temps Modernes* [August 1952], p. 359). On this same question of historical involvement, probably the most telling argument in Camus's "lettre au directeur des *Temps Modernes*" had been, that "nobody, excepting in your magazine, will have the thought of denying that, if there is an evolution from the *Stranger* to the *Plague,* it moves in the direction of solidarity and of participation" (*Les Temps Modernes,* p. 321).

An article which bears on this debate, while not referring to it, since it has been written *in memoriam,* is Justin O'Brien's "Albert Camus, Militant." O'Brien gives evidence for Camus's journalistic and oratorical militancy and for the commitment in his everyday demeanor which he had been privileged to observe personally. Yet one must conclude that Camus's steady journalistic contribution, begun early in his life in 1938, became after 1947 only an occasional voicing of opinion. And this perhaps because this one-time member of the Communist party had, earlier than Sartre, understood the—to them insoluble—dilemma of the alternatives of social evils and the totalitarianism, which as their remedy, is even worse (see *ibid.,* p. 15). Sartre himself wrote in a memorial article: "Torn by conflicts which must be respected, he had provisorily chosen silence" ("Albert Camus," *Situations,* p. 79). Camus—we know it also from his novels—was always committed to people. "Did he not say in the last year of his life that there were two places where he had been supremely happy? One was on stage either acting or directing a company of actors and the other was a newspaper composing-room" (O'Brien, p. 14).

of a person, an action, and a work." In the figure of Meursault and as the editor of *Combat,* Camus had embodied the conflicts of our epoch,[25] and had permitted us to progress in the knowledge of ourselves and of the world. "And you transcended them through your ardor to live them" ("Reply," *Situations,* p. 68).

To the theme of happiness in the coincidence of man and nature, originating with Rousseau and carried further by Breton, Camus had brought that of "the duty to be happy," so that man can be himself. Sartre interprets Camus's concept of "happiness" as being neither static nor dynamic, but as a tension which defines the present.[26] Camus has thus introduced "an altogether new shade of meaning to *morality.* To be happy, was to do the job of being a man" ("Reply," p. 69). In a world of eternal injustice—the absence of God—Camus refused "the fraudulence of the Soul and the Idea," but claimed that man had a meaning as the only being who demands one and that in creating happiness he can find it. But that would require a turning away from daily agitation and from historicity steeped in injustice:

> We can go no further: there is no place for progress in this instantaneous tragedy. An *absurdist* before the letter, Mallarmé already wrote: "(The Drama) is immediately resolved, in the time needed to show the defeat which unfolds there like lightning." [27]

And Sartre believes that the key to Camus's theater lies in this other sentence in Mallarmé: "The hero unfolds the hymn

[25] In his early review of *The Stranger* (see above, pp. 33–35), Sartre had analyzed the stylistic devices by which Camus filters out meaning from Meursault's speech and from the description of his acts, so as to manifest detachment from a world of absurdity.

The other work by Camus which Sartre esteems highly as "perhaps the most beautiful and the least understood" ("Albert Camus," p. 79), *The Fall,* also illustrates one of the modern dilemmas in the successive smugness and guilt of Clamence.

[26] One is here reminded of Meursault in his cell when he reflects that he has been happy and still is, in the light of his newly won knowledge about the absurdity of death and of society.

[27] Meursault, for one, lived a certain happiness in alienation, but only until —and that was inevitable—society and nature (death) claimed him.

(maternal) which creates him and restores himself within the theater, that it was part of the Mystery where this hymn had been buried" (cited, p. 70).[28]

Camus, in the classical tradition, remained hostile to history. But he had at last produced a synthesis among aesthetic pleasure, happiness and heroism, between contemplation and duty, "between Gidean plenitude and Baudelarian 'insatisfaction'" (p. 70), which had led him to embrace human solidarity. However, Sartre concludes, this synthesis was valid for only a particular moment in history, when both the humanism of an old culture and the contemporary absurdity and revolt were allied in the resistance against Hitler's Germany, which loomed as an evil of nature.[29] After the liberation, to be in history meant to take position man against man. Thus, in 1944 Camus represented the future, but in 1952 he stands for the past. And if history appears absurd to Camus, it is because he places himself outside of it and compares a world without justice to a justice without content.[30] For those who act and choose themselves in history there is some meaning.[31] And we cannot help doing just that, as best we can, since we are in history.[32]

[28] To illustrate: the everyday comedy of parental consanguinity or the ever-present posturing (somewhere or other) of charismatic power have certainly been dispelled in Camus's drama in *Les Justes* and *Caligula*.

[29] In *The Plague* a natural catastrophe metaphorically replaces one brought about by man.

[30] Sartre, who had disavowed Roquentin for his aloofness (see above, p. 68), now also takes issue with certain sentences in *Noces*—and indirectly with certain aspects of Meursault's "happiness"—sentences that seemed natural in the past but do not seem so at present. "We *know* that if not wealth, then at least culture, that priceless and inequitable treasure, is needed in order to find luxury in the midst of poverty" ("Reply," p. 74).

[31] We know that for Sartre the individual's choice and actions are a disclosure of knowledge and that it is his project that imparts a particular meaning to his environment (see above, pp. 67–68). Sartre had extended this phenomenological and existentialist view of the individual in the lived world to the historical arena in the "Présentation des *Temps Modernes*" (see above, pp. 77–80), and in "La Nationalisation de la littérature" (see above, pp. 80–82), and had already mentioned it in *Being* (see pp. 433–435).

[32] In practice, for Sartre, even more than for Camus, there were—in final analysis—only two political alternatives: that offered by the East, which he considers socialist, and that of the capitalist West.

Perhaps already alluding to *The Words* Sartre explains: "If you find me cruel, have no fear. Presently, I shall speak of myself and in the same tone" (p. 75). And he ends his "Reply" on a conciliatory note, with a promise to publish Camus's rejoinder, but with a vow of silence on his own part: "I refuse to fight you" (p. 78).

Camus died in an automobile accident on January 4, 1960. This event, entirely senseless, took place as if to verify the validity of a lifelong preoccupation with absurdity. That day Michel Gallimard was at his side, driving him from his home in the South of France to rejoin the life of Paris; Camus had the titles for a novel, an essay, a play—a cycle to continue, perhaps to complete, the two earlier ones of absurdity and revolt. Rarely, Sartre wrote, was it so necessary that an author live: "for us, uncertain, disoriented, it was imperative that our best men arrive at the end of the tunnel." [33] Camus affirmed "the existence of the moral fact" in our time against the Machiavellians and the realists and refused the uncertain roads of involvement. He *was* this affirmation, and as such a representative of the tradition of the moralists, whose works, holds Sartre, are perhaps what is most original in French letters. Camus, when writing, and even when silent ("What is he saying about it? What is he saying about it *at this moment?*", Sartre would wonder), constituted "one of the principal forces of our cultural domain" ("Albert Camus," pp. 79–80). And now? In a sentence reminiscent of Desnos's last poem, Sartre states: "The absurd would be this question which no one will any longer ask him, which he will no longer ask anyone, this silence which isn't even silence, which is absolutely *nothing anymore*" (p. 81).

The dialogue with Camus was of such vital significance to Sartre because Camus stood for one truth of Sartre—just as Paul Nizan [34] represented another one. Sartre, in spite of his

[33] "Albert Camus," p. 80.

[34] For Sartre's Foreword to *Aden, Arabie,* see below, pp. 257–60.

convincing case for historicity and involvement (which, however, did not have to lead him into his then somewhat simplistic choice of alternatives) showed himself able to value Camus's aloofness. Sartre himself moves between his awareness of contingency and his imperious need for commitment. And thus, Camus's later silence perhaps only anticipated a new synthesis. This aim—and this emerges clearly from Sartre's three progressively more enthusiastic critical articles—continues to exist as Sartre's temptation.

Although not dealing with literature, three articles—written from 1946 to 1950—concerned with the plastic arts and music, ought to be mentioned, since they further clarify Sartre's critical procedures in related fields. Calder's mobiles, whose girations by fits and starts Sartre describes, are seen as existing between stability and movement, between matter and life, and as both technical combinations and lyrical inventions. They suggest to Sartre Calder's metaphysics: they are sensible symbols "of that great vague Nature . . . which can just as easily seem the blind interlocking of cause and effect, like a timid unfolding, forever arrested, disturbed, crossed, by an Idea." [35]

The painter knows he is creating an imaginary object in an imaginary space (the unreality of the third dimension having brought about an early recognition of that of the other two), but the sculptor has always produced an imaginary object in real space. The viewer, then, is at a real distance from an imaginary object: at close range it reverts to its condition of carved stone. Alberto Giacometti is, according to Sartre, the first to endow his sculptures with a built-in distance.[36] Giacometti's elongated man is all essence. One does not have to move about one of his figures to get to know it; one recognizes

[35] "Les Mobiles de Calder," *Situations,* III, 311.
[36] "La Recherche de l'absolu," *Situations,* III, 289–305.

immediately its gesture, which remains the same no matter what distance or angle the viewer takes from it. Giacometti has shown man in the only truly human unity, that of the human presence behind the act. Until now, sculptors had sought vainly to create the illusion of being, but this absolute was fragmented into innumerable points of view; whereas Giacometti, who sought a "situated appearance," has found the absolute. Sartre had earlier considered Calder's mobile an absolute. In its movement it is unpredictable and "forever renewed" (like Valéry's sea), while Giacometti has succeeded in fixing distance. The absolute means to Sartre to be independent of, not relative to, man.

Music is an art which does not signify, that is, it is not an object which leads to another object. Its signs (its sonority) constitute its very object. In prose literature the sign is distinct from its object; one may forget the words and retain the theme. But in any art the meaning is never distinct from its object:

> I would say that an object has a meaning when it incarnates a reality which transcends it but which cannot be apprehended outside of it and which its infiniteness does not allow to be expressed adequately by any system of signs: it is always a matter of a totality, . . . of a person, milieu, time or human condition." [37]

Music, then, does not signify anything specific, but it is of its epoch and partakes of a *Weltanschauung*.[38] If for no other

[37] Preface to René Leibowitz's *The Artist and His Conscience, Situations,* p. 150.

[38] "[Bach] taught how to find originality within an established discipline. . . . He demonstrated the play of moral freedom within the confines of a religious and monarchical absolutism . . . [through] the infinite variations which he performs, the postulates which he constrains himself to respect." Beethoven, on the other hand, "rhetorical, moving, sometimes verbose, . . . gives us with some delay, the musical image of the Assemblies of the French Revolution" (pp. 153–54). One can readily see that these "translations" which may be relevant to the understanding of the composer add only little to that of the composition and next to nothing to musical enjoyment. In any art as "secret" as music, verbal explanation can hardly go beyond the technical discourse of musical theory. Bach may represent "originality within an established discipline" more specifi-

reason than that, simply within the limits of its medium, in the words of Malraux, "all creation is at its origin the struggle between a form in *potency* and in an imitated form." [39] Still, Sartre, with an exception made in regard to the eighteenth-century French composers, doubts the possibility of a "musical commitment" as advanced by René Leibowitz. And, though in this very article he had made all kinds of allowances for Soviet absolutism, Sartre concludes with a forceful rejection of Zhdanov's demand at a Congress of Soviet writers for didactic works.

As in the early reviews (considered in the first chapter), Sartre in the occasional articles examines the various artistic forms—the style of the first full-fledged novel by Nathalie Sarraute, the dynamic aspects of Calder's mobiles, the configuration of Giacometti's statues—in order to reach the metaphysics they express. Furthermore, until his article "The Living Gide," Sartre had never stated so clearly his contention that a literary "becoming" has the validity of a theological or philosophical demonstration. And there is now in these writings, just as in the contemporary or immediately preceding programmatic articles, a new concern with the historical implications of literature—of Gide, of the Negro poets, of Camus (and even of musical compositions). These articles represent Sartre's first attempts to focus his phenomenological and existentialist critical method on the author as he faces and reflects history.

---

cally than other composers, but he does not necessarily treat of "moral freedom within . . . absolutism."

[39] For the word in italics, see *Situations,* IV, 22.

Chapter 4

EXISTENTIALIST PSYCHOANALYSIS IN BIOGRAPHICAL INTERPRETATION: *BAUDELAIRE*

In *Being and Nothingness* Sartre had described man's freedom which he exercises in an initial choice: man is his own project. And while this is always the being-in-itself-for-itself, the impossible synthesis of fixed being and elusive existence—as established in ontology—the concrete aspect of this project varies from individual to individual. It has thus to be revealed by an existentialist psychoanalysis. In an introduction to an edition of Baudelaire's *Ecrits intimes*[1] Sartre, in line with this approach, intended primarily to demonstrate that the poet had, indeed, chosen his destiny. In the words of Michel Leiris this biography is not "the life of a saint, nor yet a clinical case history," but "the adventure of freedom,"[2] that is, the history of a consciousness.[3] Yet in conclusion Sartre will also furnish an

1 Editions du Point du Jour, 1946; written in 1944, that is, shortly after *Being*.

2 Prefatory "note" to Sartre's *Baudelaire*, p. x.

3 Simone de Beauvoir recalls that Sartre's aim to understand the moments of a life from the point of view of its totality was not recognized by the critics—excepting Blanchot—who accused him of failing to understand the character of poetry. But Madame de Beauvoir astonishes us with these lines of her own on Sartre's *Baudelaire:* "[It is] a phenomenological description; it lacks the psychoanalytical dimension that would have explained Baudelaire on the basis of his body and the facts of his life history" (*Force of Circumstance,* pp. 44–45). As

explanation for "the poetic reality" precisely as an expression of Baudelaire's fundamental choice of being and its complex manifestations.[4]

The initial choice of a person has been reached when one can describe his way of apprehending being, which is irreducible to anything further. In this search for a man's primary motivation Sartre accepts Freud's guiding principle that each manifestation, no matter how insignificant or superficial, can be related to his total personality, for man is not a collection of disparate characteristics, and nothing he does is purely accidental.[5] The aim of Sartre's existentialist psychoanalysis, which we will also see applied in his most considerable work of literary criticism to date, the *Saint Genet, Actor and Martyr,* is to decipher empirical behavior, so as to reach conceptualization. Its point of departure is experience; its pillar of support is a preontological comprehension of the person, which is intuitive and immediately given, even if not immediately understood; [6] its method is comparative and should serve to isolate the unique ontological choice from among its occasional and historical aspects.

---

will be seen, quite to the contrary, Sartre makes the most of an analysis of biographical data. And, furthermore, in this study not only does Sartre acknowledge the accepted Freudian psychoanalytical understanding of Baudelaire, limited though it is, especially by the impossibility of a dialogue with the living Baudelaire, but the main purpose of the book is to go deeper through existentialist analysis.

[4] "There is actually not a single page . . . which is not clarified by reference to *Being and Nothingness,*" observes Georges Blin in the chapter "Jean-Paul Sartre et Baudelaire" in his *Sadisme de Baudelaire,* p. 120.

[5] See *Being,* pp. 459 and 568. This principle, a premise for Sartre's *Baudelaire* (and his other major critical works) is disregarded by Georges Blin who, along with much favorable comment and support, criticizes part of the *Baudelaire* as an "abusive indictment" (p. 123). And this, in final analysis, because "in his system Sartre has not made sufficient allowance for chance, distraction, fatigue and inertia" (pp. 139–40). Also, if Baudelaire, as Blin maintains, adopted accepted mores "as a game, as a dare or a kind of bravado" (p. 127), this would still have to be related to his total personality. It would have been, indeed, "the freeest kind of choice" (p. 127) only if it had led him to face up to his own truth rather than to hide it.

[6] See below, p. 148.

Existentialist psychoanalysis follows Freud in the first principle (mentioned above) and in some others, all of which are premises necessary for further investigation. There are, then, a person's myriad manifestations, objectively discernible, which symbolize fundamental structures. Furthermore, each person is taken to have a history; it is therefore not some static and constant state of mind but the direction and orientation of his evolution, and of the difficulties he may have encountered, which are to be uncovered. No conclusions can be drawn from some "primary givens," hereditary tendencies or character traits which precede a person's history. Finally, the crucial event of this history must be considered anterior to a logical stand, for it is this event which leads to the individual's train of thought.

In contradiction to what Sartre terms "empirical psychoanalysis," existentialist psychoanalysis, first of all, firmly rejects every and any factor of determinism. The initial choice, the instant of freedom, and not a libidinous attitude brought about by early family life, is the irreducible first moment, the crucial event, of a person's history. Sartre's phenomenology does not make allowance for any subconscious structure. (Would not the "censor," postulated by Freud, have to know what to repress and what to disguise? Sartre considers that apologetic references to the subconscious or to traumatic or childhood experiences are invariably advanced in bad faith.) However, Sartre maintains, since an individual does not live at any distance from himself, he cannot have a knowledge of his consciousness; [7] it is the practitioner of existentialist psychoanalysis, for which Sartre only proposes the guiding principles, who is to provide the individual with the awareness of his own fundamental project. Such an analysis cannot interpret symbols as if universally valid,[8] but will have to understand them on an

[7] For this baffling distinction between "consciousness" and "knowledge" see above, pp. 68–69*n*40.

[8] This should meet Georges Blin's objection to the *Baudelaire,* when he states

individual basis, and may even have to reinterpret them since the person under analysis may have reoriented his basic aim during his lifetime. And this analysis focuses not only on dreams, lapses, failures, obsessions and neuroses but also on waking thoughts, on successful and normal pursuits, on style, on a preference for particular things[9] and so on.

The criterion for the success of this analysis lies in the number of phenomena it can explain and integrate, as well as in the intuition that one has reached an irreducible self-chosen motive. Existentialist psychoanalysis, wrote Sartre,[10] is still awaiting its Freud, "at most we can find the foreshadowing of it in certain particularly successful biographies." Sartre went on to express the hope that he might himself write one of Flaubert and another of Dostoyevsky. At this point, Sartre's studies on Baudelaire and on Jean Genet and the essential presently published articles on Flaubert, are such analytical biographies, all the more successful since they did not depend on some intuitive anticipation but were designed to illustrate and to round out a set of guidelines for a critical method which ought to take us a considerable step further in the understanding of literary figures and their creations.

Certain reviewers of the *Baudelaire* have suggested that Sartre's interest in the poet lies in a certain biographical parallelism, since both the poet and the critic lost their fathers at an early age and saw their mothers remarry soon thereafter.[11] But contrary to Freud and these more or less Freudian critics,

---

that "a man's experience remains inseparable from the terms in which he has related it" (*Le Sadisme de Baudelaire,* p. 135).

9 For the psychoanalysis of things, see *Being,* pp. 600–7; and above, pp. 39–41 and 71–72.

10 See *Being,* pp. 568–75.

11 An extreme reaction is that of Philip Thody (*Sartre, A Literary and Political Study,* p. 145). Thody goes as far as to see an identification of Sartre with Baudelaire and to claim that the poet is explained in terms of the critic's own experience and ideas. He simply confuses in Sartre's approach the ontological and the analytical. Sartre's ideas lead in the very opposite direction from identification when they seek Baudelaire's original choice as a point of departure for the evaluation of Baudelaire's own symbolism in his life and in his poetry.

Sartre rejects any mechanistic interpretation of the formative aspect of early family experience—as of any other—and not only does he deny its traumatic character but he makes the child's conscious interpretation of this and any other situation the decisive point of departure for the child's understanding of his being. What fascinates Sartre is precisely Baudelaire's uncanny lucidity, which, however, he used so as to become "the man who felt most deeply his condition as man, but who tried most passionately to hide it from himself" (p. 42).

Sartre's essay has no subdivisions, but one can clearly recognize three parts. A first one (to p. 99) represents, roughly, a "regressive psychoanalysis," in which—from an observation and interpretation of acts as they can be known from autobiographical statements and letters, from the prose writings, the poems and the testimony of contemporaries—one moves to Baudelaire's "ultimate possible," which is identical with the fundamental choice. A second part (pp. 99–172) can be seen to correspond largely to the "synthetic progression," in which one returns from this ultimate possibility of a person to his attitudes and "character traits," in order to see whether they can be integrated in the specific totality which a person is, or whether they lead to a reinterpretation or a revision. This is actually the process of verifying the hypothesis about this totality, which was arrived at in the first part. A conclusion (pp. 172–92) applies the insights of existentialist psychoanalysis to explain Baudelaire's poetic creation as an aspect of his project.[12]

Sartre knows that Baudelaire represents "an indissoluble

[12] See *Being*, p. 460, for the terms "regressive psychoanalysis" and "synthetic progression" in Sartre's method. Otto Hahn (see his penetrating "L'Œuvre critique de Sartre," *Modern Language Notes*, May 1965, who makes no reference to this method, observes also that the *Baudelaire* has two major parts (followed by a conclusion) which he calls the poet's "choice" and "conduct." He then subdivides the "choice" into the objectively observed in-itself and the subjectively felt for-itself; and the "conduct" into the "imaginary world" and the "relations towards others."

synthesis," of which he can only give descriptions which he calls "successive" (p. 185). He therefore presents us with five more or less complete reviews of Baudelaire's history, each time attempting a total portrait as seen from a particular structure of his life: his being, his consciousness, his aversion to nature, his relations with women, and, finally, his outward attitude towards himself and towards others. As Sartre moves from one cross-section to the next, in an ever-widening spiral, at first moving to the original choice, then rising to surface aspects, he keeps correlating more and more of his knowledge of Baudelaire. Then, in his consideration of "the poetic reality," as well as of the testimony of eye-witnesses, each of the many and often contradictory elements falls into place in an integrated totality. The axis on which Sartre's analysis of Baudelaire turns is the poet's dual choice of being.

Baudelaire must have come to realize early—he was six years old when his mother became Madame Aupick—that he was not justified in his existence, that he was expelled irrevocably from what he recalls as "the green paradise of young love's thrills." [13] Baudelaire remembers that especially among his playmates he was keenly aware of his solitude which he says he felt already then as his destiny.[14] In Sartre's opinion, Baudelaire realized his otherness, the "separation" from his mother which he called "my flaw," [15] with shame and rancor, but at the same time also with pride. Baudelaire in a moment of absolute commitment, even while affirming his deep resentment, wanted to be unique,

[13] "Le vert paradis des amours enfantines," *Les Fleurs du mal,* XLII; translated in *The Flowers of Evil and Other Poems* by Duke, p. 115.

[14] See "My Heart Laid Bare," p. 68, translation by Isherwood of "Mon coeur mis à nu."

[15] "On this point Crépet quotes a significant comment of Buisson's: 'Baudelaire was a very delicate soul—sensitive, original, tender—who had been flawed by the shock of his first contact with the world.' His mother's second marriage was the one event in his life which he simply could not accept. He was inexhaustible on the subject, and his terrible logic always summed it up in these words: 'When one has a son like me'—'like me' was understood—'one does not remarry" (*Baudelaire,* p. 17).

and to be himself the cause of his forlornness, so as not to fear its imposition from the outside.[16] Of course, Sartre can (and will) offer only circumstantial evidence for this definition of Baudelaire's original choice of himself, the ultimate possibility of which became, in self-deception, a Satanic revolt under God.

In his otherness Baudelaire lives at a distance from the world, but he also wishes to enjoy his position,[17] that is, to retrieve his uniqueness and to reach coincidence within himself. He is Narcissus always observing himself, never natural. So that with him everything is "faked," for his moods and his wishes "come into being *observed* and *unravelled*" (p. 23). "At this point the drama of Baudelaire began" (p. 25). All through life he will exacerbate his lucidity in a vain effort to see himself as others do, tense in desperate striving at recuperation of his consciousness as a thing. The impossible "Revealing, disquieting meeting,/When hearts see themselves mirrored back!" (Duke, p. 143) becomes the "I am the wound and the blade/ . . . /I am the limbs and I the rack" (Duke, p. 139),[18] in which the relation between two persons is projected into the one between his prereflective and his reflective consciousness.[19] But Baudelaire can no more seize his singularity than he can embrace himself; he lives his failure as *ennui*.

For those, Sartre says, who come to consciousness from a

[16] "Primarily a defense mechanism," Sartre writes, it is also "in a sense an *ascesis* because for the child it takes the form of pure self-consciousness. It is an heroic, an aggressive choice of the abstract, a desperate stripping of oneself, at once an act of renunciation and affirmation. . . . It is a stoic pride, a metaphysical pride which owes nothing to social distinctions, to success or to any recognized form of superiority or indeed to anything at all in this world. It simply appears as an absolute event, an *a priori* choice which is entirely unmotivated and belongs to a sphere far above any of those where failure could destroy or success sustain it" (p. 21).

[17] His entry in "My Heart Laid Bare" on his "sense of *solitude*, . . . the sense of a destiny eternally solitary" is followed immediately by: "Yet a taste for life and for pleasure which is very keen" (Isherwood, p. 68).

[18] "Tête-à-tête sombre et limpide/Qu'un coeur devenu son miroir!" and "Je suis la plaie et le couteau/. . ./. . ./Et la victime et le bourreau" (*Les Fleurs du mal,* LXXXIV, II and LXXXIII).

[19] See above, pp. 49–54, for an exposition of the two levels of consciousness and the effort at recuperation as they are described in *Being.*

world of all kinds of fixed beliefs and imperatives, there is meaning; but for those who like Baudelaire come to the world from consciousness, which has to invent the laws it wishes to obey, there is only futility. Baudelaire called his lack of conviction "laziness"; Sartre has no quarrel with the claim that it was pathological and perhaps to be classed under Janet's neurasthenia. "It must not be forgotten, however, that as a result of their condition, Janet's patients frequently had metaphysical intuitions which the normal person tries to hide from himself" (p. 32). Baudelaire had failed to reach his singularity, but he had found the universal structure of reflective consciousness. He symbolized this structure—elusive, transcendental and for him of the past, as we shall see—as the evanescent perfume that recurs in so many of his poems.[20]

Baudelaire, according to Sartre, defines man as a being who is forever going beyond something.[21] He felt the infinitude of consciousness in the determination of the present by the future, and he recognized this transcendence as "insatisfaction." This revelation and that of his gratuitousness should have brought him face to face with his freedom. Indeed, he complained of standing at the edge of an abyss and of forever feeling some vertigo; but he exerted his immense will-power [22] in an effort to hide from himself his freedom which might have severed him

[20] To cite a notable instance: "(There) are some perfumes. . ./. . ./in bold and infinite expansion/. . ./(which) unite to sing the joys of soul and sense" (Duke, p. 139). ("Il est des parfums . . ./. . ./Ayant l'expansion des choses infinies/. . ./Qui chantent les transports de l'esprit et des sens" [*Les Fleurs du mal*, IV].)

Pure stylistic criticism disregards biography and, in a kind of psychoanalysis of things, has explained the use of "perfume" as an archetype standing for memory and eternity. This method, as plausible as it is, in principle falls short of elucidating the specific use to which a term is put in a given poem, because it chooses to ignore the poet's deeper motivations. Indeed, according to Sartre too, memory and eternity are precisely the meaning the poet seeks in using this image. However, as we learn from the total Baudelaire, for him eternity is in the past.

[21] His way of seeing correspondences everywhere is part of his *élan* towards transcendence.

[22] One is reminded of Hegel's definition of will-power as a particular kind of thought.

from his mother, and from resentment and pride as his *raison d'être.*

With his acute power of cerebration, Baudelaire could not fail to appreciate (and practice) intellectual creation. But in his fear of freedom it was frequently of the re-creational variety, referring to something artificial, luxurious, already endowed with purpose by others. Baudelaire's milieu is the city, and he dwells on its more gratuitous aspects—its lights, "cosmetics, finery and clothes. . . . Baudelaire, who hated man and 'the tyranny of the human face,' discovered that he was after all a humanist because of his cult of the works of man" (p. 44).

But Baudelaire refuses that creation which would place him in the position of giving meaning to all other creations: that of a scale of values. Not men, only gods and prophets are capable of that, he wrote. Sartre contrasts Baudelaire, the man of "complete abdication," with Gide, who, "in spite of a thousand relapses, . . . has moved forward towards *his* morality" (pp. 49–50). It had never occurred to Baudelaire to contest "la famille"; he remained his mother's loving and fearful child throughout his life.[23] He accepted the severe judgment of his stepfather and of his legal tutor, he did not protest the condemnation of his poems by the court, he never truly challenged their authority and their criteria. In seeking a seat in the French Academy, Sartre notes, he behaved as if he sought judges rather than electors.[24] "If he had only once made up his mind to challenge the principles in the name of which he was condemned by General Aupick and Ancelle he would have been free" (p. 46).

Resentment and pride led Baudelaire to revolt, but in his

[23] Poignant reminders of this fact are his death in his mother's arms and the tombstone in the Montparnasse cemetery which has the name of Charles Baudelaire inscribed between that of his mother and Général Aupick.

[24] "Two chairs were then vacant, those of Lacordaire and of Scribe, and Baudelaire opted for the first one. This gesture created a scandal in the professional journals and even the popular press" ("Chronologie de Baudelaire," *Œuvres Complètes,* p. xxxvi).

fear of solitude he craved protection. He was not a revolutionary like Rimbaud, who wanted to change life, he was a rebel within a universe of secure meanings.[25] To characterize Baudelaire's dual aspirations Sartre recalls Jean Wahl's terms of "transascendance" and "transdescendance." In Baudelaire's own words: "There are in every man, always, two simultaneous allegiances, one to God, the other to Satan." [26]

After the description of Baudelaire's initial project as deduced from the outside, and constituting "a phenomenology of childhood," [27] Sartre then tries to make the poet's choice of himself intelligible from the point of view of Baudelaire's own reflective consciousness. Sartre, of course, is not looking for an unresolved Oedipus complex and denies any kind of traumatism, which would have inhibited Baudelaire for life. Since, in fact, Baudelaire was very much attached to his mother, and suffered from an early separation from her, Sartre seeks to find the seven-year old's reaction to this event, conscious no matter how obscure or complex or confused—imbedded in contradictory emotions—it may have been. "It matters little whether or not he desired his mother. I should rather say that he refused to resolve the theological complex which transforms parents into gods" (p. 55). The experience of his "flaw" was one of separateness and solitude. Heretofore he had felt that he was as his parents saw him, basking in the purpose they represented, and that even things had their rightful place since they had assigned it to them. Baudelaire continues to long for the absolute security of childhood, "because in infancy he was freed from the worry of living" (p. 57).[28]

[25] "Satanism itself . . . is a way of affirming belief," comments T. S. Eliot, who goes on to explain "that damnation itself is an immediate form of salvation—of the salvation from the ennui of modern life, because it at last gives some significance to living" ("Baudelaire," *Selected Essays, 1917–1932,* pp. 337 and 342–43).

[26] "My Heart Laid Bare," Isherwood, XLI, 73.

[27] Otto Hahn, p. 351.

[28] Later, Baudelaire extends this same attitude into adulthood. "J'eusse aimé

Solitude is the insufferable burden for the child and for the mature poet.[29] Only in bad faith can anyone try to escape it for "no man can place on others the burden of justifying his existence" (p. 54).[30] Baudelaire had recourse to self-deception for despite his pride in his singularity he stopped short of this metaphysical truth. He sought reassurance on all sides. He even used his feelings of rancor against his mother and General Aupick and other persons in authority in order to make of himself an object, even if one of scorn as a pariah. He continually tried to make them feel guilty for having abandoned him; but in preference to his independence, he indulged in a form of masochism when he elevated them to the position of judges,[31] so as to see them confer a stable "nature" on him.

Baudelaire, in selecting his jury, looked forward to being examined in the light of their criteria. And just as his God is without charity,[32] so are his judges. Even Madame Aupick, who remained linked for him to a happy and carefree childhood, had, after the death of General Aupick, to assume "in spite of herself the crushing role of judge" (p. 62).[33] Simply to accept

---

vivre auprès d'une jeune géante,/Comme aux pieds d'une reine un chat voluptueux" (*Les Fleurs du mal,* Vol. XIX); ("I wish I'd lived near a young giantess,/A sensuous cat who at his queen's feet lies"; Duke, p. 36).

[29] "He returned to the subject a hundred times in his letters to his mother. He described it as 'atrocious,' 'reducing him to despair.' Asselineau tells us that he could not bear to be alone for an hour" (p. 54).

[30] In this sense Sartre would accept Georges Blin's accusation that "Sartre condemns all those who have not chosen to be free" (*Le Sadisme de Baudelaire,* p. 126).

[31] In support, as so often, of Sartre's interpretation, Georges Blin cites from Baudelaire, in this case from a letter of May 6, 1861, to his mother: "Sometimes I have had the idea of calling a family council, or of appearing before a court" (*ibid.,* p. 109).

[32] His religious beliefs seem to have altered between mysticism and a religion without a personal God. "Even if God did not exist, Religion would still be Holy and Divine" (*Fusées,* Vol. I).

[33] To give just two examples from Sartre's documentation: After reminding his mother of a series of charming little incidents from their past, Baudelaire continues a letter to her—"Ah! those were for me the happy years of motherly love and affection . . . I was still living in you; you were mine exclusively. You were both an idol and a comrade" (May 6, 1861; Hyslop, p. 174). And by contrast from a letter written in 1860 when Baudelaire was 40 years old—"I must

their idea of good would have run counter to his resentment, his singularity and his creativeness. In his pride he wished to be his own creation and to recuperate his being, to seek confirmation of his singularity, in the gaze of the other. He aimed at possession of himself. But, "a man can only possess himself if he creates himself; but if he creates himself he escapes from himself" (p. 69).[34] One is reminded of Heraclitus's metaphor about the impossibility of stepping twice in the same stream. Still, one can possess a thing. So Baudelaire attempted to attain the impossible status of a "freedom-thing" under the severe gaze of his judges, which he provoked by doing evil while manifestly staying within their system of values, as evidenced by his reiterated "consciousness in evil."

Baudelaire opted to exercise his freedom in Evil (not in indifference or a separate set of values) and to be the fixed object of condemnation of the persons who represent the Good. He knows that his evil is without efficacity, just a fragmentary contradiction to a total system which readily absorbs it. Just as in such acts of evil so in the creation of a poem having evil as its object, "it is a work of luxury which is gratuitous and unpredictable" (p. 73). Such a poem is "a flower of evil." Sartre can now define

> the significance of his vocation as a poet. His poems are like substitutes for the creation of Good which he had renounced. They reveal the gratuitousness of consciousness; they are completely useless. . . . They remain in the sphere of the imaginary, leaving untouched the question of primary and absolute creation. . . . Each represents a symbolical satisfaction of a desire for complete autonomy, of a demiurgic thirst for creation [p. 70].[35]

---

tell you one thing which you've probably never guessed, I'm very, very frightened of you" (cited in *Baudelaire,* p. 62).

[34] Paul Valéry explains Baudelaire's originality as a poet especially in terms of his need to avoid imitating Victor Hugo ("Situation de Baudelaire," *Variété, Œuvres,* I, 598–613).

[35] In an article on Baudelaire, Maurice Blanchot notes that Sartre's evaluation of Baudelaire's personal life was equitable but that, nonetheless, his poetry was

Baudelaire's evil is his somewhat perverse eroticism, his pleasure ("volupté"). Here too he did not really compromise the good; it is only a playing with evil, some shivers of pleasure (a "frisson"), an empty game.[36] His ever-present acknowledgments of his sin, culpability and remorse are his way of expressing his inner climate of bad faith in bowing to ready-made values because they are ready-made. Torn between lucidity and self-deception Baudelaire, never venturing to the far end of either his own good or an "evil nature," forever oscillates between existence and being, between for-itself and in-itself. This frenetic flight from existence to being and from being to existence, this determination of Baudelaire "was *his* consciousness, *his* essential plan" (p. 81).

Perhaps, Sartre conjectures, at the bottom of the words "frightful," "nightmare," "horror" and others of similar connotation which abound in the *Flowers of Evil,* and of what has been observed as his "laziness," lies the poet's inability to believe in anything at all or take himself seriously, an indifference—so close to liberation—that is perhaps his real suffering.[37]

Baudelaire, like Narcissus, assimilated his reflective look to the gaze of the other.[38] Through self-punitive measures he

---

"a success . . . which has as its *raison d'être* this failure" of his life, a poetry which "draws the most brilliant truth from a fundamental imposture" ("L'Échec de Baudelaire," p. 81). Yet it is certainly not the kind of "brilliant truth" one encounters in Hugo, in Rimbaud or even in Mallarmé. Something that is unresolved or sickly manifests the poet's "dual postulation" also where he is extremely successful. It is perhaps partly in this sense that André Rousseaux remarked that Sartre's "masterful essay permitted him to understand better "what is so strange about Baudelaire" ("Le Baudelaire de Sartre," p. 2).

[36] "The supreme and unique pleasure of love lies in the certainty that one is doing evil" (*Fusées,* III, cited in *Baudelaire,* p. 76).

[37] Gaëtan Picon cites from a letter written to his mother in 1857: "What I feel is an immense discouragement, an unbearable feeling of loneliness, . . . a total lack of any desire. . . . I forever ask myself what is the use of this? what is the use of that? That is the real spirit of spleen." ("Baudelaire," *Histoire des littératures,* III, 944). Picon sees Baudelaire's work linked to his life and calls the *Flowers of Evil* "an existential creation" (*ibid.,* p. 945).

[38] See above, p. 132.

sought to live and to accentuate this division.[39] Thus he drew to himself disease and misery.[40] In his ostentatious dolorism Baudelaire expresses his resentment as a reproach to his mother and at the same time appeals for a condemnation which comprises absolution. "Suffering, he said, is 'nobility' " (p. 95). It is his way of comprehending the human condition: "In this sense suffering was the affective aspect of lucidity" (p. 96). It is also related to his "insatisfaction" which stems from his understanding of human transcendence. "If Baudelaire had gone on living his transcendence to the end, it would have led him to challenge Good itself, to move forward to other goals which really would have been his goals" (p. 98). But he only wants to live the negative aspect of his transcendence in his "dissatisfaction." Immense pride, and a sense of defeat, go through Baudelaire's work in the unexpressed cry of "*I am* Satan" (p. 99).[41]

One has generally recognized Baudelaire's major traits of character as his horror of nature, his cult of frigidity and his dandyism. But these, his ways of acting, are not the ones formed at first, even though they are his immediately and empirically observable ways of behavior. They are not independent phenomena, they only "reveal the transformation of a

[39] In *Les Paradis artificiels* an opium addict accuses himself but also finds excuses in the fact that he observes himself with "inquisitorial care": "How many other people could one find in the world of men who are as skillful in judging themselves and as severe in self-condemnation as I?" (cited in *Baudelaire,* p. 85).

[40] Sartre reproduces the four quatrains of a juvenile poem, which had appeared in *La Jeune France,* to show that it is "filth, physical wretchedness, illness and the poorhouse . . . that attracted him . . . in Sarah 'l'affreuse Juive.' " The uncharitable insolence of the poem expresses, in Sartre's view, Baudelaire's reflective reaction: he wishes to be free through his (sadistic) gaze (see *Baudelaire,* pp. 88–89).

[41] Simone de Beauvoir comments: "This is the demoniac attitude such as Jouhandeau has described it: one maintains stubbornly the values of childhood, of a society or of a Church in order to trample them underfoot. The demoniac is still very close to 'seriousness,' it wants to believe in it, it justifies it through its very revolt: it is lived as a negation and a freedom, but it does not actualize this freedom as a positive liberation" (*Pour une morale de l'ambiguité,* p. 77).

situation by an initial choice; they are the complications of this choice"; and as a matter of fact, "in each of them co-exist all the contradictions which disrupt the choice, but the contradictions are reinforced and multiplied by their contact with the diversity of objects in the world" (p. 100).

To Baudelaire, nature is bestial, virtue is artificial, "supernatural": "evil . . . is done naturally, . . . the good is always the result of art," he wrote.[42] But, Sartre notes, his demoniac evil is artificial and voluntary, and the critic cites passages in which the poet equates "natural" with "just" and "legitimate." There is, then, for the poet also a certain attraction to nature. His ambivalence is that of all those who have neither opted for themselves nor decided to follow once and for all the others' option.

Sartre, while on the whole putting little stock in Joseph de Maistre's influence on the poet, thinks that Baudelaire was ready to follow the broadly antinaturalist trend of his century, when Saint-Simon, Comte and Marx, among others, opposed a human order to natural injustice. Baudelaire's interest lies in human labor, inasmuch as it is "like a *thought* imprinted on matter" (p. 104). In untrammeled nature Baudelaire meets the gratuity of his consciousness, unlike in the city, where he prefers to dwell and where he can persuade himself that "a product of nature which has been manufactured and turned into a utensil loses its injustifiability" (p. 106). "I find unenclosed water intolerable. I like to see it imprisoned in a yoke between the geometrical walls of a quay" (cited, p. 105). It is also the proliferation in nature which runs counter to his ideal of singularity. Baudelaire displays an affinity for metals and minerals, because of their sterility and luminosity. He hated life, and steel seemed best capable of objectifying his thought in general.

[42] "Eloge du maquillage," *Œuvres complètes*, p. 1183.

If he felt a tenderness towards the sea, it was because it was a mobile mineral. It was because it was brilliant, inaccessible and cold with a pure, and, as it were, an immaterial movement. Because it possessed those forms which succeeded one another, that change without anything which changed, and sometimes that transparency, that it offered the most adequate image of the spirit. It *was spirit* [p. 109].

Baudelaire's style of living was likewise dominated by a fear of abandon to nature. Thus, he took great care to be impeccable in toilette and dress; at times he had his hair colored green. He also sought to disguise his need for food in his interminable disputes with practitioners of the culinary art. He made contradictory impressions on people: to some he seemed unctuous, to others brusque and dry; in either case he was not letting himself be natural. Finally, from his writings (*La Fanfarlo,* "Portraits de maîtresses" and other prose poems from *Le Spleen de Paris*) as well as from some biographical data, one is led to surmise that, in a form of fetichism, he preferred to the beauty of the nude, an artificial and luxurious array of dress and make-up.

Similarly, in his aversion for the natural, inspiration was shunned in poetic creation. Rather than in daring intuition and discovery, Baudelaire saw art in transformation and refinement.

When he came back, fresh like a stranger, to a poem which was already written and into which he could enter again, when he experienced the craftman's joy over changing a word here and a word there, which was derived from the pure pleasure of *arranging,* he felt that he was as far removed as possible from nature, most gratuitous and, as the passage of time had delivered him from the pressure of emotion and circumstance, most free [pp. 112–13]. Thus without absolutely denying the fact of poetic inspiration, the poet dreamed of substituting for it pure technique" [p. 112].

Baudelaire's cult of frigidity was, in some ways, another facet of his alienation from nature. Most often he was coldly polite and expected, in return, an icy reaction from others. He was seeking, as it were, the gaze of the Medusa which would freeze and solidify him. In his pride he did not want to be dominated by the stern look of a man, but he did seek it from women, whom he considered inferior. As always, Baudelaire refused to live any of his solutions to the end; he kept open a retreat from being to existence. In his life as in his poetry, the woman he adores is only a pretext[43] for dreams, in which he does not believe.

Marie Daubrun loved another man; in a letter to her Baudelaire explains that this is the reason for which he loves her with respect and profound esteem; he does not wish her to alter her attitude of unreciprocated love. In the same vein, Baudelaire left Madame Sabatier the day she believed and gave way to his entreaties. In his erotic game the inaccessible woman represents the judge; in it, frigidity stands for purity, impartiality and objectivity. At the same time he rebelled against his self-instituted judges, by recalling their images while in the company of harlots.[44] His masochistic attitude in making of himself an object of severity was reversed in his sadistic treatment of the lady's image.[45] "This large, frigid, silent, motionless form was for Baudelaire the expression in erotic terms of the social sanction" (p. 124). Altogether in such moments, Baudelaire succeeded in experiencing his dual postulation of Evil and Good. "It was not so much the incestuous love of his mother which made him seek authority in the women he desired," writes Sartre in a reduction of the Freudian interpretation, "his need of authority, on the contrary, led him to transform his

[43] Henri Peyre points out that Baudelaire, just as Shelley, needed a muse for his poetic creation (see his Introduction to *Baudelaire, A Collection of Critical Essays*, pp. 3–4). This is equally true for many other poets in different times, notably the troubadours. This explanation, while valid for all, has to be more closely examined to be relevant to each.

[44] "The thing that makes one's mistress dearer to one is an orgy with other women" (quoted in *Baudelaire*, p. 123).

[45] See above, pp. 65–67 (and *Being*, p. 364–412) for Sartre's ontology of love as a "system of indefinite reference" (p. 376) from subjectivity to objectivity, and in its exacerbated form—as here—from sadism to masochism.

mother like Marie Daubrun and the Présidente into a judge and an object of desire" (p. 123).

Dandyism was Baudelaire's deliberate and ostentatious way of showing himself to the outside world,[46] in keeping with the control he ceaselessly exercised in his protective antinatural and frigid attitudes. He tried also to counterpoise to the demands made by his consciousness the constantly renewed demands which dandyism was making on him. It also fit in with his intuition of transcendence and satisfied his need to limit it. Gratuitous in its refinement, insensibility and elegance, dandyism is "free," useless and inoffensive, on the margin but within the bounds of accepted mores. Furthermore, it corresponds to his ideal of achievement in effort. In his dandyism a posture of aristocratic superiority was not the fruit of heredity but of his own daily striving: "Baudelaire's nobility and his greatness as a man are due in a large measure to his horror of drift" (p. 134). This very special kind of effort upon himself responds to his intuition that he could recuperate his singularity in tension.

Sartre notes that only few authors, like Lautréamont and Rimbaud, and the painter Van Gogh, had the courage to live in solitude and anguish. Some like the Goncourts and Mérimée sought the protection of a parvenu aristocracy just as the authors of the two previous centuries enjoyed that of the old aristocracy. Flaubert pretended to live outside of bourgeois society in an eternal confraternity of great writers. Baudelaire felt that he belonged in it,[47] but personally was primarily interested in a more quintessential society of pure spirituality, that of dandies.

In keeping with dandy etiquette, Baudelaire was always impeccably dressed, though a little effeminately.[48] He did not

[46] See his "Dandy" *Œuvres complètes*, pp. 1177–80.

[47] "The Beacons" ("Les Phares") expresses this aspiration most clearly.

[48] The feminine aspect of his gait and of his attire may also be due, Sartre conjectures, to the poet's reliance on the opinion of others which is the lot of dependent women.

want the other to have any hold on him, and, to the contrary, wished to astound, to disconcert the stranger's gaze upon him. Thus he led it to his eccentric exterior, which, while also suggesting Baudelaire's uniqueness, protected him from any fuller recognition by the other. Once more, however, there is an element of self-punishment when, in his outlandish clothing, he lays himself open to a critical gaze; and, again, he limits its effects, since, having put up only a show, he can turn his back on his judges.

Dandyism, in which Baudelaire literally "makes himself" different from what he is, was admirably suited to accentuate his dissociation within himself and to provide him with the illusion of recuperation, of seeing himself in a mirror[49] in disguise, say in green hair, and in makeup, at a distance from himself as for others. It was the most outward manifestation of the contraries he cultivated: pride and rancor, for-itself and in-itself, existence and being, insatisfaction and transcendence, sadism and masochism, cause and object, tension and "laziness," harlots and ladies, city and nature, and evil and good.

In *La Fanfarlo* Baudelaire treats of a man who oscillates from tragedy to comedy, and in a passage of personal reminiscence he recalls that as a child he had, at times, wished to become a pope, a military pope, and, at others, a comedian. Sartre sees in Baudelaire an effort to make a poem out of his own life, to create it, to correct it, and rework it like a poem. "No one had had a profounder experience of the insoluble

[49] In an article which seems to have been written with the sole purpose of assailing Sartre, Louis Jourdain ("Sartre devant Baudelaire" [Sartre in front of Baudelaire], *Tel Quel*) dismisses Sartre's analysis of Baudelaire's consciousness to replace it with his own simplification concerning "the spiritual dimension of Baudelaire's poetics": "To explicate Sartre's undertaking it would be simpler, I believe, to abandon existentialism and to turn to the perspective of the pseudo-mirror" (No. 21, p. 91). He had earlier summed up Baudelaire in this paragraph of simple empirical description: "The theme of his work is easily discernible: to evoke beauty, beloved and condemned, with as a background or counterpoint, the imminence of the Fall and of the assumption of death" (No. 19, p. 83).

contradiction inherent in creative activity" (pp. 157–58) which consists in producing something out of oneself which one can hold before oneself as something other.[50]

When Rimbaud . . . defined his attempt by his famous 'I is another,' he did not hesitate to bring about a radical transformation of his thought. He undertook the systematic derangement of all his senses. . . . Baudelaire, on the other hand, . . . when faced with that total solitude where living and invention were identical, where his reflective lucidity was diluted into his reflected spontaneity, . . . became afraid. . . . His work as a creator merely consisted in the travestying and the ordering of things. . . . The conclusion of his act would be the poem which would offer him the image—rethought, recreated and objectified—of the emotion which he had felt. Baudelaire was a pure creator of form; Rimbaud created form and matter [pp. 158–59].

Baudelaire lived, a contemporary of Michelet, of Marx, of Proudhon and of Sand, in a time when the future gave meaning to the present. He had to make a considerable effort to turn his back on the future, as he did. Baudelaire eradicated the uncertain future from his present existence because, in spite of all his precautions, he suffered moments of extreme anguish. He lived his life in the secure past as if it had ended. Also, since the past is a person's nature, his character, Baudelaire, turning his gaze backwards, was able to see himself as others do.[51]

We may recall that for Faulkner also, in his "willful illusion," the direction of vision led to the past.[52] But, Sartre writes, for Faulkner the past can be seen through the present like a diamond block through a surface disorder: he makes a frontal attack on the reality of the present. Baudelaire was abler and craftier. He never dreamed of explicitly denying this reality; he

[50] See above, pp. 87–89, for an elucidation of the author's attempt to retrieve his being through the reader in Sartre's "Why Write?" a chapter of his *What is Literature?*

[51] See above, pp. 57–59, and the chapter on "Temporality" in *Being,* for the meaning of the past as an *in-itself* in existentialist temporality.

[52] See above, pp. 24–25.

simply refused to admit that it possessed any value. Value belongs to the past alone because the past *is* [p. 171].

For Baudelaire the values of the present were those of the past. His pleasure ("volupté") in decadence, which he imparted to his Symbolist followers, was one of retrogressing while living. For him, writes Sartre, "the present is a fall" (p. 172), which is felt in remorse and regret. He is the man he was, appropriating his essential being at a distance, but he also exists in his guilt, which for him lies in his exercise of freedom.[53]

Baudelaire's predilection for the past is related to his "poetic reality." Everyone attempts the impossible synthesis of existence and being in his particular way. What Baudelaire created in his life and his poems is what he called "the spiritual." This for him meant being in cohesion, permanence, objectivity and identity, it meant existence in some absence, in something invisible, in an extreme discretion. "This metaphysical levity of Baudelaire's world represents *existence* itself" (p. 173).[54] In his characteristic evocation of perfume, there arises a vaporized, spiritualized object of the past. The "spiritual" is a being which can be possessed by the senses, and which resembles consciousness. There are other symbols of an objectified consciousness: like shaded lights and distant music. Like perfumes they can almost be "consumed," they are thoughts retrieved. So are his poems—

each of them by its skillful rhythm, the deliberately hesitating and almost vanished sense which it gives to words and also because by an ineffable grace it is a restrained, fleeting existence exactly like a scent [p. 176].

[53] "If we want to catch a glimpse of the lunar landscape of this distressed soul, let us remember that man is never anything but an imposture" (p. 82), inasmuch as every man is a useless passion.

[54] In support Sartre cites "the admirable verses of 'Le Guignon' ["The Hoodoo"]: "Mainte fleur épanche à regret/Son parfum doux comme un secret/Dans les solitudes profondes" ("Full many a flower spreads in vain/Its perfume, for it must remain/In outer solitudes to fade" [Duke, p. 29]).

In Baudelaire's poetry "perfume" is synonymous with "thought" and "secret," [55] because they all express a transcendence, which he had also sought when he made one of Swedenborg's concepts his own in his "correspondences." Even in this ideal Baudelaire expresses his "dissatisfaction," his predilection for nonfulfillment, for Baudelaire's beauty [56] lies in a suggestion only, a suggestion of "this strange, forged type of reality where being and existence merged, where existence was objectified and solidified by being, where being was lightened by existence" (p. 179). Baudelaire has himself defined beauty as "something a little vague which leaves room for conjecture" (cited from *Fusées* on pp. 181–82). It is a moment of "dissatisfaction" where the eternal appears behind the individual, and which crosses the poem.[57] But Baudelaire, who refused the future, linked eternity to the past: [58] the meaning of "perfumes," "soul," "thoughts" and "secrets" lies in the past.

"A thing possessed meaning for Baudelaire when it was, so to speak, porous for a certain past and stimulated the mind to go beyond it in the direction of memory" (p. 183).[59] In Baudelaire the past is the eternal and also the "spiritual." This manner of existence *is* because of its past tense, and it is an object of passive contemplation, while somehow phantasmal

[55] Sartre points to passages from "Le Flacon" ("The Flask"), "Le Beau Navire" ("The Great Ship") and "Le Guignon" ("The Hoodoo"), p. 177.

[56] See above, pp. 54–55, for Sartre's ontological definition of beauty.

[57] T. S. Eliot, noting a discrepancy between the perfection of form and the unsettled state of mind in Baudelaire's poems, writes that "in the best of the slight verse of Théophile Gautier there is a satisfaction, a balance of inwards and form, which we do not find in Baudelaire" (*Selected Essays,* p. 339).

[58] See *Baudelaire,* pp. 171–72: "He asked the past to be the eternity which changed him into himself. . . . Is not the past definitive, unchangeable, out of reach?"

[59] Sartre also cites these lines from "Le Flacon" ["The Flask"]: "Il est de forts parfums pour qui toute matière/Est poreuse. On dirait qu'ils pénètrent le verre" ("Some perfumes are so strong that they will pass/Through any substances, including glass" [Duke, p. 89]). "The glass which is bathed in perfume," comments Sartre, "and which is at once sharp, polished, without memory, but which is haunted by a residual element, permeated by a vapor, is the clearest symbol of the relationship which existed for him between the thing which had meaning and its meaning" (p. 183).

and absent (like a delicate perfume, soft light or distant music). The painstaking and lengthy elucidation of Baudelaire's complex choice of being permits, indeed, "some explanation of the very particular form of Beauty which the poet chose and the mysterious charm which makes his poems inimitable" (p. 100). His ideal of being is an object existing in the present with the characteristics of the past.[60]

Sartre feels that if he could see Baudelaire live for only a few moments, he would obtain "total knowledge" (p. 185), an intuition of Baudelaire superior to the portrait he has been able to give of the poet.

> Immediate perception, indeed, is accompanied by a confused comprehension or, to borrow Heidegger's expression, 'pre-ontological' comprehension. It often takes years to make this comprehension explicit and it contains the principal characteristics of the object collected together in a syncretic indifferentiation [p. 185].[61]

[60] "Deep magic spells, which to the past belong,/But which to charm the present are bequeathed!" (Duke, p. 71.) ("Charme profond, magique, dont nous grise/Dans le présent le passé restauré!" [*Les Fleurs du mal,* XXXVIII, II.])

[61] It is a preontological perception inasmuch as it occurs almost instantaneously, before one can observe an unfolding of the phenomena of a person's being. In *Being,* Sartre had written favorably on Kretschmer's characterological studies designed to lead to a "physiognomy." "The character of the Other, in fact, is immediately given to intuition as a synthetic ensemble. . . . Here to learn is to understand, to develop, and to appreciate" (p. 350). Sometimes, Sartre holds, a work of art can transmit such a preontological intuition. He mentions the *Mona Lisa* and Houdon's *Voltaire.* "Certainly, Voltaire's smile was *significant.* It appeared at specific times, it *meant,* "I'm no fool" or "Just listen to that fanatic!" But at the same time, the smile is Voltaire himself, Voltaire as an ineffable totality. You can talk about Voltaire forever—his existential reality is incommensurate with speech. But let him smile and you *have* him completely and with no effort" (*Situations,* p. 151).

Finally, this amusing anecdote in support of Sartre's rather surprising position on first impressions—where their validity can be proved—may be interesting. Thomas Hoving, the curator of the Metropolitan Museum of Art in New York, learned early to distinguish a forgery from an authentic painting by giving great importance to his first reaction to a work. "The process is basically intuitive, but it is good to have a guideline. Write down that absolutely immediate first impression, that split second. Write anything, 'Warm.' 'Cool.' 'Scared.' 'Strong.' In six years of studying hundreds of items for the Museum [then, the Cloisters], I never ended up feeling warm about something I had written 'Cool' about, or the reverse." (Cited by John McPhee in "Profiles, A Roomful of Hoving," *The New Yorker,* May 20, 1967, p. 74.)

In the absence of the living Baudelaire, Sartre has perused the testimony of those who knew him and by examining and analyzing everything the poet has ever written, the critic has been able to correlate and integrate its successive aspects into a synthetic totality. And going beyond the achievements of his previous criticism, not only has Sartre been able to locate an author's metaphysics (Baudelaire's transcendence, satanism, temporality) and to explicate his artistry (its key words, refinement and "secret") in relation to it, but Sartre has also described the personal history—"in a retort" (p. 192)—which has led an artist to his metaphysics and to his creation. "With Baudelaire, [he has] psychoanalysed metaphysics." [62] One has rarely found so essentially individual a portrait: the illusion of close acquaintance given in the standard biography of empirical description and which is created by inviting identification on the part of the reader is here replaced by a rigorous and exacting method which leads us into Baudelaire's lived world.[63]

[62] Otto Hahn, p. 354.

[63] A new edition of Baudelaire's *Œuvres complètes,* brought out twenty years after Sartre's critique, turns out to be a tribute of sorts to it. In this new edition the chronological order established heretofore by Crépet and Georges Blin has been somewhat reversed so as not to conclude on a "failure," but on an ultimate conversion. "Yves Florenne's one concern is, indeed, to contest Sartre's affirmation that Baudelaire is the man of failure, and his monumental edition of the *Complete Works* is intended to exonerate the poet of this accusation" (P.-H. Simon, "Œuvres complètes de Baudelaire," *Le Monde,* p. 11). Needless to say, this rearrangement of certain of Baudelaire's entries cannot alter the validity of Sartre's argument—that Baudelaire was responsible for his "destiny." Furthermore, despite the relentless logic with which Sartre has pursued his research and analysis of the "imposture" of Baudelaire, the poet needs no apologetic defense against the critic. For Sartre has erected a monument to Baudelaire which shows him, indeed, neither as a saint nor as Satan, but as a man of profound intuitions, suffering doubly because his self-deception could not protect him from his extreme lucidity; and which shows him capable of transferring his attempted solutions into the imaginary by his incomparable poetry. What Sartre—in his "truth, the bitter truth"—has done for Baudelaire is to have erected to him the only monument possible.

Chapter 5

SAINT GENET, ACTOR AND MARTYR

For some months we had been hearing about an unknown poet whom Cocteau had discovered in prison, and whom he maintained to be the greatest writer of his age. At any rate, this was how he had described him in July, 1943, when composing a letter to the presiding magistrate of the police court in the 19th district, before whom the poet, one Jean Genet, was up for sentence, with nine previous convictions against him for theft already. . . . When the first section of *Our Lady of the Flowers* appeared in *L'Arbalète,* we were very much impressed. Genet had obviously been influenced by Proust and Cocteau and Jouhandeau, but he nevertheless possessed a voice of his own, a quite inimitable style of utterance. It was a most uncommon occurrence nowadays for us to read anything that renewed our faith in literature: these pages revealed the power of words to us as though for the first time. Cocteau had read the situation aright: a great writer *had* appeared [Simone de Beauvoir, *Prime,* p. 458].

Together with Cocteau, Picasso and others, Sartre addressed a petition to President Vincent Auriol and obtained Jean Genet's pardon. At that time Sartre became personally acquainted with Genet. "The whole basis of his fellow feeling for Sartre was this idea of liberty they shared, which nothing could suppress, and their common abhorrence of all that stood in its way," observes Simone de Beauvoir, who, in her spontaneous manner, enumerates as inhibitions to freedom: "nobility of soul, spiritual values, universal justice, and other such lofty words and principles, together with established institutions or ideals" (p. 459). When Gallimard was planning to publish Genet's works, Sartre was to write a preface. It became a separate volume, the first and not the least considerable of the Genet series.

The reaction of the confraternity of critics to Sartre's third major work of criticism was either enthusiastic or hostile. To write a "balanced" or "impartial" review, to give a "sober" or "objective" appraisal was just out of the question: this book is too dynamic, too profound, too upsetting, and either too persuasive or too forbidding to permit any kind of treatment of the leveling-off variety. Even in scholarly magazines the resounding epithets usually restricted to the press (which, indeed, also used them in this case), were freely displayed. We read that "everything contributes to make of this book a monument," "one of the richest books of our time." [1] That "Sartre constructs one of the most elaborate, insightful and idiosyncratic intellectual skyscrapers in the history of letters." [2] And, that "Sartre's introduction to *Our Lady of the Flowers* taken from his vast Saint Genet can only be described in superlatives: it is one of the most amazing pieces of literary analysis I have ever read." [3] Also, this "monumental study of Genet" is declared "surely one of the most astonishing books of our age." [4] Some, however, were not so easily impressed. The author of a full-length book on Sartre has remarked on the *Saint Genet* that "it would be

[1] Georges Bataille, *La Littérature et le Mal,* pp. 200 and 201.

[2] Bernard Ellevitch, "Sartre and Genet," p. 410.

[3] Lionel Abel, "The Genius of Jean Genet," p. 7.

[4] Martin Esslin, "Jean Genet: A Hall of Mirrors," *The Theatre of the Absurd,* p. 141.

rewarding to be able to maintain that it is something more than 550 closely printed pages of verbose and unconvincing argumentation." [5]

Sartre's purpose in writing the *Saint Genet* is to make the author and his work intelligible by applying to the fullest his critical existentialist psychoanalysis. The method is used rigorously and Sartre expects the reader to follow a maze of major and minor intricate sequences with painstaking attention, lest he be left behind. Yet, at times, especially at the very beginning, the book reads like a creation in *belles lettres,* when in counterpoint to lyrical phrases quoted from Genet, Sartre writes an entire paragraph which reads as from a novel of phenomenological description. The following from *Saint Genet* may serve as an example:

Genet is seven years old. The National Foundling Society has placed him in the care of Morvan peasants. Adrift in nature, he lives "in sweet confusion with the world." He fondles himself in the grass, in the water; he plays; the whole countryside passes through his vacant transparency. In short, he is innocent.

This innocence comes to him from others—everything comes to us from others, even innocence. Grownups never weary of taking stock of their belongings: this is called regarding. The child is part of the lot, between two stools or under the table. He comes to know himself through their regard, and his happiness lies in being part of the stock. To Be is to belong to someone. If property defines Being, the quiet, sober steadiness of earthly possessions defines the Good. Good as good soil, faithful as a spade, as a rake, pure as milk, Genet grows up piously. He is a good little boy, a respectful and gentle child, weaker and smaller than his playmates, but more intelligent. He is always at the head of his class. In addition, he is serious, thoughtful, not talkative, in short, as good as gold. This Good is simple: one has parents whom one worships, one does one's homework in their presence, and before going to bed one says one's prayers. Later, one likewise becomes an owner of things and one works hard and saves. Work, family, country, honesty, property:

[5] Philip Thody, *Jean-Paul Sartre, A Literary and Political Study,* p. 156.

such is his conception of the Good. It is graven forever upon his heart. Later on, despite the fact that he steals, begs, lies, prostitutes himself, it will not change. The local priest says that his is a religious nature [p. 14].

It will be noted that sarcasm is here Sartre's method of reduction of accepted mores. It is conveyed only by innuendo from the talk of "das Man"—similar to the literary device of a Nathalie Sarraute novel.[6] At other times, Sartre quotes directly from "the talk":

Because he is regarded as a thief Genet *becomes* a foundling. . . . His faults are explained by dark forces whose origin antedate his birth: "That little thief, where does he come from? Only a slut would abandon her son. A chip off the old block" [p. 28].

Sartre feels free to reconstitute moments of Genet's life, indispensable for a full understanding, and plausible in the light of Genet's own recollections and fantasies:

The child was playing in the kitchen. Suddenly he became aware of his solitude and was seized with anxiety, as usual. So he "absented" himself. Once again he plunged into a kind of ecstasy. There is now no one in the room. An abandoned consciousness is reflecting utensils. A drawer is opening; a little hand moves forward.

Caught in the act. Someone has entered and is watching him. Beneath this gaze the child comes to himself. He who was not yet anyone suddenly becomes Jean Genet. He feels that he is blinding, deafening; he is a beacon, an alarm that keeps ringing. *Who* is Jean Genet? In a moment the whole village will know. . . . The child alone is in ignorance. In a state of fear and shame he continues his signal of distress. Suddenly

. . . a dizzying word
From the depths of the world abolishes
the beautiful order. . . .[7]

A voice declares publicly: "You're a thief." The child is ten years old.

[6] See above, pp. 111–13.

[7] "Un mot vertigineux/Venu du fond du monde abolit le bel ordre" (Genet, *Poèmes*, p. 56).

That was how it happened, in that or some other way. In all probability, there were offenses and then punishment, solemn oaths and relapses. It does not matter. The important thing is that Genet lived and has not stopped reliving this period of his life as if it had lasted only an instant [pp. 26–27].

No biography of Genet was available, as there had been for Baudelaire, at the time Sartre introduced his works. Jean Genet's chronological progression therefore constitutes the armature of the book. Sartre, who was said to be hostile to Baudelaire, is certainly very sympathetic towards Jean Genet. Genet's experience of life, one-sided as it was, certainly did not take place "in a retort." [8] And the criminal did not live in bad faith, he was wont to drive with abandon to the very end of his intuitions. The defiance of prevalent social mores by this equally gifted artist was genuine. Finally, Sartre knew Genet and, conversing with him on his past, found much common ground with him. He had dedicated his *Baudelaire* to Jean Genet.

Sartre has formulated the aims of this unusual biography as follows, in his conclusion:

To indicate the limit of psychoanalytical interpretation and Marxist explanation and to demonstrate that freedom alone can account for a person in his totality; to show this freedom at grips with destiny, crushed at first by its mischances, then turning upon them and digesting them little by little; to prove that genius is not a gift but the way out that one invents in desperate cases; to learn the choice that a writer makes of himself, of his life and of the meaning of the universe, including even the formal characteristics of his style and composition, even the structure of his images and of the particularity of his tastes; to review in detail the history of his liberation. It is for the reader to say whether I have succeeded [p. 628].

Sartre sees the life of Genet as dominated by one event, with three metamorphoses in respect to this event. Genet has the

[8] *Baudelaire,* p. 192.

acute feeling of having died in shame, in an instant of transformation from innocent child to thief.[9] His ulterior metamorphoses—into an aesthetician and, then, into an author—are repetitions of the first one,[10] ritual repetitions of the original fall from grace. His time is cyclical, it is that of the Eternal Return, for Genet lives in horror and fascination of its possible recurrences. This gives to his works, especially his plays, through the replacement of individualization and plot by the acting-out of an obsession, their aspect of ritualistic rites. He continually transforms his history into mythical categories:

> If we wish to understand this man, the only way to do so is to reconstruct carefully, through the mythical representations he has given us of his universe, the original event to which he constantly refers and which he reproduces in his secret ceremonies. By analysis of the myths we shall proceed to re-establish the facts in their true significance [p. 14].

As we know, when he was seven years old, Jean Genet was placed by the welfare services in a peasant family in the Morvan. Very early the absent mother is part of his mythology. He feels unwanted in his very existence, his social demise seems to

[9] "Like me and like the dead child for whom I am writing, his name is Jean" (*Our Lady of the Flowers*, p. 257; written in the prison at Fresnes, 1942).

[10] In *Le Véritable Saint Genest,* a play by Jean Rotrou (1646), an actor becomes a martyr after having played the role in a drama. A certain Magnon had preceded Rotrou (in 1644) with *L'Illustre Comédien, ou le Martyre de Saint Genest.* The original Saint Genesius was a third century Roman actor who converted to Christianity and was baptized on stage and, later on, made patron saint of actors. His relics are today enshrined in the Church of Santa Susanna in Rome.

Since Genet wanted to become a saint Sartre had no need to refer—as indeed he has not—to any of this, when naming his volume *Saint Genet.* Yet it may be interesting to note that, according to Jacqueline Van Baelen (*Rotrou, Le Héros tragique de la révolte*) in Rotrou's *Saint Genest* "we are confronted with the sudden self-awareness of a character, who decides to assert himself against the society of which he is a part, and who thereby brings into question the values of the world which he had heretofore accepted" (p. 145). Furthermore, observes the critic, who seems not to have taken note of Sartre's *Saint Genet,* "there is at the same time a depreciation and an elevation: a depreciation to the degree that the martyrdom of Genesius is a parody, a poor imitation of Hadrian's martyrdom. . . . A true elevation . . . because now the life of a man is really at stake" (p. 157).

him only an extension of his original rejection. So, he is nothing, all the more so, since, he, a foundling, has nothing. Had he been raised in some worker's family he might have learned that one is because one does. But among owners of land, one has property because one inherits it, and one is fashioned by what one has.[11] As a child Genet reacted to his double exile by playing at being a saint, that is, one whose being does not proceed from men but from God. And he steals, not because he rebels against private property from which he feels excluded, but because he wishes to become part of it, to reintegrate himself in it. For, as he recalls, "the melodious child" is happy, he tries to be like all the others. "He is playing at possession" (p. 22). Because of his complete adherence to peasant morality, in the absence of his mother he seeks God, and, since everything is "given" to him, in theft he seeks to be as a proprietor. To the problems arising from the facticity in his in-itself, Genet, in his for-itself, is groping for a solution. One can readily see that this is in no way an automatic reaction, it is even in its milieu a rather unusual one.

Surprised in the act of "appropriation," Jean Genet, perhaps ten years old, hears himself called "thief." "A dizzying word." He is ostracized by those whom he wanted most to resemble. He is floored by a sophism which he cannot refute: he wanted

[11] See above, pp. 67–71, for the interchangeable ontological categories of being, having and doing in *Being*. Here, however, their respective importance is weighed according to the social role of the person.

Robert Cumming remarks (*Sartre,* p. 30) about these three categories, that "it is worth discerning, however remotely, the three traditional categories of *situs, actio,* and *habitus,* which are older than Aristotelianism and can be found embedded in primitive forms of language. With Sartre's analysis of 'situation' (which he adapts from Heidegger's analysis of the *Dasein*) he has in effect restored that concrete and rudimentary sense (which Being had before philosophical reflection began its enterprise of idealistic abstraction) whereby something is, if it occupies a place. . . . He is . . . reinvigorating 'having' (*avoir*) by recourse, in effect, to its primitive sense as a verb of action referring to something one holds in one's hand. . . . Sartre is now developing a reflexive analysis of human behavior as a whole, in which he is restoring, in effect, the original reference of the English be-havior to the self-possession of actively upholding oneself."

to steal, he did steal, he *is* a thief. He does not recognize himself in this accusation, but he must accept it as what he is objectively for others. Suddenly, torn from his dreams, he is told of his nature, he is notified of his essence for all time.[12]

Had he been older, say a boy of seventeen, the age at which one liquidates paternal values, he might have retorted in one way or another. But Genet is still a child, one who shares his accusers' values; a child who wished sainthood, not property, so that their accusation seems to emanate from his inner self. He suffers as if from a psychosis of influence. He will never be able to accept himself. Furthermore, in culpability, one makes the discovery of a singularity, of an otherness without reciprocity. All the others have one characteristic in common which the little Genet is made to define for them—and therein lies his "social function": he is a thief, they are not.

The righteous man suppresses the negative aspects of his attitudes: he loves his friend, but denies that he hates his friend's enemy. For him, evil is always incarnated by the "other," sometimes as something other within himself. The "gentleman" is manicheistic, he tears from himself his freedom towards evil and projects it on others, preferably on those who, because of their station in society as members of a minority or as outlaws, lack any relation of reciprocity with him, and will not remind him of his own capacity for evil. Little Jean Genet fulfilled all the requirements for becoming the focus of absorption for the fear of evil of the Morvan community in which he was placed.

[12] In *Our Lady of the Flowers* (p. 246), Darling is shown putting in his pocket something belonging on a shelf in the Galeries Lafayette. Instantly he hears an old lady ask: "What have you stolen, young man? . . . Almost immediately the colossus [the guard] was upon him and grabbed his wrist. He charged like a tremendous wave upon the bather asleep on the beach. Through the old woman's words and the man's gesture, a new universe instantaneously presented itself to Darling: the universe of the irremediable. It is the same as the other we were in, with one peculiar difference: instead of acting and knowing that we are acting, we know we are acted upon. A gaze. . . ."

Our consciousness gives us certain knowledge of ourselves, at least to a limited degree, whereas the opinion others have of us is only probable; it varies from observer to observer. But under strong social pressure there exists a kind of alienation to the other, in which we surrender our subjectivity to the object we are for the other. Thus the Indian Untouchable interiorizes what he hears said about himself, and he believes that he is untouchable. And so Jean Genet thought that it was his destiny to be a thief, he alone saw Evil not in the other but within himself as his essence. Ultimately, however, evil is always the other. Genet has thus been convinced that he is other than himself:

> The most immediate result is that the child is "doctored." He regards the existence of adults as more certain than his own and their testimonies as truer than that of his consciousness. He affirms the priority of the object which he is to them over the subject which he is to himself. Therefore, without being clearly aware of it, he judges that the appearance (which he is to others) is the reality and that the reality (which he is to himself) is only appearance. He sacrifices his inner certainty to the principle of authority. He refuses to hear the voice of the *cogito*. He decides against himself in the very depths of his consciousness [p. 46].

Genet transforms himself little by little into someone who is a stranger to himself as he interiorizes the adults' judgment of him.[13] A vertiginous word has branded him and has delivered his being into the hands of the others. A word has created his being. While for others language, as it generalizes the particular, is almost transparent, and permits communication by a hint, for the future poet there is a tight separation between the particular and the universal meaning of words: "The trick is done: we have made a poet of the doctored child. He is haunted by a word" (p. 53). But that is not all, for:

[13] Asked to explain his thefts, the young Louis Culafroy answers: "Because the others thought I was a thief." Of course, "the Mother Superior could make nothing of this juvenile nicety. He was called a hypocrite" (*Our Lady*, p. 211).

If you touch a single word, language disintegrates in a chain reaction; not a single vocable is spared. The word "thief" is everywhere, extends through everything. . . . He is blond *as a thief.* Introduce an imaginary quantity into your calculations and all the results become imaginary [p. 53].

This ten-year-old might have been suffocated completely, his being-for-itself throttled by his being-for-others. But he managed to react via his reflective consciousness to the original crisis. The great lacuna of his life—the lack of family and protection—which had marked him for disaster, now was shielding him from it: he felt that he, who was born in the fifth district of Paris, did not belong to the Morvan, he knew that he was only placed there by the welfare agency. Heretofore he had wished to be separate from man, above him as a saint. Now, when he is between ten and fifteen years old, he comes to decide —"the paradox of every conversion is that it spreads over years and gathers together in an instant" (p. 61)—that he will assume what the "crime" has made of him: *I will be the Thief.* It is an attitude of dignity, also encountered among oppressed groups when they reach a certain cultural level, at which point they wear proudly the epithet they cannot shed. So that, being a realist, Genet wishes to attain perfection in evil in this world as it is, as it has challenged him. And being also an idealist, he acts to prove that he is, indeed, the thief by nature that the others have proclaimed him to be. At this point, Sartre says, Genet had hardly any other alternative left open to him: "Only one thing has changed, the inner meaning of his pilfering" (p. 70).

But how does this first conversion appear in the consciousness of the young adolescent? Later he will recall: "I decided to be what crime made of me" (p. 71).[14] How can one decide to

[14] In his frankly autobiographical *Thief's Journal*—dedicated to Sartre and to the "Castor," the nickname of Simone de Beauvoir—Jean Genet recalls his attitude at the reform school when he was sixteen years old: "To every charge brought against me, unjust though it be, from the bottom of my heart I shall

be what one already is? Actually, paradoxical as it seems, this would corroborate the characteristic of our being as developed in *Being and Nothingness* and as restated here: "we are beings whose being is perpetually in question" (p. 72). Whereas a table is a table, "a man's a man for a' that/For a' that and a' that," only if he will renew his choice, again and again in the present and the future—a choice which, in the past, has made his essence as a "man." Genet wants to remain a thief: *I will be the Thief.*

But there is also in Genet a determination to see the "nature" of a thief fixed in his in-itself and being-for-others. Yet this "nature" he knows to be the outcome of his will to make it his. There is, then, a contradiction in Genet's choice of "willing" an evil "nature": "Unable to choose, he yokes two incompatible world systems: substance and will, soul and consciousness, magic and freedom, concept and judgment" (p. 73). Jean Genet reflects the conflict between the rationalism of the city and the naïve substantialism of the country, the belief in things. This tension will be carried over into his literary vision. For Genet will continue to hold on to two systems of values irreducible to one another: that of being, as an object in fatality and tragedy, and that of doing, as a subject in freedom and comedy. These two systems exist in a dynamic interrelation, but for the purpose of analysis Sartre treats them separately and then, from time to time, correlates them.

Since Genet is for himself what the others say he is, it is terribly important for him to see himself as the others do, for this is his way to know himself and to coincide with himself.[15]

answer yes. Hardly had I uttered the word—or the phrase signifying it—than I felt within me the need to become what I had been accused of being. . . . I kept no place in my heart where the feeling of my innocence might take shelter" (pp. 157–58).

[15] Therefore, in the *Saint Genet* Sartre turns from a psychoanalysis of things (the Husserlian "return to the things themselves" in which culminated his existentialist psychoanalysis in *Being*) back to an elaboration of his earlier understanding of "self-consciousness as consciousness of the self as something of

Yet it is not given to anyone to see himself objectively. So Genet seeks being, as in mysticism, in a state where subject and object, consciousness and being, the eternal and the particular become one. Since he never reaches this blissful coincidence when he observes himself so intently, the more he tries the less can he feel any approximation of it. He lives in a state of expectation and of absence: this is his "I," a pure, abstract will. Therefore the failure of being is continually replaced by doing. The only way he can attempt to coincide with himself is by willing his life as it is: "the fulfillment of my legend consists of the boldest possible criminal existence." [16] He wishes his "consciousness in evil" to precede his evil "nature." Thus, while he negates all other possibilities of his being and all evidence about them, he assumes his solitude, his exile and his nothingness. "That is his greatness. . . . One step further and he would deliver himself from evil itself" (p. 81).

Each theft is both utilitarian and ceremonial; he enacts the original crisis,[17] but without any witness. He is now his own cause: [18] he makes himself be a thief. He will later compare this "creation" to poetry. He does in order to be. The sophism of the "right-thinking," who endowed him with a nature because of his acts, is now reversed. He does evil for evil's sake but also in order to be; he observes himself, his acts become mere gestures as in a comedy. Genet oscillates between acts and gestures, between doing and being, between freedom and nature. The quest of being will lead Genet to homosexuality, to the exercise of a will to betrayal, and to a solitude he calls sainthood.

---

which the other is conscious" (Cumming, *Sartre,* p. 32). Concerning the being-for-others in *Being,* see above, pp. 62–68.

[16] *The Thief's Journal,* p. 185.

[17] "I am always moved whenever I learn that the miraculous unhappiness of my childhood at the Mettray Reformatory is forever perpetuated" (*ibid.,* p. 66).

[18] "Divine, in order to complete, to consummate the sacrilege, and, in a way, to surmount it by willing it, perhaps also out of exasperation, tears the flowers to shreds" (*Our Lady,* p. 89).

In his search for his being, Genet realizes he needs a mediation between what he is to himself and what he is to others. If he could possess the other, who possesses his image, might not the other be a real mediator?[19] At fifteen, in the reform school of Mettray the orphan again finds himself excluded: now, "that other society of castoffs, of dregs, that excremental society, rejects him" (p. 89). Genet, since he is desperately willing to establish some relationship with his fellow inmates, becomes homosexual and even accepts to serve in abjection as the passive "lover."[20]

Sartre's ontological description of Genet's sexual abnormality is startlingly novel but convincing, inasmuch as—unlike any explanation offered heretofore—it integrates his eroticism to his total being. Against Genet's own evaluation of his history, according to which he became a thief because he was a homosexual, Sartre maintains that

> he became a homosexual because he was a thief. A person is not born homosexual or normal. He becomes one or the other, according to the accidents of his history and to his own reaction to these accidents. I maintain that inversion is the effect of neither a prenatal choice nor an endocrinian malformation nor even the passive and determined result of complexes. It is an outlet that a child discovers when he is suffocating [p. 91].

For Sartre eroticism is part and parcel of one's being and its evolution. From among a multitude of possible attitudes, the outcast from respectability and from the underworld chose the one which responded like a sympathetic chord to his basic

[19] "There is the scene in which Erik is getting dressed in the presence of his lover: 'There were times when he desired to be the executioner so as to be able to contemplate himself and to enjoy from without the beauty which he emitted, to receive it'" (p. 87).

[20] In Sartre's ontology, love, as we have seen (above, pp. 65–67) as a particular aspect of the being-for others, is an effort at recuperation of one's being through the other. To love, therefore, means to make oneself loved, which is usually a mutual effort of both partners. Among pederasts, however, only one aspect of the normal relationship prevails: the active partner seeks only to make himself loved without recognizing any reciprocal demands by the passive partner.

choice of himself: to will what the others tell him he is. Genet was in a pre-homosexual situation: the crucial event early in his life was a violent surprise which took him from behind; the gaze of the other which froze him into a thief was akin to a violation. His acceptance of shame and culpability had earlier led him to substitute his objectivity for his subjectivity in a general inversion of all values. And it is from the other at his back, who possesses his image, that he may retrieve it. In his eroticism Genet reenacts the situation of his original fall.

But these supposedly powerful "super-males" in their very indifference towards their "girl-queens" and in their brutish stupidity are finally reduced to mere objects, of whom Genet in his lucidity is "constituent consciousness" (p. 136).[21] Thrown back to his solitude, Genet moves somewhat closer to liberation from both good and evil. For his pederastic experience leads him back to his starting point. But "this new solitude is deliberate, it has been pondered, it is based on experience of the world and on the failure of love" (p. 154).

At this point Sartre can give a remarkable *explication de texte* (pp. 136–42) of a Genet reminiscence, of the kind so often encountered in all his works.[22] In a cell with twenty other accused men, but by mistake the only one to wear prison garb, Genet is the butt of the derision of the others, who also have their language in common against him. One prisoner is asleep, and everyone plays at pulling a handkerchief from that man's

[21] That is, "a free and exasperated consciousness, which supports, all by itself, an imaginary world" (p. 128). Genet writes in the *Journal* about Stilitano: "Still very good-looking, despite the heaviness of his features, wearing an expensive woolen suit and a gold ring, he was being led by a ridiculous, mean-tempered, tiny little white dog. It was then that this pimp was revealed to me: he held his folly in leash, his curly, frizzy, coddled meanness" (p. 69). Later on, therefore, Genet realizes that "Stilitano was my own creation and that its destruction depended upon me" (p. 114). Similarly, Genet dominates the overpowering Armand when he becomes aware that he is "devoid of the slightest spirituality" (p. 119). As for the irresistible beauty of Bernardini, Genet remains under its spell while noting: "I even think I created it." (p. 170).

[22] Hazel E. Barnes aptly calls *Our Lady of the Flowers* "a novel within an autobiography" (*Humanistic Existentialism*, p. 349).

pocket. When it is Genet's turn, he faints. He is transported to the far end of the cell. The others laugh at him. Then, Genet has a "supernatural moment," in which he sees the world reduced to people playing, and himself exiled from these "graceful pupils of lightfingered theft." This cell reveals to him its essence as "prison of the world."

In Sartre's understanding, to Genet this situation evokes, symbolically, the double exile suffered in Mettray. Rather than being assimilated to the others by success, Genet chooses to fail as a buffoon. In this make-believe theft Genet can act out the solution he wanted to give to the original theft, that is, suicide, for which fainting is a make-believe substitute. It represents the death of "the melodious child dead in me long before the ax chops off my head"; [23] so that, when he regains consciousness, he has a revelation of himself as someone who does not share the human ends of the world. Play and prison, says Sartre, have been the favorite symbols of those thinkers who have placed themselves on the outside of society in considering human activity: namely, Pascal, Nietzsche and Kafka. However, Genet is not at a distance from it all: the bourgeois values of the Good still haunt him, and for him it is only "Evil which is a Ballet." And, mere actors, these "gracious thieves" depend on the onlooker for the existence of their graceful appearance. To become essential to this performance Genet's consciousness had to remain at a distance. As he put it in his reminiscence of the event: "I was, through my monstrous horror, exiled to the confines of the obscene." In Sartre's interpretation, abjection is Genet's method, like Descartes's doubt or Husserl's reduction, a conversion which leads to an existence, wherein Genet is master of himself and of others since he accepts them only if he is the one to give consciousness to their existence:

[23] "L'enfant mélodieux/Mort en moi bien avant que me tranche la hache" (*Le Condammé à mort, Œuvres complètes,* II, 180).

A work of Genet's, like Hegel's phenomenology, is a consciousness which sinks into appearances, discovers itself in the depths of alienation, saves itself and relegates things to the rank of *its objects* [pp. 141–42].

The interest and tension of Genet's works lie in the resultant contradiction between two forms of unhappiness, one of which is prereflective and noble, the other being abject and reflective; the first despises the second, the second dissolves the first. Wishing to be—as a saint, whose being does not depend on society—and to do—as a criminal, whose antisocial deeds he glorifies as those of a warrior—he is both a master who is and a slave who does. Thus he exclaims in *Our Lady of the Flowers:* "Oh those males, I hate them lovingly!"; and in *Funeral Rites:* "I love him out of hatred" (quoted on p. 143). He hates them because he must become abject when he tries to become what they are, when he loves them.

In his novels these small-time underworld figures become enveloped in a tragic veil, for Genet disposes of a capacity for creating myths in transforming acts into gestures, ceremonies and language, while his corrosive, analytical mind intervenes to have their cruel beauty depend explicitly on his own consciousness.[24] It is his way of "digesting a too coriaceous reality." Sartre sees Genet's "grandeur" in this effort, when in black despair he reaches beyond "everyday reality to attain beauty without in any way renouncing a ruthless lucidity" (p. 149).

Distance from the other through abjection has led Genet back to his starting point, his double exile, but he is now capable of seeking a solution within himself. At about eighteen he tramps through a good part of Europe as a thief, a prostitute and a beggar. Heretofore he wanted to see his evil nature and retrieve it from the others by assuming it. Genet now sees

[24] All of Genet's novels avowedly are set in his own consciousness: "So Divine is alone in the world. Whom shall I give her for a lover?" (*Our Lady*, p. 113).

himself as an object only of God. The country people had designated him for Evil and suffering, but Genet now thinks of them as signs of an election for a "sacred drama." [25] He is resigned not to see, not to comprehend his Evil, but he wishes to be conscious of being seen as such by God.[26] For like his protagonist in *Our Lady of the Flowers,* Genet now seeks God's gaze to consecrate his pursuit of evil, sacred because of his suffering. He feels like a prereflective consciousness whose reflective consciousness is in heaven. In this worst of all possible worlds, Genet also can exclaim *I is Another;* the Other, according to Sartre, being God (pp. 162–63).[27]

Sartre now sums up Genet's first three stages of seeking being. In the first crisis of alienation he decides that he will be the thief the others say he is. He abandons his consciousness of himself in deference to his consciousness of the other. His is only a "nonthetic consciousness (of) self." [28] In the second

25 Genet has repeatedly expressed his belief that the word "la sainte" (the saint) is the most beautiful one in the French dictionary.

26 "Much solitude had forced me to become my own companion. Envisaging the external world, its indefiniteness, its confusion, which is even more perfect at night, I set it up as a divinity of which I was not only the cherished pretext, an object of great care and caution, chosen and led in masterly fashion, though through painful and exhausting ordeals, to the verge of despair, but also the sole object of all this labor. And little by little, through a kind of operation which I cannot quite describe, . . . it was within me that I established this divinity—origin and disposition of myself. . . . I dedicated to it songs of my own invention. At night I would whistle. The melody was a religious one. It was slow. Its rhythm was somewhat heavy. I thought I was thereby entering into communication with God: which is what happened" (*Journal,* p. 74).

27 This should not surprise us, for to Sartre the fundamental project for any man is to become God (see above, pp. 53–54). But since Genet is considered to be suffering from a psychosis of influence (see above, pp. 157–58), that is, from the obsession that another possesses his mind, it would seem that in Genet Sartre found an acute form of the general ontological project, when he distances himself from the others—the society of the Morvan—to place himself under the one Other—God. Sartre will discuss Genet's claim to sanctity and his sophisms in the following chapters.

28 That is, as Sartre explained in *Being* (see pp. liii-liv), his prereflective consciousness, filled with the outside world, does not reflect on its own existence, but is still somewhat aware of itself. "Every positional consciousness of an object is at the same time a non-positional consciousness of itself." But to describe the latter structure "we can no longer use this expression in which the "of self" still evokes the idea of knowledge." Hence the parentheses around "of," for the

stage, Genet returns from the others to his solitude. The pimps, the supposed "hard ones" and murderers, are only appearances to whom Genet, without any reciprocity, gives a being through his imagining consciousness. From his being-for-others he reverts to his being-for-itself. In a third phase, he subjects himself to himself as to an Other, the God of Evil.[29] He makes his prereflective for-itself an object of an "outside" reflective for-itself. But, just like Divine of *Our Lady of the Flowers,* Genet cannot truly believe in God,[30] and, in utter loneliness, he returns to subjection as a pederast. From now on, "he goes round in circles, . . . from essence to existence, and from existence to essence, from poetic glorification to corrosive lucidity" (p. 167).

Sartre goes on to examine (in the chapter "A Daily Labor, Long and Disappointing . . .") what evil and good represent ontologically and how Genet lives and understands them. Genet's descent into abjection was seen as his methodical doubt and his phenomenological reduction; it also places him outside the realm of accepted norms of morality within or above the underworld.[31] In betrayal he will reach the far end of suffering, for which, at last, he is his own cause. Thus, continually, he hurts others and hurts himself. Also, to some degree, in his defiance he tries to shame society, just as did Baudelaire in his conduct towards Madame Aupick.

An exclusively psychoanalytical interpretation of his attitude would beg the question: to be sure, the intelligent solicitude of

---

nonthetic consciousness is not an "intentional" consciousness *of* itself. (For the concept of intentionality, see above, p. 5).

[29] "Abandoned by my family, I already felt it was natural to aggravate this condition by a preference for boys, and this preference by theft, and theft by crime or a complacent attitude in regard to crime. I thus resolutely rejected a world which had rejected me" (Genet, *Journal,* p. 75).

[30] See *Our Lady,* pp. 173–74.

[31] "I treated myself to a sumptuous lunch [with the ransom money]. Pépé [whom Genet has betrayed to the police] must have been dying of hunger in jail, but I thought that by means of this crime I had freed myself of moral preoccupations" (*Journal,* p. 68).

> decent people did its utmost to burden the child with every possible complex. Rancor, feeling of inferiority, overcompensation, Genet has known them all. But we will understand nothing about his case if we are unwilling to recognize that he undertook, with exceptional intelligence and vigor, to carry out his own psychoanalysis. It would be absurd to explain him by impulses when the fact is that it is against these impulses that he wants to regain his autonomy. . . . Jean Genet is a thief who wanted *to change his motives for stealing* and who thereby transcended his original situation. His astounding effort to regain freedom in Evil deserves therefore to be explained by his object and not by a *vis a tergo,* which, in point of fact, he escapes [p. 176].

The Good is defined by society and by religion, it is universal, it is as irresistible as the evidence of logical discourse. But Evil is without a general cause; [32] it is defined only by an individual and exists only through him.[33] For "the Being of Evil is both the Being of Nonbeing and the Nonbeing of Being" (p. 172), since the Good is equated with upholding being. Evil exists only relatively to Good; there is no absolute Evil.

Since to will Evil, then, results in some measure of Good, Genet fails in his endeavor.[34] He cannot reach Evil; all he can do is will it. In his lucidity, "not only does he attempt the worst, but he demands the radical failure of his attempt" (p. 188). Unlike Baudelaire or Lautréamont, Genet does not invoke Satan, he knows God always wins, he is not manicheistic. His pride refuses any evasion. He plays at *loser wins* when "he is the being who makes himself exist through *his will to be impossible*" (p. 204; words in italics are my own translation, *cf.* Sartre, *Saint Genet,* p. 175). So that "this child who wishes to purify himself through crime" only manages to make of Evil

[32] Sartre exclaims: "Just try to make universals of theft, crime and lying!" (*Saint Genet,* p. 177).

[33] Genet describes in the *Journal* how Erik, trembling and terrorized, kills a child without any motive (cited as an example in *Saint Genet,* pp. 169–71).

[34] We have seen that as a criminal he threatens but also serves society as a focus of absorption of evil, and that in betrayal of his fellow criminals, he again serves society while negating it in utter abjection.

"the instrument of his own punishment" (p. 173). In his failure to become Evil, Genet moves from evil as resentment, which is just sulkiness, to evil as self-torture, which becomes pure ascesis, to gratuitous evil which manifests his freedom. Genet keeps turning from one to the other:

"Evil," he writes, "is achieved little by little, through a discovery of genius which makes you drift far away from men. But most often by a daily labor, long and disappointing" [p. 174].

He then tries to reach Evil in betrayal,[35] but this ultimate evil causes him extreme suffering. It is a parasitic crime, since it rests on another one, in a sense—a "reflective crime." Indeed, in his lucid reflective consciousness, as a passive homosexual, as aesthete and as poet, too intellectual and too sensitive, Genet is never genuinely and entirely on the side of his fellow criminals; [36] in a way he actually dominates them, so that, guilty in the eyes of the "right-thinking people," he is also suspect to the outcasts. Objectively, treason is worse than criminality. The murderer becomes other to society, and it can preserve itself by excluding him from it. But through betrayal the entire society becomes other under the unexpected gaze of the other in its midst.[37] The outcasts acknowledge it as the worst calamity when they prefer murder to betrayal.[38] A criminal and traitor, the outsider Genet becomes his own cause "as an ascertained impossibility of giving [himself] being" (p.

[35] " 'You'll get a hundred francs each time' [continued the inspector]. Darling accepted. He liked selling out on people, for this dehumanized him. Dehumanizing myself is my own most fundamental tendency" (*Our Lady*, p. 82).

[36] Darling and Our Lady "were not witty, their remarks had no finesse" (*ibid.*, p. 126).

[37] This may also go to explain the revulsion against adultery even among the unconventional.

[38] Guy is ready to kill but shrinks back in horror from the thought of "giving" a fellow thief. So that Genet, who had begun to reveal himself to Guy in order to find "a companion and support in vileness," now needs all the power of maneuver, denial and persuasion which, says he, "conferred upon me my mastery of language," to extricate himself from his self-exposure as a traitor. (See *Journal*, pp. 205–9).

205); but he still does not reach the person whom he was seeking all along in the mirror, in the eyes of the other and in his relationship with "the hard ones."

However, for the first time in his life he exists. *"Lived by Genet,* [betrayal] becomes sacrilege, poetry, paradoxical ambiguity of the instant, ascesis" (p. 200). He deliberately violates religious injunctions. Moreover, since like French sociologists he sees society at the origin of the sacred and since he feels excommunicated from it as from the Church, his betrayals trample its laws and go beyond accepted evil as the saint goes beyond the call of duty. "To betray" is also poetic, for it "is to engender a destiny by means of words" (p. 201). For Genet it is a "cathartic crisis and the paradox of the instant" (p. 202), this moment of betrayal, at which the "just" ones are forced to become the accomplices of the greatest evil (betrayal) in order to eradicate a lesser one (an ordinary crime); and after which the cajoling representative of society comes to despise Genet even more. Genet, after a momentary appearance of reciprocity with the Good, dives into the utterly inhuman. At this ultimate point, he can say: "I am really all alone." [39] What he seeks the most in the betrayal of fellow criminals and of loved ones is the horror this causes to himself. For "betrayal . . . is an ascesis which little by little dissipates the phantasmagoria and leads by degrees to a horrible nirvana of despair, darkness and self-hatred" (pp. 202–3). Betrayal is failure and destruction.

Genet willed evil in crime and failed. He subsequently willed failure in betrayal; but then his acts became gestures and being became appearance. "Now, the law of appearances and gestures," writes Sartre, "is Beauty" (p. 214). [40] For beauty is in a form which elicits an imaginary intention, it is an

[39] Like Lefranc at the end of *Deathwatch.*

[40] See above, pp. 54–55, for Sartre's definition of beauty in *Being* as the imaginary value in-itself-for-itself.

appearance, which is to reveal essence.[41] But, also, "appearance is satanic, because it caricatures being and because it is all that man can produce by his own means." Altogether, then, in a sense, the Imaginary can be called Evil: "It is the destruction of being, conceived as the creation of appearance."[42] "We shall see," Sartre concludes, "that this last formula can be rigorously applied to Genet's aesthetic" (pp. 178–79). Since he dreams about his acts for a long time beforehand and while committing them, and since the moment of absolute Evil is reached when one dreams about a crime, Genet's acts are both criminal and poetic.[43] "For Genet the other face of the Beautiful is Evil" (p. 535).

As we have seen, from early childhood on, Genet wanted to become a saint. Sartre devotes a chapter ("To Succeed in Being All, Strive to Be Nothing in Anything" [44]) to a description of sainthood as an objective and social fact and—an intricate process—as a subjective determination, as it appears in Saint Theresa of Avila, in Jouhandeau and in Genet. Historically, sainthood is for Sartre bound to an aristocratic society of consumption: "Aristocrats have made gold useless by applying it to the walls of the churches. The Saint makes the world useless, symbolically and in his person, because he refuses to use it" (p. 222). His is what Sartre calls the sophism of the no: extreme denial is wealth, refusal is acceptance, and God's absence is the blinding manifestation of His presence. From Saint John of the Cross's mysticism it takes little more, in Sartre's view, to reach

[41] One might say that betrayal is to crime what imaginary art is to utilitarian craft.

[42] One is here reminded of the Old Testament injunction against any imagery of God, man or beast (Exodus xx. 4; Deuteronomy v. 8; etc.).

[43] "My solitude in prison was total. . . . At night I would let myself be borne along by a current of abandon. The world was a torrent, a rapid of forces come together to carry me to the sea, to death. I had the bitter joy of knowing I was alone" (*Journal*, p. 97).

[44] From Saint John of the Cross.

Genet's sophisms according to which sin is God's open door, nothingness leads to being, and to love is to betray. Even though we live in a productive society, much of the old has survived, especially in religion which is syncretic. In the feudal hierarchy of the underworld, "Genet plays the role of a clerk: he is the only one who knows how to read, like the chaplain amidst the barons" (p. 225).[45] He interiorizes, as it were, their drama.

Sartre sees in Plato an anticipation of Christian asceticism:

> We know the principle of *The Symposium:* the philosopher must die to his body in order to rise to the contemplation of the True and the Good. Let us interpret this to mean that we must renounce our particularity in order to attain the intuition of the Universal [p. 226].

This pure universality is taken to be God; the saint is the one who elevates himself towards it. There is, then, a certain hatred of oneself as of something particular.[46] In an agricultural and artisan society, the concept of the universal had, indeed, to be conquered beyond the individual. Today the terms are reversed; it is the individual which is to be reached within the universal all around us. Genet is equally removed from either pursuit. Genet, just like Jouhandeau, Catholic and pederast, who recognizes himself a sinner, knows that he has excluded himself from the universal. Both of them, then, attempt in a practice of renunciation a destruction of their given singularity

[45] "Talent is courtesy with respect to matter; it consists of giving song to what was dumb. My talent will be the love I feel for that which constitutes the world of prisons and penal colonies" (*Journal,* p. 97).

[46] "He who is truly humble must sincerely desire to be scorned, persecuted and condemned without reason, even in serious matters" (Saint Theresa of Avila, quoted in *Saint Genet,* p. 227).

Genet goes one step further, in a twisting of the Christian position: "I shall first incur the scorn of men, their judgment. I distrust the saintliness of Vincent de Paul. He should have been willing to commit the galley slave's crime instead of merely taking his place in irons" (*Journal,* pp. 192–93). But, as Sartre notes about Genet's attitude: "We discover that he was faking his humility in the depths of abjection. . . . The Saint was close to God *despite* the scorn of others, our author *because* of this scorn" (p. 249).

in favor of a singularity of their own volition, which sets them apart.[47] Therefore, while the process of detachment is ascensional and reversible in Theresa, Nietzsche and Gide, it is descensional in Genet and Jouhandeau, and it is irreversible, since they do lose everything. However, for those who, like Saint Theresa and Jouhandeau, believe in God, transcendence allows them to regain more fully what they have given up in their abnegation, while Genet moves towards lesser being.

The "destitution" of the saint, actually, exists only for the others, for the saint is filled with the positivity of Being; but Genet lives it to the hilt. "The canonized Saint, the Sinner and the diabolical Saint all demand that they be arraigned and blamed for acts which they have not committed" (pp. 240–41).[48] In this humility, the risk, however, is not equally shared. In the case of the saint, humility is secure and akin to pride: the approval of God has been substituted for that of one's fellow man. God judges being whereas man looks at appearance, and the saint chooses being over appearance. Thus, his ascetic elevation is true, not so his humility and abnegation. Jouhandeau, who risks eternal damnation, can also hope to be granted pardon in view of his constant striving, and also because Evil is a condition of the greater Good. Only Genet's humility, "renunciation" and abjection are entered into without recourse. Their acrobatics, says Sartre, take place above a net, Genet's do not.

Altogether, Christian ethics present us with a contradiction. Objectively, in ascesis as proof of our love of God, we abandon our possessions in indifference, but subjectively, in a desperate struggle. "I am not presenting these contradictions in order to

[47] "Nothing exalts me more surely than reprobation" (Marcel Jouhandeau, *Treatise on Abjection,* quoted on p. 229).

[48] Sartre goes on to quote from *The Way of Perfection* of Saint Theresa: "We are always full of faults." And from the *Treatise on Abjection* of Jouhandeau: "It means that there is a certain amount of truth in it [the accusations leveled against him]." And Genet: "It staggered me to know that I was composed of impurities, I became abject" (p. 240).

condemn Christian ethics: I am far too convinced that *any* ethic is both impossible and necessary. I am describing" (p. 247). We shall see how Sartre seeks, in his subsequent writings, the resolution of this dilemma in the praxis of commitment.

The drama of the bourgeois homosexual is that of guilt in nonconformity while he is otherwise well integrated in society. As an agnostic, Proust argues—by invoking a psychological determinism—that the normal Swann is undermined through his jealousy as much as the baron de Charlus through his perversion. The Protestant Gide seeks to overcome social taboos when he claims the rights of spontaneity and nature as against those of the supernatural. Unlike Gide, Jouhandeau continued to hold to the dogmas of his faith; he could not claim freedom to follow his unnatural bent but only seek condemnation in abjection as the one hope of salvation.

While Saint Theresa let herself be accused of sins she did not commit, and while those of Jouhandeau are not at all serious, Genet in betrayal has committed the worst of crimes, without any ulterior hope of redemption. This difference between Genet and Jouhandeau can be seen in their respective styles. While Genet, with "a short, hard word . . . stamps his will to the irremediable," the style of Jouhandeau, "one of the finest of our time, with astonishing resources—displays at times a suspicious oiliness, a flabbiness, a glass transparency, a hideous amiability." In each of his sentences "a word, a supernumerary word, which represents Good, creeps into each of his sentences; sometimes it is simply the tense of the verb." Genet wrote: "Je devins abject" (I became abject)"; Jouhandeau would have written: "J'étais devenu abject" (I had become abject) (p. 258).

For Genet, as we know, the choice of being, the cause of his crimes, was a *cogito,* a way of placing himself above essence through the exercise of the vertiginous freedom of the condemned; but as he followed the road of crime, it did become his essence.[49] Then, he wanted it to be an object of God's sight. Just as Descartes had substantified thought, "a thinking substance," so Genet could say: "I do Evil, therefore I am. I am an evildoing substance" (p. 266). Genet maintains within himself the conflict between doing and being, like a religious community that distinguishes between good works and faith, activity and contemplation, discursive and intuitive reason, and the categorical imperative and passive beatitude. "Genet's originality lies in his wanting to be and in his being the nonsynthetic unity of his contradictions" (p. 273).

How did the world look to Genet during his first metamorphosis, when he was from fifteen to twenty-five years old? Sartre has so far tried to render the child and adolescent Genet intelligible by isolating his initial choice and by setting up some logical categories which proceed from it, in what he calls a "chemical analysis."

Now (in the chapter "Cain"), Sartre attempts a portrait of the young Genet, syncretic because of his "religious nature," a synthesis of how the world appears to Genet at this stage within his contradictory fields of reference. There is at first a description of his inner climate and, then, of "his" external universe: his attitudes towards the world of tools, nature, miracles, lan-

[49] Sartre maintains that crime can be classified as a statistic and fully explained by sociologists, by criminologists and by psychiatrists, while "a technical invention, a work of art, have a positive content which remains irreducible. After you have explained Rácine by his environment, by the age, by his childhood, there remains *Phèdre,* which is inexplicable. But as the evil action wills itself as pure destruction, when you have reduced its perpetrator to being only a *case,* only an illustration of contemporary society, there remains no residue; the crime is the criminal's failure" (p. 260). This reasoning is surprising, for it would presuppose that Sartre now considers crime and the criminal fully determined and understood in each and every case by the laws established in the various disciplines mentioned. Actually, however, Sartre's study of Genet shows precisely the highly individual and often entirely unforeseeable metamorphoses of the criminal Genet. So also it is not only Phèdre but Racine as well who, in his freedom, in final analysis, remains inexplicable beyond his choice of being. It is Sartre who has shown that freedom is freedom precisely because it cannot be reduced to any other category.

guage, history and reason. After what was primarily the "regressive psychoanalysis" of Genet, we are now given the synthetic progression";[50] for in the *Saint Genet,* as earlier in the *Baudelaire,* Sartre pursues his phenomenological and psychoanalytical descriptions and the resulting developments in logical discourse to the limit. Yet at the same time—with the existentialist conviction of the primacy of experience—he is determined to find "what has actually been experienced" in its "nondifferentiation" (pp. 273–74), now, however, rendered comprehensible in its complex manifestations. Genet's "emotional climate" is not geared towards some physical euphoria. Once his prereflective consciousness had become one of a hostile world, the child's *élan vital* had lodged itself in his reflective consciousness, often in his imagination. Genet has preserved a considerable optimism which is anterior to his experience and which it has not been capable of stamping out.[51] His imaginary flights render his misery more horrible, but through them he can live at a distance from it; yet without getting used to it, for he wishes to be aware of his suffering since it is to him a sign of his election. In his optimism he believes in a cause of his existence. It is not he who is out of order but the universe, and precisely in its inexplicable aspects it is sacred. Genet himself, inexplicable in his misfortune, is sacred;[52] he feels that his exile is visited upon him because he

[50] See above, p. 130, for the definition of these terms from *Being* as they are applied in the *Baudelaire.*

[51] "But what will prevent my destruction? Speaking of catastrophe, I cannot help recalling a dream: a locomotive was pursuing me. I was running along the tracks. I heard the machine puffing at my heels. I left the rails and ran into the countryside. The locomotive cruelly pursued me, but gently and politely stopped in front of a small, fragile wooden fence which I recognized as one of the fences which closed off a meadow belonging to my foster parents and where, as a child, I used to lead the cows to pasture. In telling a friend about this dream, I said, ". . . the train stopped at the fence of my childhood," (*Journal*, p. 186).

[52] "Saintliness means turning pain to good account. It means forcing the devil to be God" (*ibid.,* p. 185). Sartre cites Mircéa Eliade's *Histoire des religions,* in which *sacer* is shown to have meant in antiquity both "accursed" and "holy" and *haghios* both "pure" and "soiled." A similar ambivalence of the sacred is

bears some higher destiny which he has set out to discover in horror and enthusiasm. "As Camus sees it, the thin crust of meaning sometimes melts, disclosing the raw reality which signifies nothing. In the eyes of Genet, it is reality which tends to be effaced in favor of meaning." For Genet, underworld figures or prison guards are angels, that is, etymologically, envoys sent to him by someone. So that, Sartre concludes, "metaphysical intuition of the absurd leads to nominalism; that of Genet orients him towards a vague, Platonic realism" (p. 280).

Genet perceives the profane outer world like everyone else, but he differs from others in the significance he assigns to it. "The industrial products that make up the urban landscape are the social will bottled and canned" (p. 282). We are surrounded by mute, more or less specific, injunctions to use, to do or to abstain. They are addressed to everyone, but "Genet is the chosen victim of these mineral gazes. . . . The finality of utensils arraigns him" (p. 284).

He reacts to the world of tools in three manners simultaneously. As always, he wills to refuse what is refused to him. He reduces the human imprint on tools to just another natural fact. But since that way he risks eliminating social reality altogether, he also appropriates things while destroying them by breaking into homes, and, at best, transforms items of use into goods of exchange.[53] Genet variously describes in his novels the many different ways thieves have of enjoying their intrusions, all of which have little to do with the gain they may obtain; such actions being rather expressions of some pathological desires. To Genet himself, Sartre reminds us, they represent reenactments of his first "appropriation" which was to make him a proprietor. This way also lies perpetual dissatisfaction. Genet, therefore, in order not to succumb to the positive

---

supposed to have prevailed in the paleo-Semitic and Egyptian worlds (see *Saint Genet*, p. 280).

[53] "I am steeped in an idea of property while I loot property" (quoted, p. 286).

power of tools, often chooses to distort their utility in a diabolical manner. In *Our Lady of the Flowers* Genet actually writes about himself: "It was the sisters' clothes that gave Culafroy the idea of running away. All he had to do was to put into action a plan that the clothes conceived by themselves" (quoted, pp. 288–89). To this "vague Platonic realism" (whereby the thing represents an innate Idea) Sartre opposes what may be called an existentialist analysis of things (in which meaning is given to them by a particular individual) in this description:

To the nuns, these garments propose traditional acts which were long ago determined by the Church. Through them and through the intermediaries of the dressmakers who made them, all of Christian society addresses itself to the sisters. Every morning they find in their robes the image of their sacrifice and of their dignity; the garments reflect to them their integration into the community of Christ and their rejected, neglected, yet ever-present femininity. Culafroy, as a prisoner, as a young boy, has nothing to do with a skirt and a coif. Nevertheless, he lights up these objects with his guilty desires: as a prisoner, he wishes to escape; as a boy, he dreams of a secret femininity. Society responds to his wishes with a twofold prohibition: thus, it is not society that addresses itself to him through the intermediary of these garments. And yet social exigencies, animated by his desires, begin, all by themselves, to concern him. The buttons are there to be buttoned, the skirt to be slipped on. Buttoned *by him,* slipped on *by him.* At the very moment when these imperatives address themselves to Culafroy, they cease to be social by becoming objective. They are secret solicitations—valid for him alone—that are borne spontaneously of the garments. The gown and the headdress outline the image of a false femininity and of an escape without danger. The gesture is the thing; it waits; it is a magical power. If Culafroy dresses up as a nun, he will be possessed by outlandish behavior; an outcast and homosexual nun will establish herself within him to govern his movements. But he will know the perverse joy of turning against men their own instruments. In order to escape from the just, the most decried of children uses the sacred garments that the just respect. The ideal thing would be to kill a blacksmith with his own hammer (p. 289).

What people usually seek and "find" in the harmony of nature, Sartre holds with Marx, is the "order" of their social universe.[54] Indeed, thoughtlessly or maliciously equating free man to determined nature, they point either to immutable order in recurrence, or to blind and brutal conflict in nature in order to argue for a given social order or to apologize for some human barbarism. Genet, who feels excluded from society, cannot integrate himself in nature.[55] "But even if he is in the open country . . . the site refuses to contain him" (p. 293).[56] Only in his imagination could Genet feel akin to nature.

Those phenomena in society or in nature which point to our forlornness and limitation are the ones which Genet experiences as specially destined for him. He terms them miracles, and they can be both horrible (as was the pantomime of theft he witnessed in the prison) or poetic. These miracles show him

[54] In nature—as an escape from society—the aversion to society persists as a negative moment in a total human existence. This escape is therefore short-lived.

[55] With the exception of that of betrayal, all major themes of Genet's *Welt als Vorstellung*—the world as a representation—can be found in this passage from *The Thief's Journal* (pp. 62–64): "Chased by the municipal guard . . . I traveled alone. Occasionally, I would meet or overtake another tramp. Without even sitting down on a stone pile, we would tell each other which village was more friendly to beggars, which mayor less inhuman, and we would continue on our solitary way. . . . I was alone. I walked humbly along the outer edge of the roads. . . . By this shipwreck, sunk by all the woes in an ocean of despair, I still knew the sweetness of being able to cling to the strong, terrible . . . negro. . . . Toward evening my feet would be sweating, . . . I would therefore walk in the mud. The sun filled my head with a lead ballast which served as thought and at the same time emptied it. . . . I remember that I offered all my woes to God. In my solitude, remote from men, I came quite close to being all love, all devotion. . . . Between them and me there will be even fewer bonds, and the last will be broken if to their contempt for *me*, I oppose my love of *them*. . . . I was dry, [yellow] and sad. . . . As a young Frenchman on that shore, from my solitude, from my beggar's state, from the dust of the ditches that rose up in tiny individual clouds about each foot, renewing themselves at every step, my pride derived a consoling singularity which contrasted with the banal sordidness of my apparel. . . . It was during the summer of 1934 that I trudged along the Andalusian highways. . . . The dogs would scent me—my odor further isolated me—they would bark whenever I left a farm or arrived at one. . . . I dàred not even notice the beauty of that part of the world—unless it were to look for the secret of that beauty, the imposture behind it, of which one will be a victim if one trusts it. By rejecting it I discovered poetry. . . . All this beauty, however, is meant for me. . . . It is so conspicuous in order to show how woebegone I am."

[56] Cumming reminds us that in early antiquity occupying a *situs* was considered being (see above, p. 156).

his destiny in a lightning moment, in a symbolic repetition of his original crisis, and happen with the fatality of sacred time, for the outcome of his life had been decided long ago, when he was forewarned by the villagers that perpetual prison terms and violent death were his lot.

"It was on seeing red velvet chairs and gilt-framed mirrors in a green field that Genet felt one of his strongest poetic emotions" (p. 299). Like Rimbaud, like Mallarmé, he was struck by the contradiction between society and nature that this spectacle contained, a contradiction which reflects that within man, part nature, part antinature. When Genet faces so poetic an object, he feels relieved of his own tension, as if this object were to bear it for him. "In Genet, the highest pitch of lucidity coincides with the fright of the dream, and the most acute consciousness of misfortune with the quietism of aesthetic contemplation" (p. 302).

Language is part of nature when we discover that it has its own laws and resistances to be observed and followed. It is a tool when we use it to communicate with one another. And it can be miraculous when it creates of itself puns and visions. Genet has taken a complex attitude towards language in which he resumes his positions towards society, nature and the supernatural.

Our language has aged because of the huge upheavals in society since World War I. Brice Parain, Leiris, Bataille and Ponge [57] have therefore been somewhat alienated from language because of what Sartre calls "a slight and discontinuous maladjustment" (p. 303). In the case of Genet this alienation is radical and permanent. For this boy who is other to himself, language becomes that of the other. Its signification exists only for the other. Using a perfectly normal sentence, he sends a

[57] See above, pp. 37–38 (Parain), 36–37 (Bataille), and pp. 39–41 (Ponge) for an exposition of Sartre's articles on some of their writings and on the problem of language.

salesman for a book he does not want, so that he can steal the one in front of him. Even when he tells a salesman that he wants to buy something (that he cannot steal), he pays for it with stolen money; and while he does not lie, he plays a role, he is a *comédien.* He recites the words of the honest man just as the actor in Diderot's *Paradoxe du comédien* coldly observes himself intonate those of Hamlet or Britannicus. Either as a true thief who lies or as a false bourgeois who speaks the truth, for Genet "the Word is the Other" (p. 311). In theft (as in homosexuality) intimate reality becomes pure appearance and appearance becomes reality, so that language, which is supposed to reveal, actually deceives.

For Genet ordinary prose is that of the other; but could he not use the dialect of the underworld as his own? Indeed, slang permits the outsiders to communicate with one another without recourse to the language of the society which represents them all, threatens many with jail and some with execution. Their speech is not a new invention, its main device being distortion of dictionary words, by often only a slight shift in meaning, or by the more extensive use of adjectives as nouns. Since these words also refer to things mentioned in normal speech, evoking the same essence by a concrete term [58]—but indirectly—they have something allusive and poetic about them; and in their obliqueness they seem modest despite their manifest vulgarity.

> To talk argot is to choose Evil, that is, to know being and truth but to reject them in favor of a nontruth which offers itself for what it is; it is to choose the relative, parasitism, failure [p. 314].

One might add that here, through abjection on the verbal plane, dominant society is rendered unreal, just as through the "sublime" chosen by Preciosity in the seventeenth century.

Genet, however, as a "girl queen" was not allowed to use

[58] "Bureaucrate," for instance, becomes "rond de cuir" (cushion).

slang, the language of the "hard ones." [59] Like Divine he knows references to himself as feminine are at best valid for the others. In his double exile, both common prose and the dialect of the underworld lose for him their value as means of communication; but by the same token they do not pass unnoticed as they do for those who use them simply to signify. He hears slang as the voice of the male. Genet in his writings uses it as a revenge against society, and at the same time he betrays the outsiders by the use he makes of their language, sometimes only of a single word.[60] Sartre writes that one can describe Genet's use of words from the point of view of both "lawful and unlawful" language ("faste et néfaste"). One can, for instance, apply Blanchot's analysis of Mallarmé's choice of terms from poetic language ("la langue faste"):

"This single word is only the beginning of the shift since, by means of the signification, it again renders present the object signified, the material reality of which it has set aside. It is therefore necessary, if the absence is to continue, that the word be replaced by another word which removes it further and the latter by another which flees it and this last by the very movement of the flight. . . . We gain entrance . . . into an order where every figure is a passage, a disquiet, a transition, an illusion, an act that has an infinite trajectory" [quoted on p. 317].

Genet is not yet a poet. He knows three languages—the accepted one, slang and the dialect of the "girl queens"—but he cannot truthfully speak any of them, for he is a thief to society, a "girl queen" to the thieves, and a traitor to all. Devoid of reciprocity with anyone, he speaks to himself, or rather, to the other within himself. Genet, who owns nothing

59 "Slang was for men. It was the male tongue" (*Our Lady,* p. 90).

60 His cellmates tell him, "we're making the pages [beds]," to which—in his mind—he adds "of the palace" thus restoring "the pages" to its original sense and inverting "make" to its sexual slang meaning. He may have answered, "yes, let's make the pages." Seemingly an answer that establishes contact and understanding between him and his cellmates, but actually an escape into his own imaginary world. (See *Saint Genet,* p. 317).

but words, degrades reality to appearance, and makes of appearance his reality. In abjection he leaves the world of prose, and becomes a poet.[61] "It is the vertigo, the want, the nothingness, and the negation which mark the poetic emotion" (pp. 325–26). Genet experiences again and again the power of a word, as during his original crisis. Genet when about twenty to twenty-two years old is a poet but he does not know it himself, for he addresses his word- or sentence-poems only to himself; they are attempts at salvation in a dialogue with himself. He magnifies his abjection through incantation and prayer so that he can endure it. We find little narrative or anecdote in his writings of this period, but words that attempt to preserve the sacred amidst what is unspeakably profane.

Sartre gives an *explication de texte* of this single line of octosyllabic verse by Genet: "Moissonneur des souffles coupés."[62] It would seem to mean that impassible nature is seen as fused with some frightening episode of a man's experience, but closer examination shows that the reaper has vanished into the past along with the "cut breaths." A line that because of the absence of any verb neither negates nor affirms, and that seemed at first not to mean anything, in final analysis comes to mean: nothing. Genet seeks only the word, not its signification.[63] He has created a thing. To Sartre a word signifies when it is a substitution for an absent object, when it is

61 "I now perceive in it [my work] . . . a will to rehabilitate persons, objects and feelings reputed vile. Naming them with words that usually designate what is noble was perhaps childish and somewhat facile. . . . I have forgotten those boys: all that remains of them is the attribute which I have sung. . . . I wanted them to have the right to the honors of the Name" (*Journal*, p. 96). We know of course that from the start Genet has transfigured their pitiable reality into magnificent archetypal essences of Evil.

62 See *ibid.*, pp. 330–338, for this "harvester of cut breaths." See also Genet's own reminiscence (in *Journal* pp. 39–41), to which Sartre turns after a most painstaking and objective analysis of this "cluster of sound."

63 Genet writes in his "Letter from the author" prefacing Pauvert's edition of *The Maids*, that he aimed to produce a "gap" between reality and appearance in this "play on a play," to manage thus to abolish the characters in favor of signs as distant as possible from what they were originally to signify (p. 13).

transcendent. A thing, however, has a "meaning," a quality in its being which is also that of other like objects, present or absent, visible or invisible, a transcendence which has become immanent in that thing. The word may lead to an intuition of being, the thing itself is. The word "perfume" signifies, the perfume is. Genet's first poem is like a thing, a "poem-thing"; the *signification* of words has been transformed into a *meaning:*

When we first encounter it, it is inert and voluminous, like a carriage or a wig; it indicates nothing; it refers only to itself; it is at first only a sounded rhythm that imposes itself on our breathing; and it is only after repeating it as a refrain that we discover in it a vague and, as it were, natural savor. It would be a waste of time to look for logical organization in it; it expresses, without differentiating, the countryside and fear, the diurnal mystery of Nature: all things interpenetrate [pp. 332–33].

The young Genet does not believe that he has a history. He has not changed from his reform-school days, when he was fifteen years old, to the time of his first theft with forced entry at twenty-five. His reflection and his abjection are born of a belief that the original theft has stopped his development and has stamped his life into a mold in which he repeats himself. There is no progression from *Our Lady of the Flowers* (written in 1942) to *Miracle of the Rose* (written in 1943) and to *The Thief's Journal* (published in 1949). Nothing ever happens to the character representing him in his books. The people he meets are archetypes. He has seen the prototypes of his black knights in the underworld or in prison, or he has "fed on the serial stories which are the *chansons de geste* of these plebeian heroes" (p. 342). They antedate Genet's existence, and in his novels they exist only as types.

In another of the many *explications de texte* (pp. 342–55) by which Sartre advances and demonstrates his critical understanding of Genet's work and of his life history, we are shown the mechanism by which the author reduces an individual to a gesture and a symbol and by which he has a particular event take on the meaning of a repetition of a sacred ritual. In the *Journal* Genet describes how he notices a boy in Antwerp, who spits into his hands and rubs them as if preparing to do some work, which he is not. This gesture and the fact that he wears a broad belt, a symbol of manliness, distinguishes this boy. His beauty, like that of Stilitano, of Bulkaen, of Mignon and all the other heroes of Genet's fiction and reality, only conveys to Genet the fatality of crime. Genet knows that Stilitano only imitates a criminal figure of prestige, and what Genet likes about his imitation is precisely its character of a gesture, that is, of a posture already held by others. This "geste" is sacred, it transmits to its imitator the power of the original doer. Genet notes himself: "I sometimes try to imitate the discovered gesture. I note the state that it makes me know" (cited on p. 354). In Genet's erotic relationships, however, his identification with another seems to be more than a symbolic gesture:

I aspired at the time to being embraced by the calm, splendid statue of a man of stone with sharp angles. And I felt that peace only if I could completely take over his qualities and virtues, when I imagined I was he, when I made his gestures, uttered his words, when I was he [cited on p. 355].

To Sartre this means that since Genet is other for himself (x), he wishes to become another (y), in order himself to feel as another (y) that other one (x) whom he is. For this very reason his love is not lived, he does not lose himself to reach another person as in a normal relationship, he can only return to himself, he does not change. So that when Stilitano—in *The Thief's Journal*—leaves Genet for another boy there is no crisis; Genet simply lets a certain Armand take his place. Even Divine— in *Our Lady of the Flowers*—is more concerned with jealousy towards other "girl queens" than with love for her partner.

His loves do not even leave a true remembrance; what remains is purely imaginary. Genet himself explains: "Pretexts for my iridescence, then for my transparence, and finally for my absence, the lads I speak of evaporate. All that remains of them is what remains of me" (cited on p. 356). Again he has willed the situation the others have created; the indifference shown by the pimps towards him, he has returned against them.

For ten years—from fifteen to twenty-five years of age—Genet is put in apprenticeship, escapes, steals, is sent to reform school in Mettray, escapes, begs, tramps through France, joins the Foreign Legion, deserts it, flees to Barcelona where he steals and prostitutes himself, tramps through Spain, Italy, Central and Eastern Europe, crossing borders illegally and getting to know a goodly number of prisons on the way. Yet nothing changes him. As it is for a member of some primitive society, his time is cyclical, that of the eternal return, and it is therefore not irreversible. This adolescent does not acknowledge a historical process in his life nor will the author in his novels or plays.

Genet writes of himself that he is both the weakest and the strongest of men. He is the weakest as the object of society and of the "hard ones"; and he is the strongest when he outwits them as a "saint." This position depends on a number of sophisms which he has elaborated in his mind. He tries to "derange the mind" as Rimbaud tried to "derange the senses," and he succeeds in doing so—for a while—by circuitous reasoning. The impossibility of acting in pure Evil finds its counterpart in that of knowingly reasoning in error. That is precisely what Genet is attempting and Sartre defines it as his perversion (p. 363).

Genet actually builds his reasoning on the celebrated argument of Epimenides.[64] He wills his exile, the world's refusal of

[64] Of course, it could not stand the test of the simple rules governing a syllogism. It runs as follows: Epimenides says the Cretans are liars, he is Cretan, he is therefore a liar, hence the Cretans are not liars; thus, being Cretan, he

him, his evil and nothingness; but to refuse the world which refuses him is to accept being, which he does in his "miracles." So that to seek nothingness becomes a way of reaching being. Or, simply, when Genet seeks failure and obtains it, this is a success. But too lucid to believe his own rationalizations, Genet reaches the depths of his suffering: he seems to abandon the belief in sanctity. But could not this extreme sacrifice give him a "saintly consciousness" in the eyes of the Other and be rewarded?

Genet does not resolve his conflicts (to negate what is false so as to affirm what is true, and to destroy in order to build) but keeps two fields of reference between which his thoughts oscillate in an ever more frenetic swing back and forth. The positive pole is blind conformity, the negative one is negation of everything. There is absolutely no progress possible in this repetitive process of thought and no experience can breach it. There is, however, the fear of becoming old with which he cannot reason and which he imparts, much later when he becomes an author, to Divine in *Our Lady of the Flowers.* At times, Genet must also have feared, like some of the prison inmates in his novel, that flight into imagination could undermine him completely: a "hero" tells his stories, but now and then "he gives himself away," he needs to return to reality, and perhaps "he is afraid to fall to the depths of imagination to the point of becoming himself an imaginary being." [65] Yet both of Genet's postulations (to will the world and to will its total refusal) are already in the realm of imagination. "To refuse," writes Sartre, "is not to say no, but to modify by work" (p. 374). Genet's refusal is without any efficacity; it is a mere gesture. Genet is an actor, *un comédien,* in spite of himself.

Sartre sees in Genet's first play, *The Maids,* "the most ex-

must be telling the truth, wherefore the Cretans are liars, so he lies, and so on and so forth.

[65] *Miracle de la rose,* p. 217.

traordinary example of the whirligig of being and appearance, of the imaginary and the real." [66] Genet wishes to push appearance to its extreme. Two actresses play themselves, one another and "Madame" (who also appears briefly). Furthermore, Genet wanted the maids' roles performed by young men, with a poster next to the stage advising the spectators of this fact all through the performance.[67] Thus, "Genet *betrays* his actors. . . . Illusion, betrayal, failure: all the major categories that govern Genet's dreams are here present" (p. 655).

Theatrical appearance, which almost passes for reality, is used to show its unreality. In his second play, *Deathwatch,* Genet has men portray a similar back-and-forth between reality and appearance, and there Maurice (the "natural" assassin) and Lefranc (who suffers utter solitude) form what Sartre calls in one of his chapter headings "The Eternal Couple of the Criminal and the Saint [*la Sainte*]." In both plays, the mostly absent lady of the house (in *The Maids*) and the always absent Monsieur (in *Deathwatch*) represent the indifference of the pimp. To the degree that the maids love their employer they wish to become one, in conformity, but to the degree that they hate her they revolt, though only in their dreams. Moreover, each one also sees in the other herself as other. It is in order to will their servitude that they play each other's role, and in order to will everything as it is, that they each in turn play "madame." In this most false of appearances (thrice removed from reality: an actor plays a maid who plays another role) genuine being is reached, for the actor actually plays the role of an actor. Finally, each play is a black Mass, the rite of a murder (attempted or executed).[68] In short, Sartre shows how Genet's

[66] Appendice III, *"The Maids,"* in the *Saint Genet,* p. 654.

[67] As a concession to Louis Jouvet who directed the play at *L'Athénée* in 1946, this requirement was dispensed with.

[68] Genet writes in the "Letter from the Author" preceding Pauvert's edition of *The Maids:* "The highest modern drama has been expressed for two thousand years and every day in the sacrifice of the Mass" (p. 14). He then goes on to explain that "one of the functions of art is no doubt to substitute the efficacy of

very problems of being and the principle of his sophisms (truth is a lie, and a lie is the truth) are incarnated in these plays.[69]

We are now able to understand Genet's adventure. This energetic, active little man has dedicated himself to the mad undertaking of becoming what he already is and of destroying what he cannot prevent from being. Immediately his will volatilizes in the imaginary. Since it wills what cannot be willed, it is therefore dreaming that it wills it. Doomed by nature to remain ineffectual, his destruction and his approbation take place *symbolically*. The day he chose to will his destiny, Genet decided, unwittingly, to make himself a symbol, to express himself by symbols, and to live amidst symbols [p. 381].

When Genet wakes up to the fact that all he succeeds in doing is to play-act as *comédien* and that his interpretation of himself is only imaginary, he is going to will his dreams as a poet. But before he discovered that he could speak to others as a poet, he spent several years (from about the age of twenty to twenty-six) speaking only to himself. He suddenly realized that the kind of dreamer which he was all along was evil, for his imagination was reducing being to nothingness which paraded as being.[70] In this, his second metamorphosis, Genet therefore moves from an ethics of Evil in crime to an aesthetics of Evil in gesture. Sartre is thus led to discuss (in the chapter "Strange Hell of Beauty") the imaginary pursuit of value in aesthetics as an Evil which undermines Being, which is equated with the Good by the "spirit of seriousness." [71]

---

beauty for religious faith." And this beauty ought to have "the power of a poem, that is, of a crime" (p. 15).

[69] "I go to the theatre so as to see myself on stage (recreated in a single character or by means of a multiple character . . .) such as I couldn't—or wouldn't dare—see or dream myself to be, and such, however, as I know myself to be" (Genet, "How to play *The Maids*," introductory note to the Barbézat edition of the drama, p. 10).

[70] Sartre had himself become aware of the difference between perception and imagination in his *Imagination* (see above, pp. 12–14) and had elaborated on it in *The Psychology of Imagination* (see above, pp. 19–23).

[71] It will be remembered that Sartre calls *l'esprit de sérieux* the escape from

It is precisely when Genet knows that his long daydream has been a lie and a sham that he tries to dwell upon it. And—in this he is highly unusual—he seems capable of embroidering on his imaginings while at the same time perceiving them for the nonreality they are, of maintaining and enjoying for long intervals the tension between these mutually exclusive structures of consciousness. Most wretched among the wretched, Genet in the Barrio Chino of Barcelona, fully aware of his condition,[72] manages to protect himself for a time by dreaming up a fabulous existence.[73] He thus creates of himself a false image, just as he is a false female.

Only as regards the image, Sartre points out, can one affirm that to be is to be perceived (*esse est percipi*)—its being depends exclusively on the dreamer. In his prison cells or on the roads and in the slums of Europe as a lonely outcast, Genet, cerebral and lyrical, evil and religious, oscillates between acid knowledge and aesthetic magnification.[74] He still spends a great deal of energy in sustaining his daydreams.[75] Indeed, in onanism, he is able to have his imagination produce a real event in which, furthermore, he satisfies his fundamental contradiction.

---

recognition of fundamental contingency by making oneself believe that one's pursuits are a necessary and sufficient cause for existence. On this self-deceiving conduct, see *Being,* p. 626.

72 "1932. Spain at the time was covered with vermin, its beggars. . . . I was thus a louse, and conscious of being one" (*Journal,* p. 11).

73 "In his solitary eroticism the leper consoles himself and hymns his disease. Poverty made us erect. All across Spain we carried a secret, veiled magnificence unmixed with arrogance. . . . Thus developed my talent for giving a sublime meaning to so beggarly an appearance. (I am not yet speaking of literary talent)" (*ibid.,* p. 20).

74 "The tapestry known as "Lady with the Unicorn" excited me for reasons which I shall not attempt to go into here" (*ibid.,* p. 39). The lady is portrayed (on a series of tapestries in the Musée de Cluny) between a unicorn and a lion. Genet recalls that, frightened during an illegal border crossing by his recollection of Vacher, the mass murderer, he created himself "a fable-like fauna" (*ibid.,* p. 40). It is as if Genet had invoked the innocent unicorn to protect himself from the ferocious lion.

75 "Bulkaen is God's finger, Harcamone being God since he is in heaven (I speak of the heaven that I create for myself and to which I devote myself body and soul) . . ." (*Miracle de la rose,* p. 195).

He can see himself as both the criminal and the saint when the former violates the latter.

In passing, Sartre gives us an ontological explanation of the pederast's "elegance" and bad taste.[76] Extremely loud colors, violent perfumes and unusual combinations are expressions of an *antiphysis,* of sheer appearance. We are shocked by "bad taste" because it points to man's ability to transform nature, and, we might add, to exceed social norms. But while the ordinary enjoyment of the gadget, also an industrial product, is humanistic since it appreciates human labor, the homosexual's predilection for the artificial is due to the fact that it is mere appearance, that is, false by definition as is the pederast's existence. "In matters of great importance the vital element is not sincerity, but style," wrote Oscar Wilde, whom Sartre calls the "prince of aesthetes" (p. 410), and who termed "style" what Genet calls elegance. We can readily see that it will be easy for Genet to project elegance and style into words: "A false woman harboring an imaginary passion for an appearance of a man and adorning herself in order to please him with appearances of jewels: is not that the definition of the homosexual?" (p. 394).

It will be remembered that the object of freedom is the ideal value in-itself-for-itself,[77] which, while it is out of reach, is also the aim of the artist who, in his search for beauty, prefers appearance to the reality of being. In their fear of such a negation, the "righteous," however, have assimilated the Good to being and have persuaded themselves that values are objective structures of reality. It is true that sometimes we all perceive "beauty" as one imagines it: as when contemplating natu-

[76] "To achieve harmony in bad taste is the height of elegance. Stilitano had unfalteringly chosen a pair of tan and green crocodile shoes, a brown suit, a white silk shirt, a pink tie, a multicolored scarf, and a green hat. It was all held in place by pins, links, and gold chains, and Stilitano was elegant" (*Journal,* p. 106).

[77] See above pp. 51–55 and *Being,* pp. 194–195.

ral scenery which seems brought about expressly by some value and created to manifest some finality.[78] Actually, at such moments, the being of the landscape is transformed into what is only an appearance in our imagination.[79] Someone who throughout life wishes to see being as appearance is an aesthete. Genet perceives in the same way as one imagines:

"I kept moving forward among the same flowers, among the same faces, but I sensed, from a kind of uneasiness that was coming over me, that something was happening to me. The scents and colors were not transformed, yet it seemed to me that they were becoming more essentially themselves. I mean that they were beginning to exist for me with their own existence, with less and less the aid of a support: the flowers. Beauty too was becoming detached from the faces. Every child who passed tried to hold it back, but it ran off. Finally it remained alone, the faces and flowers had disappeared. . . . Strange hell of Beauty" [quoted on pp. 409–10].

Beauty, as nonbeing, cannot be fulfilling, but through it Genet can assume his resentment against those who *are*. For Beauty as well as Evil undermine being, and Beauty imagined by those who hate is akin to Evil. Genet's aim as author will be to transform the "righteous" into an aesthete, and thus to lead his enemy—rather than by attacking him through criminal evil —by the attraction of beauty away from his "spirit of seriousness" and to appearance.

The criminal act in the reality of Genet's existence, corresponds to the gesture in his aesthetic imagination. Genet, writing about Divine (and therefore himself) in *Our Lady of the Flowers,* notes that "all her acts were served by gestures that were necessitated not by the act but by a choreography that transformed her life into a perpetual ballet" (cited on pp.

[78] This experience is at the origin of the pantheistic interpretation of nature, without validity for Sartre.

[79] Natural beauty seems to indicate value preceding being, which could only emanate from the *Ens causa sui* (a Being which is its own cause), God. Artistic beauty points to value as emanating from the artist's being.

411–12).[80] Genet forever moves from ignominious reality to superfluous bazaar-luxury, which he has learned to appreciate from popular song and literature; and to his luxuries always clings the misery in which they have been displayed.[81] Similarly, when he succeeds in winning us over with some artful literary make-believe he is also ready to rebut us with some bitter truth which expresses his hatred for his readers.

Genet, who tried to make things unreal by gestures, becomes aware of the fact that language can render this service more easily. For Genet, excluded from language as from the goods of this world, words have the being of whatever object they name. And he will usually declare something from the world of misery to be from that of luxury, on the order of "the prison is a palace": "Genet restores to the verb an ontological power" (p. 427). He does that both by demonstrating his conviction that this is so and by enunciating it as if it were a tautological truth. His art consists in preparing us for such substitutions, in moving us to the point where we understand "becomes" when we read "is." Genet employs two devices in his lyricism. One is magnification, by which he elevates simple pimps to the ranks of assassins, and common traitors to that of saints by naming them to such a high calling. The other is a device of transubstantiation; again by the use of words. "Harcamone est une rose"; the persuasiveness of such a preposterous statement ("Harcamone is a rose") lies in the sonorous *o*. This process of

[80] Sartre gives an *explication de texte* (pp. 412–17) of such a gesture (in *Our Lady,* pp. 193–94): Divine, having accidentally lost her diadem, which lies shattered on the floor, crowns herself with her false teeth, whereby she affirms and renders unreal her utter misery in a terribly real but illusory gesture.

[81] In much the same way is his ethics bound up with betrayal. This shocks the unsuspecting reader just when he has been convinced of Genet's true feelings: "I told Salvador that I couldn't stay at the hotel that night and that a former member of the Legion was offering me his room. He turned pale. The humility of his pain made me feel ashamed. In order to leave him without remorse I insulted him. . . . He gave me a woebegone look, but it was charged with a poor wretch's hatred. I replied with the word: 'Fruit.' I joined Stilitano who was waiting for me outside" (*Journal,* p. 33).

transubstantiation also dematerializes his heroes, so that they finally take on the shape of heraldic figures. Having produced a system of sophisms and a rhetoric to undermine being, Genet succeeds in projecting in his language the vertiginous and negating appearance of beauty.

In 1936—he is twenty-six years old—Genet returns to France from his adventures abroad. Until now only a beggar, a prostitute, a stool pigeon and a petty thief, he meets and collaborates with a professionally competent robber who is skillful in using tools when breaking into places and also laboriously active. "I had the revelation of theft," reminisces Genet, who tries to seduce us into believing him when he states: "I went to theft as to a liberation, as to light" (cited on p. 435). Sartre makes of this statement the title of his next chapter, in which he downgrades Genet's claim that his turning to an "artisanal" pursuit had alone freed him from his dream world. Why then, argues Sartre, would he have become an author? Why was he obliged to become an author in order to solve his problems, all of his problems, in the way he ultimately did? "Genet merges the concrete person with the most abstract determinations of activity" (p. 439).

It is true nonetheless that in his new criminal professionalism Genet is not only gesturing; he now also acts, he even labors, at a "trade." From the hierarchical society of those who are the "hard ones" or the "girl queens" by heredity, as it were, he has moved to a society where one becomes because one does. Genet has partly moved from aristocratic to professional values, from mysticism to rationalism. But, largely, he remains in the field of the imaginary, and Evil continues to haunt him. Now, however, the pretense of "working" deepens the conflict between his reality and the game of fantasies that he plays for himself.

At this time Genet comes to feel that he has grown too old for his feminine role, a realization towards which he has been prompted also by his active role as a professional thief. Sartre bases himself on intentional self-portraits from Genet's later novels (*Our Lady of the Flowers, Miracle de la rose, Pompes funèbres* and *Querelle de Brest*) and on Genet's own reminiscences and statements, in order to elucidate the conditions of this change of attitude. It would seem that Genet agreed only reluctantly, as a necessity, to assume an active homosexual part. Since he had been spiritually violated during his original crisis, and wished to reenact this experience, this now meant a radical reversal of roles. He could no longer abandon himself to his dreams when he had to impress a younger partner as a "super male." "The condition of an aging fairy is a strange one. Though physiologically male, that is, possessing male sex organs, he is forced to *play at being a male,* that is, to play what he is, as Solange the maid plays at being a servant" (pp. 445–46). While Gide had tried in the *Corydon* to establish homosexuality as something natural, to Genet it was always unnatural and Evil, and he liked it for this very reason. Now, however, as an active partner, the character of his pleasure has become forced and imaginary.

Now Genet has to assume the role of those criminal "heroes" who dominated him. He must now play the role of an independent "sovereign" and suffer the consequences: isolation and anguish, which tend to bring him closer to reality just as had his activity as a burglar. His acts interfere with his dreams, and he has to take a reflective attitude towards his imaginary world. It cannot satisfy him any longer, and he is brought face to face with a new choice. His rendering unreal of reality in his own imagination has proved to be a failure. Could he instead try to realize his imagination? Don Juan and Don Quixote have never existed but are real to the reading public of the world. If Genet were to lead society to accept his dreams it would lend objectivity to them. Divine, "the Giddy one," seduced others by her gestures, and the aging Genet will do likewise by the construction of traps, of objects—his books—through which the imaginary enters into the world of reality: "The paradox of a work of art is that its meaning remains unreal, that is, outside the world and that nevertheless it can be the cause and the end of real activities" (p. 455). The private imagination, the world-objects of the aesthete will have to be projected into the artist's literary work.

Poetry was an apprenticeship towards the prose of Genet, "who has reinvented literature" (p. 473). It is not that his poems are worthless; Sartre finds them seductive because of "a kind of rough, primitive richness" (p. 478). But Genet's poetry leads towards prose since he simply links his "sound-clusters" into transparent and signifying (hence nonpoetic) units. In a close analysis of Genet's early poems (in the chapter "A Mechanism Having the Exact Rigor of Verse") Sartre can demonstrate how they are crystallizations of Genet's experiences and how they lead to his prose solutions, composed at a juncture between his past as an aesthete and his future as an author.

After a first poem, written, typically enough, so that he might "be moved" (p. 459), and so that he might hear himself as another, Genet writes a poem (eight years later at the age of twenty-eight) in order to antagonize others, and this is a turn towards being understood by them. Genet himself relates this event as follows:

"I was pushed into a cell where there were already several prisoners in 'city clothes.' You're allowed to wear your jacket while you're still awaiting trial. But though I had filed an appeal, I was made, by mistake, to wear the prisoner's outfit. That weird getup seemed to be a jynx. They despised me. I later had the greatest difficulty in overcoming their attitude. Among them was a prisoner who composed poems to his sister, idiotic, sniveling poems that they all admired. Finally, in irritation, I said that I could do just as well. They challenged me and I wrote *The Condemned Man.* I read it to them and they despised me even more. I finished reading it amidst insults and jeers. A prisoner said to me, 'I write poems like that every morning.' When I got out of jail, I made a particular point of finishing the poem, which was all the more precious to me for having been despised" [quoted on pp. 460–61].

Of course, Sartre does not seek the causes of an act; he considers that he has explained an act when he can uncover the fundamental themes which the individual expresses through it, often in some new syntheses. In this case—as in his life and in the prison cell in which the world had appeared to him as a play in a prison—Genet again feels doubly exiled, which feeling we recognize as the first leitmotiv that directs his life. He sees himself as a marked individual even among fellow prisoners; for all of them he is the other, he is "the foundling," and so he can see himself designated in his original culpability. There is here also his second leitmotiv, that of fatality: the prison administration has, cruelly or carelessly, abandoned him, just as had his mother; accused unjustly or not, he wears the garb of the convicted, he is what the others see in him. And God is testing him by placing him in a position of culpability in regard to the others in the cell. This leads to the third leitmotiv which reverses the first one: the others are guilty. They hate in him their own image, they fear their own convictions and prison sentences. He is their negation. They take towards him the attitude the "righteous" have towards feelings within themselves, when they cast them out and project them on others. As always, all of this is a play of appearances and mirror reflections, for Genet is not yet tried and either he or the others may escape conviction. What is new to this situation is that Genet picks up the gauntlet, addresses himself to his cellmates and creates an object, a poem.

Through a "martyr's reflex" (p. 463), through a fascination for the bad taste shown by this assembly, Genet invites their ugly reprobation by his superior verses. These people were evil in applauding a maudlin poem, they will be more evil still in hissing better ones; and they will crown him with their hate.

He deliberately provokes his cellmates, for he is reciting *The Condemned Man* which treats of crime, homosexuality and the death penalty. With his imaginary object Genet produces a real and brutal reaction. He is despised, he has an experience which through his sophisms becomes akin to his sainthood and asceticism in crime. "Similarly, St. Theresa wished to be slandered in order to raise herself above men and to remain alone in the presence of God. Genet's God is himself, himself as Other" (p. 465). Once outside of prison, alone, he takes up the poem again to rework it: it is dear to him because of the heinous reaction it provoked. He only read it to the others so that they would confer his singularity on him. The poetic act is still only a gesture; its aim is the martyrdom of the poet.

The first two stanzas of the poem, which Sartre analyzes (pp. 467–71), contain a number of truly poetic "sound clusters." The first line, almost entirely monosyllabic and forcefully rhythmic,[82] leads to others which are repetitive. Their meaning is of the magnifying variety: "prison is palace." To communicate his lyrical intuitions, Genet chose to present and connect them by intermittent prosaic explanations. He thus transcribes, translates, as it were; and logical signification takes precedence over the immanent poetic meaning. Moreover, his verse is derivative: Sartre cites examples to show how some poems read like an imitation of Cocteau, some others of Valéry, of Verlaine, or of Mallarmé. But, unlike Mallarmé who, says Sartre, wished to "reveal Nothingness as the immediate meaning of poetry," Genet wished to "commit a *murder,* that is, to show us the real, its derealization and finally the unreal as the gulf in which the real is swallowed up." Whereas Mallarmé "used

[82] The first stanza: "Le vent qui roule un coeur sur le pavé des cours/Un ange qui sanglote accroché dans un arbre/La colonne d'azur qui entortille le marbre/Font ouvrir dans ma nuit des portes de secours" (Genet, (*Œuvres complètes,* II, 179). ("The wind that rolls a heart on the pavestones of courtyards/ An angel that sobs caught in a tree/The column of azure round which twines the marble/Unlock in my darkness emergency exits" [translated in *Saint Genet,* p. 467].)

half-extinguished words that illuminated each other with their reciprocal gleams; Genet chooses dazzling words whose lights extinguish each other reciprocally" (p. 476). Furthermore, certain of Genet's images are empty abstractions and communicate this character to all the others.

Genet had two conceptions of poetry which corresponded to the contradictions which were besetting him—namely, his fatalistic belief in his destiny and his quest to find that other he was for the others; and, on the other hand, his will to assume this condition. His inner conflict was basically similar to that of Baudelaire who also oscillated from freedom to fatalism. They both pursued the impossible dream of creating a poem that would be the outcome of both the most accomplished and lucid labor and of compelling inspiration. Sartre sees here the problem of modern poetry[83] to which Mallarmé and Rimbaud, Valéry and Breton have given solutions as divergent as are thesis and antithesis.

Between the poems *Funeral Dirge* and *The Galley* Genet had begun to write *Our Lady of the Flowers.* Here he had to address himself to others, to make himself understood, precisely since he wished to lead his readers astray by charming them into accepting Evil. So Genet came to assign to prose his voluntary tendencies; and by the same token he should have been able to free his poetry from exposition and explanation and thus to assign to it the images of his fatalism. But it was too late. He could not escape from his own logical and voluntary discourse; instead, he would write novels, in which poetry suddenly explodes and volatilizes prose (see p. 478).

So far Genet's masterpiece among his prose works has undoubtedly been *Our Lady of the Flowers.* This book, so original it cannot readily be classified,[84] is analyzed by Sartre as

[83] A problem which Apollinaire terms that of poets "naturels" or "raffinés" (in a letter to André Breton, March 12, 1916). Robert Lowell, similarly, speaks of "poetry raw or cooked."

[84] In this respect one might say that Genet's work is as baffling as Rabelais's

representing in its very writing the author's progress towards an awareness of himself as an author, that is, as representing Genet's metamorphosis from aesthete to artist. The novel, Sartre points out, is rent by ambiguity. Its heroes are doomed by destiny while their author intervenes with willful freedom, which, surprisingly, not only disconcerts but also entices the reader.[85] And utter dissolution is presented triumphantly. The writing of the book—in the jail at Fresnes with a pencil on some brown paper the inmates were to make into bags, without any hope of publication—was in itself an act of considerable optimism. Genet, alone in his cell, wrote in order to dream. "No other book, not even *Ulysses,* brings us into such close contact with an author" (p. 484). It represents the gradual exorcising of his Narcissism and the conversion of the aesthete into an artist.

Genet's criterion for fashioning his characters and for lingering in their company is simply the erotic pleasure with which they can provide him. Moral or physical verisimilitude are largely replaced by fantasy, born of the fascination they exert on Genet. The reader, who remains dubious about the reality of Our Lady of the Flowers, of Darling, of Gorgui and of Gabriel, is attracted by the seductiveness they have for Divine. But, in Divine, Genet also tries to come to grips with his fear of aging. And in Ernestine he expresses both his hatred of women, since his mother had abandoned him, and his desire of feminin-

---

and some of Diderot's creations. In Genet the poetic magnification has the same disruptive effect on a work that is supposedly a novel as the sheer exuberance of language in Rabelais and the potent but unresolved ideas in Diderot.

85 "It is my own destiny, be it true or false, that I am draping (at times a rag, at times a court robe) on Divine's shoulders. Slowly but surely I want to strip her of every vestige of happiness so as to make a saint of her. The fire that is searing her has already burnt away heavy bonds; new ones are shackling her: Love. A morality is being born, which is certainly not the usual morality. . . . Divine is not beyond good and evil, there where the saint must live. And I, more gentle than a wicked angel, lead her by the hand" (*Our Lady,* p. 99). (The last sentence reads in French: "Et moi, plus doux qu'un mauvais ange, par la main je la conduis" [*Notre-Dame,* p. 40].)

ity; she does what Genet would like to do. Altogether, "except for the Marquis de Sade and two or three others, very few novelists take out their passions on their characters out of sheer cussedness" (p. 490), as does Genet in regard to both his magnified and his more realistic creatures.

When writing, Genet is drawn away from self-serving reverie. Words universalize, they lead to communication with the other. Even if only pronounced aloud in solitary confinement, their sound has a presence which mental images have not. For this narcissistic convict there are subject words and object words which serve to reproduce the wish that Genet-Darling will subdue Genet-Divine. But there are also those words which sound like blasphemy, uttered in defiance of the "righteous." When they are put on paper, he can read them afterwards; and when he realizes that they still lack dimension, he can try to have them read by others, who will give reality to the scandal he wishes to produce.[86] While writing, Genet begins to reflect on formulations,[87] and even on the course of his dreams, which means that he is also awake, more nearly assuming the role of an artist conscious of his creation, even though he is mainly concerned with his own pleasure. But

> this development of onanistic themes gradually becomes an introspective exploration. The emotional pattern begets the image, and in the image Genet, like an analyst, discovers the emotional pattern. His thought crystallizes before his eyes; he reads it, then completes and clarifies it. Whereupon reflection is achieved, in its translucent purity, as *knowledge* and as *activity*" [p. 499].

Sartre contrasts the poetic imagination of Rimbaud and of Nietzsche, which is expansive and humanistic, with that of

[86] See above, pp. 87–88, for Sartre's position on the author-reader relationship, in *What is Literature?* Only the reader can objectify the writer's imaginary creation.

[87] "I shall speak to you about Divine, mixing masculine and feminine as my mood dictates, and if, in the course of the tale, I shall have to refer to a woman, I shall manage, I shall find an expedient, a good device, to avoid any confusion" (*Our Lady*, p. 71).

Baudelaire and of Mallarmé, which tends to contract and seeks to prove the existence of a stable and quasi-theological order. Genet belongs to the latter category: he has to posit the Good before he can violate it. He leaves no room for the accidental, his vision is hierarchic and essentialist, the anecdotal represents the eternal.[88] There is no history, no progression; each event is a ceremonial and ritual reenactment. In his art he has linked truth and myth, and, as an empiricist and a Platonist, he gives to his book a strange and naïve air of "mirror of the world." Like all artists, Genet becomes "a real creator of an imaginary world" (pp. 517–18). He started writing to please himself and, failing that, writing has led him to address himself to readers.

Sartre focuses on Genet's art in the chapter "On the Fine Arts Considered as Murder." The theme of Genet's novels is always a crime and his books are symbolic murders. Genet who could not have himself loved, wills himself hated. In his work he has created a "mad object" in order to make of himself an object of horror. Neither looking in the mirror nor being possessed by someone, nor, in turn, actively possessing someone, permitted him to become for himself the other he was for the others. At last, by the creation of an "object trap," he forces the others to see him as he wants to be seen. At last he is the other, he is the thief recognized by all.

Sociology, psychopathology and criminology, among other disciplines of the social sciences, have explained crime from the outside, by whatever is visible of crime and of criminals. The poet uncovers the invisible, the human significance and the

[88] ". . . populous streets on whose throng my gaze happens to fall: a sweetness, a tenderness, situates them outside the moment; I am charmed and—I can't tell why—that mob of people is balm to my eyes. I turn away; then I look again, but I no longer find either sweetness or tenderness. The street becomes dismal, like a morning of insomnia" (Genet quoted in *Saint Genet*, p. 505). Sartre comments that if Genet found an order in this fortuitous moment, it is because he had put it there in the first place. In his books generally, Genet can satisfy his desire to create a universe and be the man who discovers its laws.

See also above, p. 15 and pp. 31–32, for such "Aristotelian" experiences in *Nausea* and *Choix des élues*.

freedom of doing. What social science considered a determined statistic [89] is rehabilitated as the gratuitous luxury of the volition of evil. When Genet thus manifests evil, he shocks "the righteous" by its unwarranted singularity, irreducible to science and to law, and by making them realize that evil resides within themselves. Though objects of horror, Genet's works have gained a considerable reading public, because of his uncanny artistic ability to cast a spell that traps the reader before he can react with indifference or revulsion.

In art the world is presented to us as if it were a human creation; beauty is an invitation to feel oneself as a part of the world, and to accept evil as an inevitable aspect of such a totality. Thus, "by the beauty of his style, of his images, by the aesthetic depth of his inventions, by the rigorous, classical unity of his works" (p. 535) Genet, in an exercise of formal beauty, leads us to follow him step by step into a world he set in motion, one which has an ugly ethics. He uses the first person, or, if this device is too alienating at the outset, he changes to the first person at an appropriate moment in his story, in order to have the reader substitute himself sympathetically for the author. He has himself possessed by his readers. Genet, in whom the others were thinking (*I am a thief*), now, in bitter revenge, thinks in the others, his readers who endow his experience with their own emotions.

Genet wants to achieve still more: the reader must come to recognize that this thief (who is guilty) is a saint (beyond the scope of human culpability). The reader is invited to adopt the author's magnifying judgments. To this end, a language for-

89 Such an attitude is not limited to the social sciences, for as Sartre already noted in his article on Dos Passos (see above, pp. 25–27)—then, however, with some measure of approval: "We get [in Dos Passos] a glimpse of an order beyond the accidents of fate or the contingency of detail, an order more supple than Zola's physiological necessity or Proust's psychological mechanism, a soft and insinuating constraint which seems to release its victims, letting them go only to take possession of them again without their suspecting [it], in other words, a statistical determinism" ("John Dos Passos," pp. 101–2).

merly stacked against Genet is rephrased to his greater glorification.

Writing is a religious act, a rite suggestive of a Black Mass, and Genet does not dislike pomp: his sentences are difficult and rich, loaded, shimmering, full of gold, resuscitated constructions (inversion, ablative absolute, subject infinitive) ; he likes to stretch out a sentence until it breaks, to suspend its course by parentheses: deferred and awaited, the movement better reveals its urgency; at the same time, he uses syntax and words like a great lord, that is, like someone who has nothing more to lose; he does violence to them, he invents constructions, he decides insolently how they are to be used, as in the following admirable sentence: "Je nomme violence une audace au repos amoureux des périls" ["I give the name violence to a boldness lying idle and hankering for danger"]. At times precious to the point of oddity, at times incorrect, he never lets his prose be overshadowed by the object; it pushes itself forward, makes itself conspicuous and does not allow the reader to overlook it [p. 542].

The reader whom Genet's art may have moved close to accepting the preposterous proposition that "the thief is a saint [*une sainte*]," or at least to believing that he has been given to experience the lives and loves of the underground (in the Dostoyevskian sense) , this reader has fallen prey to a deception. "Genet's art is a mirage, a confidence trick, a pitfall" (p. 536) . According to Klossowski, who bases himself on the Church Fathers, the devil "must borrow a being other than his. As he himself is only a negation, he needs another existence to exercise his negation." To read Genet, says Sartre, is to enter into a pact with the devil: it is to give voice and feeling to "the leaves" of the book, which, actually, are "the dead leaves" which Satan offers for souls. For once we have finished reading one of his novels "we shall know no more than we did before about prison or ruffians or the human heart. Everything is false" (p. 558) .[90]

[90] Sartre's statement is perhaps extreme. But, actually, it is through Sartre's critique of Genet that we get to understand the complexity of pathological criminal and social conduct, while Genet's books give us largely a charmed view of his world.

Genet has simply succeeded in getting his readers to sustain, in the author's place, lies against truth, evil against good, nothingness against being. And, concludes Sartre, the unpardonable crime is to induce others to evil.

The only subject of the one novel Genet has written five times [91] is he himself. At long last Genet exists opposite himself, and as a pure consciousness he can now observe himself as an appearance lodged in the others. His dream-image of himself has been fixed in poetic prose and has been given objective reality by his readers. This was not only true for the avowedly autobiographical *Thief's Journal* but, as the critic has shown all along, for *Our Lady of the Flowers.* Sartre devotes the remainder of this chapter to an analysis of *Pompes funèbres* as a prime example of Genet's autobiographical art.

In all his books what actually takes place is a progressive dissolution of the external world and of their many heroes as they are replaced by the author's magnifying, reflective consciousness of them. In *Pompes funèbres,*

> the widower [Jean Genet] is in agony because he wants to stop suffering without ceasing to be himself. Genet seeks and finds the poetic resolution of this conflict: that is the entire subject of the book [p. 562].

He will absorb his dead lover (Jean Decarnin) by identification, but only as the other, whom Genet has been for himself all his life. Genet lives his mourning to the utter limit, to its perfection, "to the point of transforming the actual sorrow into an Eidos [essence] of sensibility" (p. 564). He transforms his gnawing, prereflective suffering into a reflective knowledge of it, an Idea. In the novel, at the outset there was an open tomb, at the end there is only Genet. "This process of involution characterizes all his books" (p. 564). In this book, from beginning to end the story of a funeral, during which suffering takes the form of an endless soliloquy, Jean Decarnin, just like Stili-

[91] *Our Lady of the Flowers, Miracle de la rose, Pompes funèbres, Querelle de Brest,* and *The Thief's Journal* (from 1942 to 1949).

tano in *The Thief's Journal,* from persona becomes archetype of an evildoer, then idea, then only some mystical quality of the universe, and finally nothing.

Yet Jean Decarnin did exist; he died fighting the Nazis during the liberation of Paris in 1944. But Genet transforms real events so that he can reenact through them his personal sacred drama.[92] The necrophilia in *Pompes funèbres,* as in all his books, really stems from his own 'death' "before the ax chops off my head." Sartre sees the cult of the dead as a profound vice, since their disappearance makes of this feeling of piety something imaginary. But, at least, normal people hold on to it in spite of its unreality in order to maintain their loyalty to the deceased; Genet, however, who did not care for the living Decarnin, does love the dead one, because of the very unreality of this passion. In death, nature has operated the transformation of an individual from being to appearance, an appearance which will exist through Genet.

All the other persons on whom the characters are modeled are likewise reduced to serving as participants in Genet's ritual drama. The executioner is the masculinization of Genet and represents his rancor and sadism; Paolo is Genet in his despair; Riton is brought into the story to show Genet as betraying Jean in utter masochism; Madame D. is Genet's mother in her guilt, the maid in her humiliation. In the Nazi Erik, Genet can express his admiration for brute force (perhaps also his resentment of France). With Erik and Riton who destroy one another on the last page, Jean Decarnin and Jean Genet, whom they incarnate, vanish also. "The work cancels out: there were only dead leaves" (p. 581).[93]

92 "Why am I limited in my choice and why do I now see myself depicting the third burial as in each of my three books?" (*Pompes funèbres, Œuvres complètes,* III, 10).

93 "The little maid returned to her room. . . . When she woke up, late in the night, a moonbeam, coming through the window, was making a light mark on the worn-out carpet. She got up and quietly, piously, she placed her daisy on that tomb. Then she undressed and slept until morning" (*Pompes funèbres,* p. 162).

Sartre compares this book to a ballet in which every couple repeats the ballerina's steps, since each person is only a different modulation of the original theme. It gives to the novel the rigorous unity of a fugal composition: a dovetailing of the characters and the themes of good and evil, life and death, being and nonbeing. It reminds Sartre also of a medieval composition in its use of analogies and its images of an underworld hierarchy in which each figure represents all the others. "You can conceive the magnificent counterpoint of *Funeral Rites* [*Pompes funèbres*]: symbols, analogies, substitutions, inversions of theme, anacruses." This counterpoint represents Genet's interior search of being. It resembles his ballet *Adam Miroir*, "the Thief's *ars poetica*" (p. 583).[94] Genet has succeeded in placing himself in the book; the book is Genet, who is to himself his only subject and his artistic criterion.

Sartre holds that in writing his novels Genet has practiced a self-psychoanalysis for some ten years which has at last freed him from his obsessions. "My victory is verbal and I owe it to the sumptuousness of the terms," writes Genet,[95] who, while infecting his readers with his own problems, has himself been able to come to terms with them.[96] It is true that his novels set

[94] Sartre writes (*Saint Genet*, p. 583) that this counterpoint, at the conceptual level, has as its constituents the "reflection-reflected" (consciousness perceiving) and the "reflection-reflecting" (consciousness reflecting on its perception), which are the prereflective and reflective structures of the for-itself. He had defined them in *Being* (p. 78) as "the obligation for the for-itself never to exist except in the form of an elsewhere in relation to itself, . . . a perpetual reference of self to self, of the reflection to the reflecting, of the reflecting to the reflection . . . given within the unity of a single act." And Sartre adds (p. 173) that "what defines the reflection for the reflecting is always *that to which it is presence*."

In this context, it is interesting to note that Lucien Goldmann (as developed in the course of a lecture of November 1, 1967, at Columbia University in New York, "Jean Genet, Sociologie théâtrale") found in the plays of Genet, as an ever-present structure, the ritual of the dominated playing at being dominating, once they have taken stock of their situation. It is as if Genet's liberation in consciousness, achieved in his novels, was later followed by the positing of a social liberation in his plays.

[95] *Journal*, p. 49. Sartre takes this as the title for the next-to-last chapter of the *Saint Genet*.

[96] "This journal is not a mere literary diversion. The further I progress, reducing to order what my past life suggests, and the more I persist in the rigor

in motion archetypes which ritually reenact Genet's crisis, as is pointed out above. But Sartre also detects a shift in Genet's attitude towards them. There is a show of self-pity in *Our Lady of the Flowers,* absent from the later novels. *Miracle de la rose,* written when the author-thief had acquired skill and some self-confidence as a burglar, shows a vision that is more dispassionate. *Pompes funèbres,* dedicated to the memory of a Resistance fighter fallen in the days of the liberation of Paris, even represents an experimentation with the Good by the mature Genet, now more nearly normal erotically. The obsession with his original crisis weakens with repetition: [97] his first two novels lead him from fantasizing on his life to the reflection on it and on his work as an artist which will constitute his third novel and his autobiography.

Having progressed from private daydreams to notations on the written page, Genet had come to grips with reality. For this magnificent thief and false saint had to judge his artistic effect on others first by the impression they made on himself, and he thereby gained a degree of reciprocity with the others. Genet, who had exhausted himself in the vain effort to become what the others saw in him, now, in his works, becomes an object for them and becomes in their eyes what he wants to be. Indeed, one's in-itself always exists in the consciousness of the others.

Where "la sainte" had failed, the poet succeeds. For he has created what Sartre considers a sacred object. Genet leads the

---

of composition—of the chapters, of the sentences, of the book itself—the more do I feel myself hardening in my will to utilize, for virtuous ends, my former hardships. I feel their power" (*Journal,* p. 52).

[97] One should say that it was not traumatic in the strictly Freudian sense—for Genet was always conscious of it—but he acted towards it as if it had been such an unsurpassable event in his life. Actually, and this supports Sartre's criticism of Freud's concept of the subconscious, most people work out their supposedly traumatic experiences by symbolic repetition, an acting-out of their obsession which sooner or later permits a reflective attitude towards it (usually called learning from experience); and from this distance arises the possibility of a solution. Genet represents a particularly extreme, complex and striking case of this general tendency.

reader to identify with the subjectivity of his characters and, then, intervenes and becomes the subject ("I name violence" or "I shall speak of Divine") who makes an object at once of his characters and of his readers. A cynical freedom imposes itself on the freedom of the reader, who, already caught in the process through this identification, comes face to face with his own secret bad conscience within his good one.

"An object becomes sacred insofar as it incorporates (that is, reveals) something other than itself. A sacral stone is a thing and yet in its depths a thing is revealed." [98]

Genet's books, mere objects, reveal us as, one might say, guilty reader-objects under the gaze of the cunning poet. Sartre now deepens the distinction he had made between prose and poetry in *What is Literature?* [99] and sees in the lack of transparency of poetry something akin to a sacred pronouncement.

[The writer of prose] who is *profane* by nature, recognizes his readers' freedom exactly insofar as he asks them to recognize his: prose is based on this reciprocity of recognition. The poet, on the other hand, requires that he be recognized by a public which he does not recognize. The writer of prose *speaks* to the reader, attempts to convince him in order to achieve unanimous agreement on one point or another; the poet speaks to himself through the mediation of the reader. The writer of prose uses language as a middle term between himself and the Other; the poet makes use of the Other as an intermediary between language and himself. Between the writer of prose and the reader, language is canceled so as to further the ideas of which it has been the vehicle; between language and the poet, it is the reader who tends to be effaced in order to become a pure vehicle of the poem; his role is *to objectify speech* in order to reflect to the poet his creative subjectivity in the form of sacred power [pp. 594–95].

[98] Quoted from Mircéa Eliade, *Traité d'histoire des religions*, p. 25, in *Saint Genet*, pp. 593–94. We have seen that in Semitic, Greek and Roman terminology sacred terms were expressions of awe towards either the sublime or the abject (see above, pp. 176–77).

[99] See above, pp. 84–86.

Once Genet has succeeded through his books in being the thief for others, he, who was always desperately essentialist, can now begin to exist freely as a creative artist and can in the process finally leave his past behind him. "In carrying commitment to an extreme, he again becomes available" (p. 597), that is, at the far end of free commitment lies the freedom to experiment. His largely autobiographical books, part experience, part fantasy, are moral experiences in which he pursued his own potentialities for evil to the limit.[100] Actually, however, this constant profanation of ethics was a way of showing considerable concern for it.[101] Genet had moved from experience to dream, from dream to an ultimate experience of evil; of accidental occurrences he then makes a pure event in his verbal experience. "His work is the imaginary aspect of his life and . . . his genius is one with his unswerving will to live his condition to the very end" (p. 612). He has put his ethics in words and in this cathartic experience, he delivers himself from involvement: now he wills neither evil nor good.[102]

Now the magic of crime has been dissipated, and Genet does not like his books—the last stage of his verbal ascesis. He had sought the glory of a thief and found that of a poet. In so doing, he resolved his obsession with sanctity. But just as the poet had buried the saint, so the man passes over the poet. At the end of a long and painful and passionate struggle, Genet takes possession of his alienated consciousness: he sees himself as all do and

100 "Creating is not a somewhat frivolous game. The creator has committed himself to the fearful adventure of taking upon himself, to the very end, the perils risked by his creatures. We cannot suppose a creation that does not spring from love. How can a man place before himself something as strong as himself which he will have to scorn or hate? But the creator will then charge himself with the weight of his characters' sins" (*Journal*, p. 187).

101 "Sooner or later it will have to be recognized that he is a moralist" (Jean Cocteau, quoted in *Saint Genet*, p. 600).

102 "By the gravity of the means and the splendor of the materials which the poet used to draw near to men, I measure the distance that separated him from them. The depth of my abjection forced him to perform this convict's labor. But my abjection was his despair. And despair was strength itself—and at the same time the matter for putting an end to it" (*Journal*, p. 186).

as no one does. And the righteous have also changed: through the prestige they have bestowed on his work they have recognized the evil within themselves. "The secret failure of every triumph is that the winner is changed by his victory and the loser by his defeat" (p. 613).

Sartre concludes his weighty volume with an afterthought: "Please Use Genet Properly." The title of this last chapter may be whimsical but the ideas expressed are as challenging as those in most of the book. With Genet, homosexuality and treason enter within the boundaries of the "human" world. "Horror is *recognition*" (p. 630), and the startled reader can no longer consider them outside of his own domain.[103] He is our truth as we are his.

In these last pages, Sartre gives voice to preoccupations which will lead him to write the *Critique de la raison dialectique*. Thus he notes that the dizzying speed of scientific progress is making the future an obsessive presence. And history will judge us severely—as Genet does now.

Because of our subject-object relationships, perfect reciprocity is impossible, and therefore "the most clearly expressed and understood thoughts conceal an incommunicable element" (p. 636). There is at either extreme of communication the passion of the ultimate solitude of a Genet or the martyrdom of collective solidarity which Sartre likens to that of Boukharine.[104]

[103] Neither Proust nor even Gide quite achieved this. Sartre recalls Proust's admission to Gide that he regretted presenting the gracious aspects of homosexuality as those of normal relations in *Within a Budding Grove,* while reserving the exposure of its ugly aspects as those of the admittedly abnormal ones in *The Cities of the Plain.* One may add that Gide's discretion and aesthetic distance tended to counteract the shock of his revelations.

[104] In his argumentation Sartre actually goes so far as to reaffirm Merleau-Ponty's sophism according to which Boukharine, subjectively in opposition to the government of the Soviet Union, was objectively a traitor to it (and therefore to the Russian revolution). (See above, pp. 118–119.) And Sartre, who has the benefit of hindsight, calls Boukharine a "[rotten] member of a revolutionary community" (*Saint Genet,* p. 546). These statements implicitly consider as apodictic truth something which Boukharine denied, namely, that Stalin embodied the intent and purposes of the Russian revolution.

Sartre invites us to look into the mirror Genet holds up to us. If we are to overcome our subject-object dichotomy, we ought, at least in imagination, to travel to the far end of one or the other pole of reference.[105]

The biographical method[106] Sartre developed to comprehend Genet is more complex than that which he used in his *Baudelaire*. For Genet's life is more complicated in its metamorphoses and Sartre had further perfected his critical apparatus. From the "retort" of Baudelaire's milieu he has moved with Genet to "the world as a play in a prison," from an ambiguous posture between being and existence, to a frenetic race to an extreme pole of existence. In the process Sartre has again illuminated a work from the inside by uncovering the workings of an original choice, but in the *Saint Genet* he could demonstrate a positive progression through willed metamorphoses to an ultimate liberation from false values.

Sartre's regressive-progressive analysis allows the elucidation of early events by their later unfolding,[107] and the pinpointing of a life's synthesizing event in an early original choice. The chronological progression of Genet's life from early childhood

[105] It is to be noted that in the plays of his latter period, Genet has continued to place himself outside of what might be called the establishment, thus maintaining his position of solitude.

[106] In an article ("The Relevance of a Writer's Life") on the New Criticism of the 1930s and early '40s which established the "biographical fallacy," as its doctrine, Carlos Baker cites René Wellek to the effect that "no biographical evidence can change or influence critical evaluation." Baker comments that "in a way he was perfectly right" (p. 2) for we do not know anything about Shakespeare let alone Homer. It is obvious that in these cases ignorance left the critic no other choice but to disregard biography. Later in the article Baker quotes Wallace Stevens who stated—and this was not obvious to the New Critics —"that a man's sense of the world dictates his subjects to him and this sense is derived from his personality, his temperament, over which he has little control and possibly none, except superficially" (p. 31). We know Sartre went a step further by insisting on the freedom of the author at work in fashioning his "sense of the world" in his life and his work. Intelligent biographical evaluation can definitely be an indispensable and integral part of a critical understanding of a work of art.

[107] That "adventures" have a beginning and an end, that is, that they are recognized as such, only by hindsight, is already one of the discoveries of Roquentin (see *Nausea*, pp. 57–63).

onwards has been explicated through relevant aspects of his later work, which, in turn, becomes fully intelligible only from the point of view of Genet's early conversion and metamorphosis.[108]

Sartre at times interrupts the description of this totalizing process in Genet's life (the movement toward fulfillment of his original choice) to insert certain artificial cross-sections, in order to explicate, in isolation, particular objective and subjective factors. There are, then, numerous *explications de texte* which have as their point of departure purely linguistic and structural analyses.[109] Sartre also develops what may be called an objective ontology of homosexuality by comparative analysis of Oscar Wilde, Proust, Gide, Jouhandeau, Cocteau and others. He elsewhere applies a psychoanalysis of things in connection with the questions of elegance and style, and works out a sociology of taste. He derives a general concept of sanctity from the writings of Saint John of the Cross, of Saint Theresa of Avila and also of Jouhandeau, before going into the merits of Genet's very private conception. Similarly, attitudes to language in Genet are compared to those of Parain, Bataille, Ponge, Blanchot and Leiris. When conclusions concerning these and many other such factors are reached, they are integrated into Sartre's understanding of the totalizing process of Genet as he interiorizes such objective positions in his unique way. But, on the other hand, Genet also exteriorizes his subjectivity—and his readers cannot but be changed by his reevaluation of everything, for not before Dostoyevsky, nor since, have the lower depths of man been exposed in like manner—and Sartre gives us a number of phenomenological descriptions of this outward movement.[110]

[108] One example among many is Sartre's *explication de texte* of *The Maids,* which was discussed above, pp. 187–89).

[109] As for instance that of the "reaper of cut breaths" (see above, pp. 183–84).

[110] See for instance *Saint Genet,* pp. 536–539 for a description of how Genet's "I" becomes our own.

It is not an exaggeration to claim that Jean Genet can see himself thanks to the *Saint Genet* as another sees him, in a way that no one has ever been able to do. And, conversely, perhaps no author's work has become so thoroughly intelligible as that of Genet after Sartre's critique. Sartre has held on to both his Kierkegaardian existentialist suspicion of theory, which has made him often proceed by patient phenomenological description, and to his thorough knowledge of philosophy and the social sciences, in a movement toward encompassing "the indefiniteness of the lived." In describing the moments when objectivity is interiorized and subjectivity is exteriorized through the workings of an individual's free consciousness, Sartre has, indeed, been able to incorporate and to go beyond both Marx and Freud.[111]

A fine observer of modern criticism, Robert Ellrodt, has argued that even with Sartre's existentialist psychoanalysis

> one would fall back into the monotony of which Freudian psychoanalysis is accused: to explain *everything* in terms of sexuality and sometimes of a complex, is to explain *nothing* any more, since all the diversity of psychological life then escapes this explanation. In spite of a great wealth of concrete observations, it would appear that Sartrian psychoanalysis does not avoid this danger. The study on Baudelaire gives evidence of this: the concrete observations are admirably precise, but the principle of explanation, the fundamental project, is unifying only by virtue of its extreme generality. With a similarly defined original choice as the point of departure, innumerable personalities, all different from Baudelaire, can be constructed.[112]

It should be noted, however, that even the mere addition of a "principle of explanation," no matter how broad and all-inclusive, would be a valuable addition to our critical arsenal; especially so, if it is one capable of integrating earlier findings.

[111] See above, p. 154, for Sartre's announced intention of showing in the *Saint Genet* the limits of their respective methods of analysis.

[112] *Les Poètes métaphysiques anglais,* II, 405.

But unlike even the young Marx,[113] who minimizes the role of individuality, and unlike Freud, who reduces the importance of the social and historical factors in man, Sartre insists on the necessity of phenomenological description, on some "concrete observation," through which and through which alone general determinations taken from practically any discipline can lead to some measure of understanding of the irreducible individual. For Sartre, the truth of Genet, to the degree that one can approximate it, does not lie in a simple definition of his choice of being, but also in any of his lived moments—a particular day in a prison cell, for instance, or specific actions and reactions to others, or his way of dreaming about his situation. In Sartre, "the admirably precise" concrete observations are inseparable from theoretical formulations. The man who wrote that one must everywhere oppose Kierkegaard to Hegel,[114] and, in a sense, equally opposed Hegel (and Marx) to Kierkegaard, seeks generalizations as useful guides of investigation and of over-all comprehension but also focuses on concrete moments of lived reality in phenomenological descriptions. Because he is both philosopher and descriptive writer, Sartre in the *Baudelaire* and especially the *Saint Genet* has succeeded in explicating to a degree hitherto unknown two absolutely unique "personalities" and authors.

[113] In the same article in which Marx wrote the famous "the root is man," he placed this man almost exclusively in his sociological context as, for example, in this passage: "the head of this emancipation is philosophy, its heart the proletariat" ("Zur Kritik der Hegel'schen Rechts-Philosophie" [Paris, 1844], pp. 614 and 621 respectively).

[114] "Here as everywhere we ought to oppose to Hegel Kierkegaard, who represents the claims of the individual as such. The individual claims his achievement as an individual, the recognition of his concrete being, and *not* [*Etre*, p. 295] the objective specification of a universal structure" (*Being*, p. 239). Sartre accuses Hegel of an epistemological and ontological optimism. Hegel cannot stop "the scandal of the plurality of consciousnesses" (*ibid.*, p. 244).

Chapter 6

EXISTENTIALIST ANTHROPOLOGY: "FLAUBERT" AND LATER ARTICLES

"The Situation of Existentialism in 1957"—such was the title of the article which a Polish magazine asked Sartre to contribute to its issue devoted to French culture. Significantly, it appeared as "Existentialism and Marxism," and was soon after presented in a modified form to French readers under the title "Questions de méthode" (translated as *Search for a Method*). These methodological considerations came to be incorporated as a first part of the *Critique de la raison dialectique,* preceding the extensive descriptions of man in society and in history that constitute the bulk of the work.[1]

The avowed purpose of this one volume of the *Critique* was to provide Marxism with an anthropology.[2] A second volume, only projected, was supposed to establish, by reflection on the

[1] The *Critique* was written under considerable stress. It seems that the author was rushing forward headlong, leaving corrections and revisions in the care of Simone de Beauvoir to whom he dedicated the book (see her account in *Force of Circumstance,* p. 385). At the time Sartre was preoccupied (and personally threatened in more than one way) by the Soviet repression of the Budapest uprising (1956) and the last and most atrocious stages of the French-Algerian war.

[2] Already in *The Emotions* Sartre had noted the need for anthropology "as a basis for any psychology" (p. 13).

findings of the first—if this were at all possible—the significance of history and a rationalist dialectics (see *Critique,* p. 755).[3] That endeavor would, of course, always remain a perpetual search for answers, of which present-day "Marxism"—given its apriorism and formalism—is incapable. Yet existentialism, Sartre states, cannot hope to go beyond Marxism, which is a *totalization* of the knowledge accessible to us in our historical period, that is, a movement toward "the unification of everything that is known" (*Search,* p. 4). Existentialism is, in his opinion, only an ideology within Marxism. The task of an existentialist anthropology,[4] then, is to render the objective structures of sociology and of history intelligible as the lived moments of the participating and reflecting individuals and to transform, or at least to revitalize, Marxism by endowing it with a concern for individual concreteness.[5]

Sartre's work is in its actuality the answer to his somewhat Kantian question: "Do we have today the means to constitute a

[3] Sartre accuses Engels of having "killed" dialectics twice: when he suppressed the moment of human freedom and when he placed it in nature where only mechanistic, that is, causal, relationships prevail (see *Critique,* p. 670). Hence "rationalist dialectics," which involves man's choice, is opposed to Engels' materialist dialectics (see also p. 281, on this "false idea" of materialist dialectics which is widespread).

[4] Sartre writes "anthropologie concrète" (*Critique,* p. 59), since it aims to integrate sociology and psychoanalysis.

[5] An immediate result of the publication of the *Critique* was Adam Schaff's *A Philosophy of Man* (1963). In it the Warsaw University philosopher noted that "we are operating on ground still largely unexplored by Marxist thought," and that, furthermore, "none of the problems raised are capable of complete and final solution" (p. 6). Unfortunately, his introductory remarks notwithstanding, his refutation of Sartre is in the aprioristic tradition of the epigones of Marx. Schaff claims that "Marxism teaches that the individual attitudes are social products, and that, in adopting the attitudes he does, the individual 'belongs in reality to a particular form of society,'" so that he does so "in the sense of the social conditioning of his personality" (p. 29). Schaff's reading of Marx becomes perfectly clear when he states that "even his [the individual's] loneliest thoughts are socially formed and conditioned" (p. 67).

In the light of the foregoing, the following news item—while true—should be hard to believe, and represents a sad commentary on Sartre's efforts in Eastern Europe: *Le Monde* reported (December 11, 1965, p. 4) that Professor Schaff's "Marxist humanism" was condemned by the Polish Workers Party; it seems he had "centered his attention unduly on the individual."

structural, historical anthropology?" (*Search,* p. xxxiv).[6] He has attempted to have his philosophy[7] encompass anthropology,[8] just as he had reintegrated psychology and psychoanalysis into philosophy, when he replaced the experimental and statistical method with phenomenological intuition and description and ontological considerations in his early monographs and in *Being and Nothingness.*

Sartre's purpose in the *Critique,* then, is not to write a history, a sociology or an ethnography. It is rather, "in a parody of a title of a work by Kant, to set up the basis of the 'Prolegomena to a future anthropology'" (*Critique,* p. 153). Sartre holds to Hegel's concept of a truth which becomes, and becomes a totalization in a historical process. Of course, for Sartre the totalizer is man, not the Absolute Mind. Sartre also believes that Marxism is history become conscious of itself (at least up to our epoch). He accepts its concept of history as a history of class struggles. But against contemporary Marxists who refuse to differentiate, who suppress the particular while repeating that "man makes history on the basis of the conditions he finds," he insists that it is not the conditions but men who make the history.[9] Man is, then, by reason of his *praxis* (directed action in the social arena), a totalizer creating a totality, but he does so also in his lesser capacity as a totalized man (as a product of other men's actions). The best definition of his

[6] In the last lines of the *Critique* he affirms: "We have laid the foundations of a structural anthropology" (p. 755).

[7] He characterizes philosophy as "a method of investigation and explication" (*Search,* p. 5).

[8] He himself has most succinctly defined his aim when he writes that "the man of anthropology is an object, the man of philosophy is an object-subject" ("Anthropologie et Philosophie," p. 3). Let us recall that the "anthropology" of Montesquieu and of Rousseau was almost entirely speculative and subjective and that of Engels (in *The Origin of the Family, Private Property and the State*), equally interesting, was still so to a large degree. It is obvious that simple empirical anthropological description is meaningless without a "totalizing" concept and that the merely speculative approach has to be tested against research in the field if one wishes to move from hypothesis to a comprehensive theory.

[9] See *Search,* pp. 27–28, 48–50, and 87.

endeavor in the *Critique* has been given by Sartre himself six years after its publication:

Each person is at all times totalizer and totalized, and philosophy represents the effort of totalized man to retrieve the meaning of this totalization. . . . Inasmuch as philosophy is an investigation of man's *praxis,* it is at the same time an investigation of man, that is, of the totalizing subject of history. . . . What is essential is not what one has made of man, but *what he has made of what one has made of him.* What one has made of man are the structures, the signifying wholes, studied by the human sciences. What he makes is history itself, the actual surpassing of these structures in a totalizing *praxis.* Philosophy is situated at the juncture. . . . The philosopher is the one who attempts to think this surpassing.[10]

At the close of *Being and Nothingness* Sartre had promised an ethics. This promise was prompted by his realization of the necessity for the free for-itself to commit itself. In the *Critique,* this commitment, now inevitably in the arena of history, is precisely what is investigated as *praxis,* as the individual's relation to history. And to Sartre it is this *praxis* that reveals truth, to which, obviously, ethics is relative rather than being aprioristic and normative. This ethics has still not been spelled out, but the character of the commitment, literary and otherwise, is better defined, as is shown later in this chapter.

The reception given to the *Critique* was almost entirely negative.[11] This is not the place to refute it. Suffice it to say that the comprehension of man in history, which Sartre gained in

[10] "Jean-Paul Sartre répond," p. 95.

[11] A criticism that goes to the heart of Sartre's endeavor was leveled at him by Ludwig Marcuse "Der Künstler und die Ideologie," pp. 14–19) : "he has courageously [and naïvely] founded a Marxist relativism" (p. 18) . One must, indeed, ask if it is possible to found a concrete anthropology within a nonexistentialist and normative philosophy such as Marxism. The answer—in Marx's dialectics—is that a class, for example, is a very different thing to each individual while also being the same thing. There is, then, a class both as an objective structure and as the locus of a highly personal, even unique, experience.

Raymond Aron, similarly, considered that in the *Critique* Sartre was "trying to achieve some impossible reconciliation between Kierkegaard and Marx"—that is, between the individual and the general— ("Sartre's Marxism," p. 39) .

Aron and Ludwig Marcuse see in Marxism only the latter-day facile generali-

the *Critique,* permitted him to broaden the scope of his method of literary criticism, especially in the series of articles on Flaubert. It is therefore necessary to give a minimal exposition of the very difficult *Search for a Method* and the "Théorie des Ensembles Pratiques" ("Theory of Practical Structures") in order to facilitate an understanding of his latest critical writing. Philosophy led Sartre to literature and literature, in turn, led him to enlarge on his philosophy. A concern for an understanding of Flaubert's creativity is apparent in many pages of the *Critique* and some descriptions of aspects of Flaubert's biography illustrate its developments. Thus, in a sense, a summary of this work leads us into the heart of the literary criticism which he later developed fully. For (unlike present-day Marxism),

> the existentialist method . . . wants to remain *heuristic.* It will have no other method than a continuous "cross-reference"; it will progressively determine a biography (for example) by examining the period, and the period by studying the biography. Far from seeking immediately to integrate one into the other, it will hold them separate until the reciprocal involvement comes to pass of itself and puts a temporary end to the research [*Search,* p. 135].

Sartre's point of departure remains Cartesian in the *Critique*[12] as it was in his monographs and in *Being and Nothingness;* it is not Marx's point of departure, which lies in the productive process.[13] And the structures of Sartre's anthro-

zation, and a good rebuttal to both has actually been provided by Hans Heinz Holz when he made reference to the Hegelian dialectic of the specific and the general, which Marx himself has followed ("Sartres 'Kritik der Dialektischen Vernunft' "). He notes that "history and existence remained separate categories" in the *Roads to Freedom.* In the *Critique,* however, "the analysis of the individual's existence is maintained and justified as preparatory and auxiliary to a universal dialectic precisely because the latter integrates the former" (p. 973).

[12] "The epistemological point of departure must always be consciousness as apodictic truth (of) oneself and as consciousness of such and such an object" (*Critique,* p. 142)—now of social structures in a historical process.

[13] See *ibid.,* p. 143: "The order of [critical] experience . . . must be regressive." It starts from the concrete experience of the individual. In a late 1969 interview ("Itinerary of a Thought"), Sartre comes to minimize his own concept of individual freedom and the subjective moment in *praxis.* However, will he indeed attempt to render history intelligible (in the projected second volume of the *Critique*) by focusing on the lived world, now opaque due to the downgrading of consciousness?

pology are in a sense those of his ontology transposed (with due regard to the infinite complexities of the interrelationships now envisioned) into the historical arena. The individual's project now becomes a social *praxis.*[14] Society offers to the individual a more or less open or restricted field of future possibilities, which he internalizes as they enter his mind as motivations for his conduct. He, in turn, externalizes his choice in his *praxis:*

> *Praxis,* indeed, is a passage from objective to objective through internalization. The project, as the surpassing of objectivity toward objectivity, and stretched between the objective conditions of the environment and the objective structures of the field of possibles, represents *in itself* the moving unity of subjectivity and objectivity, those cardinal determinants of activity. The subjective appears then as a necessary moment in the objective process. If the material conditions which govern human relations are to become real conditions of *praxis,* they must be lived in the particularity of particular situations [*Search,* p. 97].

For today's Marxists, Flaubert's realism is a reflection of the social and political evolution of the middle class of the Second Empire,[15] but they do not stop to seek the genesis of such a representation. We do not know why Gustave Flaubert lived in isolation, why he chose to write, nor why he did so differently from Duranty or from the Goncourts. "The child becomes this or that because he lives the universal as particular" (p. 58, see

[14] Lionel Abel ("Metaphysical Stalinism," p. 142) notes that Marxism "can turn up a certain kind of datum about an individual, his class connections; psychoanalysis, a different kind of datum. . . . The question is . . . whether there is any specific datum which Sartre's Existentialist approach . . . is suited to uncover? I do not think so." Sartre's "datum" is obviously the ontological project that becomes the anthropological *praxis,* which encompasses family and class in a highly individual manner.

Sartre stated explicitly in 1961 (concerning the ontological difficulty of seeing oneself as other), that "what I say about the individual is valid for any social group as well" ("Beyond Bourgeois Theatre," p. 132).

[15] Hegel himself had already given such a sweeping sociohistorical definition of the *Bildungs—und Entwicklungsroman* and had, actually, anticipated the Realist novel as well. (See *Vorlesungen über die Aesthetik,* pp. 215–217.) But he did not claim to characterize any particular work or one or the other novelist by such a general definition, as has been done by even respected Marxist critics from Plekhanov to Lukacs.

also pp. 57–63); and when Flaubert got to know his class, he did so within the context of a particular family, as is always the case. In this one, his mother descended from nobility; his father, the great surgeon, was the son of a village veterinarian, and his older brother Achille, considered by far the more talented of the two, was early the object of Gustave's hate. Gustave despised the professional careers his middle-class milieu was holding out to him and, altogether, lived his condition of a bourgeois in alienation.[16] Sartre writes that roughly three phases can be distinguished in his early steps to go beyond his situation, which he resented intensely (particularly his brother's brilliance and resemblance to his father, whose cherished son he was). At home, out of spite, Gustave refuses to emulate Achille; in high school, hampered by something that remains unformulated, Gustave is only a fairly good student, a scandal in the Flaubert family, especially in comparison to Achille's excellence a few years before; Gustave, then, agrees to the study of law, a career which he detests because it manifests his inferiority to his brother. From childhood to his nervous crises in adolescence, these phases are not simply repetitive, but a movement of ever more intense efforts to surmount his situation. He succeeds in finding an issue when he decides to become a writer (see pp. 105–8). Elsewhere, Sartre states: "Flaubert writes in order to deny his status as a retarded child, . . . in order to have himself appreciated by Doctor Flaubert." He writes in order to recuperate a language, which, Sartre holds, the child had lost when he was three years old, "undesired, overprotected, passive." [17] By the time Flaubert wrote *Madame Bovary* —that is, objectified himself in language, which is a *praxis*—[18] a certain *hystérésis*, a dual history, was at work: that of his

[16] Sartre describes the adolescent's literary and personal project fully in the articles on Flaubert which are considered below.

[17] "Anthropologie et Philosophie," p. 11.

[18] "Language is a *praxis* as a practical relationship of one man to another" (*Critique*, p. 181).

personal peregrinations and that of a historical reality (see *Search*, pp. 63–65). Briefly, Gustave Flaubert's private pessimism and aesthetic mysticism came to be the expression of a young generation's wish to justify its defeatism after a lost revolution.[19]

The hopeless goal of ever attaining the absolute value in-itself-for-itself is now in the *Critique* termed a totalization, which is perpetually in course. It is a *praxis,* a totalizing activity, of individuals, and also of groups of people in a historical process, when they seek a unifying synthesis of a multiplicity of relationships.[20] "As a civilized person . . . , I totalize myself from a millenial history onwards, and within the limits of my culture I totalize this experience" (*Critique,* p. 144). In other words, I am what I have absorbed, but I have done so and given meaning to it in a unique way.

And there are partial totalizations. For example, for a definite interval in Flaubert's life, "from December 1851 until April 30, 1856," Sartre advances, "*Madame Bovary* made the real unity of all Flaubert's actions" (*Search,* p. 159). This unifying activity gave meaning to the author's existence, and thus, concludes Sartre, "it is *Madame Bovary* which sheds light on Flaubert, and not the reverse" (*Critique,* p. 284). A comprehension of the real aim of the agent, and hence of the agent

[19] Another example of the internalizing of an objective historical situation through a subjective *praxis,* which, in turn, externalizes, that is, renders objective, the agent's own project, is provided by Sartre in his fragments of a work in progress on Tintoretto ("The Prisoner of Venice" and "Saint Georges et le Dragon"). The painter did so in a context entirely different from that of the author, and in his own unique manner. He, the first painter of our secular epoch, with his radical and obsessive style felt the need to impose on the patricians and merchants of "the Queen of the seas" their own truth: "[Venise] cursed in him her own anxiety" ("The Prisoner of Venice," *Situations,* p. 48).

[20] One may perhaps consider many of the efforts of Braque, of Juan Gris and of Picasso, among others, as attempts to see totalities. These modern developments, and Sartre's keen awareness of these structures at all times—in literary, artistic and other realms—are particularly relevant in a period when extreme specialization, alienation and differentiation coincide with a leveling-off process due to mass production, mass transportation and mass living.

himself, is afforded by his *praxis* as it reveals itself in its results. Sartre's new emphasis on overt action is behind the shift in point of view from the Baudelaire, wherein an examination of the author's writing was somewhat incidental to his over-all biography, to the *Saint Genet* and the articles on Flaubert, where Sartre starts out, whenever possible, with an *explication de texte* of their works.

In *Being and Nothingness* Sartre had described how one's for-itself is limited by another's for-itself, the being-for-others being one's recognition of this relationship; but its social implications were not developed much further. In the *Critique* we meet the two structures of "the other" in society: seriality or the group. People whose only "unanimisme" lies in the fact that they wait for a bus or work, as one among many, in some office or factory, are of the former category. The term denotes *production en série*—mass production. The solitude of the man in a serial relation to others lies in reciprocal isolation. People, here, are objects of what Sartre calls the *pratico-inerte,* the in-itself, as it were, which is society, as opposed to the for-itself which is man as an agent in that society. People are objects of things which incarnate some imperative, things on which man —as a subject—has inscribed meanings, such as an assembly line, a tool, or the mass media, all of which threaten to engulf the uniqueness of their existence. Their alienation resides not only in the relationship to things rather than to people but in the fact that people who service machines can be readily replaced by others. "There are serial ways of behavior"; which means that "*the series is a manner of being of individuals towards one another and towards the common being* and this manner of being transforms them in all their structures" (*Critique,* p. 316).

In response to an action by *le tiers* (a third party) [21] seriality

[21] The one whose role defines the seriality of the others—the employer, for instance, compared to the employees.

can be surmounted and fused into a group at particular revolutionary moments (the crowd, united against Versailles, in front of the Bastille, for instance).[22] The group tries to suppress the inertia of things and conditions, and its common *praxis* becomes an *exis,* a more or less permanent tendency. To insure the latter, the group takes an oath (like the Tennis Court Oath or the acceptance of party discipline) and advocates intragroup terror to maintain its coherence (p. 450).[23] Yet there looms as a possibility to all of its acts a counterfinality, a result different from that anticipated, either because of unforeseen or unforeseeable consequences in the purely social arena or some unexpected or unavoidable ecological transformations. Usually the counterfinality appears to the individual or to the group as caused by the other, whom he had to imitate or to ward off in order to survive.[24]

Even Flaubert, passive and independent as a bachelor and an artist, and as an owner of land, is fully aware of the fact that "his unearned income and the value of his property change (or may change) from year to year and, one might almost say, *in his very hands.*" Thus, "this inner being inasmuch as it is possessed by materiality now discovers that it is conditioned by all that is exteriority" (p. 262). To such an extent can man be

22 Sartre's group in fusion is "l'apocalypse" of Malraux's *Man's Hope.*

23 In an appraisal of the *Critique* as vehement as it was hasty, despite its length, Serge Doubrovsky ("Jean-Paul Sartre et le Mythe de la Raison dialectique" noted a radical change in point of view" (p. 697) between *Being* and the *Critique.* He correctly pinpointed this shift, manifested in the vocabulary itself, as one from project to *praxis;* but he concluded, for reasons which cannot be enumerated here, and which remain unconvincing, with the forecast that "a philosophy of 'totalization' will legitimize totalitarian politics" (p. 887).

Doubrovsky was thus echoing—no doubt without his knowledge—the cry of "metaphysical Stalinism" raised earlier by Lionel Abel (see above, p. 7). Both forgot that what Sartre defends, rightly or wrongly, in his descriptions of political structures, is the intra-group terrorism of revolutionary movements (the Hungarian or Algerian ones perhaps being cases in point). His position is not an apology for the Soviet dictatorship which, in fact, he criticized by name (see *Critique,* pp. 485 and 629).

24 For example the actions prompted by competition, or that of the Chinese peasant who cuts down trees and sees his land inundated through the actions of all the "others" who eliminated the forests.

dominated by "wrought matter" which makes its various demands on the owner, the user or the worker.

> Everything is discovered in *need:* that is the first totalizing relationship of this material being, a man, with the material ensemble of which he is a part. This relationship is *univocal* and interiorized [*Critique,* p. 166].

Somewhat as "lack" and anguish at being superfluous are conditioned by man's facticity and contingency, "need" is conditioned in the social realm by "scarcity," the scarcity of goods which threatens men as "supernumerary" and makes one the enemy of the other after millenia of history. In "wrought matter," matter transformed and made consumable by man, he finds the objectification of his alienated *praxis:* he has to live the exchange of goods like a duel (see p. 225). The concrete unity of a class consists in its negation of the other.

The class being, as a *pratico-inerte* being, as an objective condition, is a "signified" being. Yet each life so signified, so determined, remains unique; it has an individual destiny, but only in the way it realizes itself in this "structured field of possibilities" (p. 294). At this point, Sartre seems to come close to some form of determinism. It would make its appearance first of all as a family influence: "To be born is to produce oneself as a particularity of the group and as an ensemble of functions (positions and powers, debits and credits, rights and duties)" (p. 493). But Sartre points also to the fact that, while the parents have indeed decided for the child as to whether, for example, he will be religious or atheistic, that parental decision

> cannot but mark him [the child] to the degree that he will freely interiorize it and that it becomes, not the inert boundary assigned to him by his father, but the free limitation of his freedom by itself [p. 492].

Sartre sees as one aspect of the serial bourgeois ideology in Flaubert's time a certain "hardened ideological violence." He cites Saint-Marc Girardin's cynical attitude after the revolt of the silk weavers of Lyons, when, while recognizing their miserable condition, he exclaimed: "the proletarians *are our barbarians!*" The bourgeois justifies his privileges by pointing to the civilizing task of his culture and claims the right of vigilant oppression against the new barbarians. There were hundreds of similar articles at the time which expressed this attitude of fear and of anger. It was internalized as inert hate, a permanent social anxiety and abstract vanity by their bourgeois readers:

> We encounter [these attitudes] again in the bad moods of Flaubert (a small landowner living outside Rouen) in the form of set outcries, of written outcries: like all people of his ilk, he "devours" workers, *without even knowing them,* and without the relationship between exploiter and exploited being directly involved; simply because for the propertied classes as a whole, the action of the groups causes seriality to be lived as a kind of complicity [pp. 703–4].[25]

Altogether, scarcity is the fundamental relation of our history, and represents an "individual relationship and social milieu" (pp. 202–4). It manifests itself to man as the fundamental characteristic of his environment. Interiorized as a threat to one's existence, as a negation by the other or of the other, it becomes "the inhumanity of man" (pp. 206–7) and thus, "*objectively* man is constituted as inhuman and this inhumanity is translated into *praxis* through the apprehension of evil as the structure of the other" (p. 218).[26] Sartre sees history as made by man when through his *praxis* he seeks to satisfy his "need" in a world of "scarcity." And contradicting Marx, who, while indeed often wrongly termed an economic determinist, does assign to the economic factor a decisive role in an over-all sociohistorical determinist concept, Sartre states: "The eco-

25 Sartre adds in a footnote: "He also 'devours' the bourgeoisie, but I will show in another work, that he does so with less of an appetite."

26 We have already met Evil as a characteristic of the other, or as the other within oneself, in the *Saint Genet* (see above, p. 157).

nomic motif is not always essential, and, sometimes, cannot even be detected" (p. 218). And at any rate, whatever its importance, it has to be freely internalized. Of course, Sartre recognizes that, at times, especially for many, this field of possibilities can be severely limited. Yet just as the situation represented an individual's milieu which he tended to live or to transcend through his project, so does he through his *praxis* determine *"for any given period* the field of possibles" (*Search,* p. 135).

Sartre's concern for the individual's relation to history was dramatized in *The Condemned of Altona,* just as *No Exit* was the tragedy of the being-for-others. *The Flies,* to some extent at the threshhold of history, actually dealt with religion as mystification. In the absence of any "significance" to history, which the second volume of the *Critique* was supposed to investigate, one may view history as a contingent facticity, as is an individual's life, a point of view exemplified in *The Devil and the Good Lord.* Yet through almost all of Sartre's work, including the *Critique,* runs the theme of social commitment in the historical arena as a moral endeavor. In final analysis, in the face of "scarcity," "need" leads to the fact that "ethics manifests itself as an imperative of destruction: one must destroy evil" (*Critique,* p. 209).

The foregoing exposition of the *Critique,* simplified to the utmost, and therefore unavoidably distorting Sartre's thought, has perhaps nonetheless shown his ability to develop sociohistorical structures as the workings of men rather than as abstract entities. This return to man, following his Husserlian return to things, makes possible a much closer understanding than heretofore of an author's writing, as it appears in a complex interrelationship with the entire spectrum of tendencies and influences in the spheres of both his private and public life. In the *Search for a Method* Sartre actually gives us what might be called his method of existentialist biography, and an illustration of it in references made to Flaubert.

We know that for Sartre "the *methodological* principle which holds that certitude begins with reflection in no way contradicts the *anthropological* principle which defines the concrete person by his materiality." And this because "the *revelation* of a situation is effected in and through the *praxis* which changes it" (*Search,* p. 32). In this *praxis,* which totalizes a life vertically (in the course of the individual's personal progress from birth to death), Sartre sees "short circuits" at particular stages of one's life, at which horizontal syntheses bring about transversal totalizations (the recognition and absorption of objective social structures into the individual's life). To give an example: the child grows within his family and, at times, is confronted with the collective landscape which surrounds him (see pp. 78–82). The two axes are interrelated and autonomous, and the same act is liable to encompass the horizontal synthesis and the vertical totalization in a dialectical relationship. To Sartre, dialectics, neither mechanistically materialist nor idealist, starts on its course as a *result* of the confrontation of projects (see p. 100) of individuals with one another, with things or with nature.

"Let us suppose that I wish to make a study of Flaubert," writes Sartre; how would he go about it? In a summary outline (*Search,* pp. 140–52), he proposes first to establish differentially—the term is Merleau-Ponty's—the manner in which Flaubert distinguishes himself from all others in a similar situation, for in such a difference lies his singularity. In a regressive analytic search he would proceed, as it were, outward in, to study the following phenomena: "I myself am Madame Bovary," the author's statement of identification felt to be true by contemporaries, among them Baudelaire; the dream entertained by this so-called father of Realism during his travels in the Near East of writing "the story of a mystical virgin," which would have been a symbolization of his own cult of art; and finally his characteristic dependency which, at the time, was called "feminine." (Later in life his doctors were to taunt him as a nervous old woman.)

Our problem then—without leaving the work itself; that is, the literary significations—is to ask ourselves why the author (that is, the pure synthetic activity which creates *Madame Bovary*) was able to metamorphose himself into a woman." [pp. 140–41].

A first step leading to an answer is the analysis of the author's style, which is to be undertaken differentially, and therefore as yet without any recourse to biography. Stylistic particularities present us by themselves with secret presuppositions embedded in the work, for style is related to a *Weltanschauung*. Contemporary opinions may now enlighten the critic further. Baudelaire had an intuition about the identity in the fundamental meaning of both *The Temptation of Saint Anthony* ("a diarrhea of pearls," as Louis Bouilhet put it), which treats of the big metaphysical problems of his time, and *Madame Bovary,* seemingly a dry work. The question raised earlier has only become more complex; Who is Flaubert to objectify himself within a few years both as a mystic monk and as a somewhat masculine woman?

Now it is time to turn to biography, that is, facts recorded by contemporaries and verified by historians. It is true, says Sartre, that the works, as the author's objectification, are more complete, more of a totality, than the story of his life, even though they cannot reveal the secrets of a biography. Thus, Sartre feels that *Madame Bovary* sheds light on Flaubert's *Correspondence,* and not the other way around. But it is at this point too early to comprehend that novel. At present this puzzling book, actually both lyrical and realistic, provides us with only a hypothesis and yields a method of research into the author's life. The work shows Flaubert as narcissistic, onanistic, idealistic, solitary, dependent, feminine and passive. These characteristics lead to some social structures (Flaubert as a landowner and stockholder) and a unique childhood drama. These "regressive questions" have brought us to the child's family "as a reality lived and denied by the child Flaubert." We find to define this reality two kinds of information: objective (class character, type of family, individual aspects of members of the family) and subjective ones (Flaubert's declarations about his parents, his brother, his sister and others). One must, however, incessantly return to his work since it contains a biographical truth (which cannot be so readily found in the "correspondence itself, falsified by its author").

"The meaning of the lived experience" of Flaubert is, on the level of general conditions, that of the intellectual petty bourgeoisie as it was formed during the *Empire* and as it evolved within French society. The literary critic should therefore analyze the rise of capitalism as the rise of the small-family enterprise, the return of the landed aristocracy, the contradictions within the political regime, the pauperism of an undeveloped proletariat and other factors, in order to reconstitute the overall character of such petty-bourgeois families at that time. One would then compare Flaubert's family to that of Baudelaire ("higher" in rank), to that of the Goncourts ("aristocratic" due to the purchase of titled land late in the eighteenth century), to that of Louis Bouilhet and others. Furthermore, one would have to determine the relationships scientists and professional men (like Flaubert's father) had with industrialists (like the father of his friend Le Poittevin). Thus, moving from the general to the particular, "the study of the child Flaubert, as a universality lived in particularity, enriches the general study of the petite bourgeoisie in 1830." Especially since in this case the ramifications are rather far-reaching: Flaubert's grandfather was a Royalist village veterinarian, his father married a noblewoman, and he became a landlord and was acquainted with industrialists. Sartre, who has studied the total situation of Flaubert's childhood, sees at this level the basic contradiction in the child's life: the opposition of the bourgeois analytic mind to the synthetic myths of religion. But he warns the researcher to approach the given in a spirit of absolute empiricism, to learn rather than to find the expected; all the more readily since "he has at his disposal a philosophy, a point of view, a theoretical basis of interpretation and totalization" (*Search,* p. 165). The critic's methodological point of view only permits him to integrate such data into meaningful wholes, once these data have been established.

By itself, the regressive analytic search could have yielded only isolated insights, in spite of the constant back-and-forth motion between the various levels of reference. Now the critic can retrace the movement of progressive totalization, by following Flaubert's project which, in an enriching surge forward, encompasses these fields in his experience and objectifies them. This project Sartre has found to be the escape from the petite bourgeoisie, which actually leads him to alienation from himself. But it is not only negation, it also aims at the "production of himself in the world as a certain objective totality." Flaubert's solution is not only to write [27] but to write in a certain way, while also remaining within the framework of a certain contemporary ideology. He should in the end be found to have constituted himself "inevitably and indissolubly as the author of *Madame Bovary* and as that petit bourgeois which he refused to be" (p. 147).

But one may have failed to reach this conclusion; the final objectification may not agree with the initial project. Sartre, then, would return to the regressive analysis to find possible moments of deviation in the course of the author's life, to reexamine its coherence and incoherence. *The Temptation of Saint Anthony* expresses Flaubert's project in pure form and

[27] See above, pp. 221–23.

with all its contradictions. But his friends, Maxime du Camp and Louis Bouilhet, consider it a failure and ask Flaubert to tell a story in the next work. This represents a moment of deviation. Flaubert writes an anecdote in which he places everything, Saint Anthony, himself, heaven and earth—a "monstrous, splendid work . . . in which he is objectified and alienated, . . . *Madame Bovary*" (p. 148).[28] A return from the work to biographical detail thus reveals accidents and deflections from the original project while confirming it.

"We shall define the method of the existentialist approach as a regressive-progressive and analytic-synthetic method"; consisting also in "an enriching cross-reference between the object [Madame Bovary] (which contains the whole period as hierarchized significations) and the period (which contains the object in its totalization)" (p. 148). What has often been explained as "realism," namely, in Sartre's terms, the simple inert juxtaposition of epoch and object,[29] now should instead be seen in terms of a live conflict. Sartre, thoroughly anticlassical, states that only "in a study which is going to be long and difficult" can one hope to understand the work, the author and the public.

Flaubert's readers preferred him to Duranty and decided that he, who hated Realism, was the true Realist, as compared to Duranty who had issued Realist manifestoes. One may now ask why his contemporary readers were looking for Flaubert's kind of Realism, "that admirable faked confession, that disguised lyricism, that implicit metaphysic?" (p. 149); and why

[28] One would wish, even in this outline of research (which the author himself calls" 'schematized' outrageously" [p. 107]), some further elaboration of this view on *Madame Bovary;* and there are a few more informative assertions from the *Critique* which are quoted below. In his articles on Flaubert, however, Sartre is able to show conclusively how Flaubert, especially in two of his very early writings, experimented with a representation of himself either projected outward into a universal context or focused inward on his own intimacy.

[29] An "explanation" invoked especially in support of the idea that the *Sentimental Education* represents Flaubert's despair after the failure of the Revolution of 1848.

they relished "as an admirable character portrayal of a woman (or as a pitiless description of a woman) what was at bottom only a poor disguised man?" A definition of the kind of Realism the reading public preferred at that time would shed light on the historical period which sought its image in it. At any rate, this public success is the moment of "the misunderstanding" (p. 150), when Flaubert's work is alienated from him and when it becomes an object in a historical action.

The objectification of the experience of particular, well-defined conditions takes as many diverse forms as there are individuals—in other words, this particularity is a manifestation of freedom. Those, however, who accuse Sartre of making a fetish of liberty are actually adherents of a mechanistic philosophy, as is vulgarized "Marxism." Its proponents would *"reduce praxis,* creation, invention, to the simple reproduction of the elementary given of our life"; they explain a work, an act, an attitude, by the factors which condition it. This is, actually, "the wish to assimilate the complex to the simple, to deny the specificity of structures, and to reduce change to identity." This mechanistic "Marxism" is a return to scientific determinism. "The dialectical method, on the contrary, refuses to *reduce;* it follows the reverse procedure. It surpasses by conserving." (p. 151).[30] It is the initial project and the eventual synthesis in a work which point to the modalities of the conditioning. Thus, for example, Flaubert's childish fear of death is only revealed in his choice to become an author. "What we call freedom is the irreducibility of the cultural order to the natural order" (p. 152).

For Sartre what matters is to substitute "history for all economic and sociological interpretations, that is, in general, for all determinisms" (*Critique,* p. 687). Theoretical conceptualization is only the moment of abstraction in the process of

[30] One should note that Sartre's phenomenological descriptions, one of the tools in his analytic-regressive method, also *reduce,* but in a Husserlian sense (in order to isolate the particular and the concrete), while the dialectics in his synthetic-progressive method *conserve.*

comprehension which takes place through *praxis.* The role of what Sartre calls the existentialist ideology of authentic Marxism is to "reintroduce the unsurpassable singularity of the human adventure" (*Search,* p. 176) into its now distorted concepts.

In this Sartre, precisely, is not only Kierkegaardian. "Kierkegaard has as much right on his side as Hegel has on his" (p. 12). Kierkegaard insisted on "the *primacy* of the specifically real [grief, need, passion, the pain of men] over thought, [on the fact] that the real cannot be reduced to thought." Kierkegaard thus noted "the incommensurability of the real and knowledge" (p. 12). Sartre believes that Marx has resolved this dichotomy, "since he asserts with Kierkegaard the specificity of human *existence* and, along with Hegel, takes the concrete man in his objective reality" (p. 14). Sartre defines this issue in his own terms when stating that "the solution of the conflict between Hegel and Kierkegaard lies in the fact that man is neither signified nor signifying but *at one and the same time* . . . signified-signifying and signifying-signified" (*Critique,* p. 103), that is, an individual who is made by and makes history.

Sartre, who in the *Saint Genet* maintained that his method marked an advance over Marx and Freud,[31] is now in the *Critique* too modest in the appraisal of his own contribution to the elaboration of an anthropological philosophy. He brings to Marx's social and historical categories existentialist psychoanalysis and existentialist biography, which make use of phenomenological description, and which, because of his double postulation of the project and the *praxis,* permit the grasping of the subjectively concrete within the objective structures. Therefore, it is rather Sartre who at last has resolved the conflict between Kierkegaard and Hegel (similar to that between Pascal and Descartes, between intuition and rationalism). Thanks

[31] See above, p. 154.

to Sartre's philosophy, literature and criticism, "nausea" has become thinkable as the feeling which informs us of our contingency, as does anxiety or vertigo of our freedom, shame or pride of the presence of the other, *praxis* of society and of the inert around us, literary style of one's metaphysics, and "the period flavor [which] is a shudder of revulsion" [32] of our historical predicament.

Sartre ought, on the whole, to shed his deferential attitude towards the "socialist" countries of the East and the "communist" parties in the West. If Marxism is today in the hands of people from whom Sartre must rescue it, this can hardly be due to the fact that it is a "lazy Marxism," since he himself recognizes it also as a "paranoiac dream" (*Search,* p. 53). The case of Professor Schaff, who initially tried to cope somewhat courageously with Sartre's *"Search for a Method,"* which appeared first in his country as "Existentialism and Marxism," is a case in point: [33] powerful new interests, antithetical to Marxism, are at work to modify its content.[34] Sartre has written that "the intellectual, . . . a product of bourgeois universalism, is within the bourgeoisie *the only one sensitive* to the contradictions of humanism" (*Critique,* p. 741). It is, indeed, not any official "Marxist," as self-appointed spokesman for the working class, but Sartre who is profoundly "sensitive" to the ideological problems of our time as they affect us in so many ways in philosophy and literature.

The "Flaubert" at present is a large fragment of "a work in progress." [35] It is not only in the *Critique* that Sartre had

[32] Concerning *The Condemned of Altona,* see Cumming, *Sartre,* p. 46.

[33] See above, p. 217.

[34] Sartre himself has told of this "humanist" slogan on Warsaw street walls: "Tuberculosis slows down production" (*Search,* p. 178). Unfortunately, he refused then to ask himself for whose benefit the production runs.

[35] The entire fragment consists of two parts: "La Conscience de classe chez Flaubert" ("The Class-Consciousness of Flaubert") and "Flaubert: du poète à l'artiste" ("Flaubert: From the Poet to the Artist"), published in *Les Temps Modernes,* Nos. 240–45, and comprising some 254 pages.

concerned himself with this author previously. Already in *Being and Nothingness* (pp. 557–63) he had discussed the writer's vocation and rejected the psychological explanations given, for example, by Bourget, in such terms as: "The effervescence of his young blood was *then* turned into literary passion as happens about the eighteenth year in precocious souls. . . ."[36] "Open any biography at random," comments Sartre, and this is the kind of description which you will find more or less interspersed with accounts of external events and allusions to the great explanatory idols of our epoch—heredity, education, environment, physiological constitution."[37] Sometimes the relationships established in this manner are not just ones of temporal sequence but are meaningful, and yet they remain general, as do those between chastity and mysticism, or between weakness and hypocrisy. Thus Flaubert has not been "endowed" with his ambition. "It is meaningful; therefore it is free. Neither heredity, nor bourgeois background nor education can account for it." The reader of the subsequent *Critique* sees a consistency with this Sartre of 1943, who also wrote at that time that "to be, . . . means to be unified in the world." The irreducible, that is, unique unification which *is* Flaubert is "the unification of an original project."

The mode of "unification" specific to the writers of the middle of the last century, those whom Sartre calls the first modern ones, was already indicated briefly in Sartre's *Baudelaire:*[38] "Baudelaire's cult of being different reappeared

[36] Paul Bourget, *Essais de psychologie contemporaine: G. Flaubert,* as cited by Sartre.

[37] In commenting on Sartre's later "tantalizing" fragment on Flaubert, a respected contemporary critic has noted "the cluttered brilliance we have come to expect of Sartre" (Roger Shattuck, "Genesis of the Artist," p. 4). It will be recalled that Sartre had, indeed, himself promised "a study which is going to be long and difficult," but it is not "cluttered" nor forbidding to a reader of the *Critique.* Furthermore, this same critic, writing half a century after Bourget, states that "the hardest thing to ascertain is whether the molting process . . . [in Flaubert] is self-induced, as Sartre would have us believe, or represents a *natural* stage in the *life-cycle* of a writer of his *temperament*" (*ibid.,* p. 18, italics mine).

[38] See pp. 140–44.

in a Flaubert or a Gautier." They did not want to be bourgeois and thought of themselves as belonging to some sacred and eternal confraternity of the arts,[39] which dispensed them from having to come to grips with their contingency and forlornness.

Sartre's purpose in the Flaubert articles is to seek the key to Flaubert's dualism (lyricism and realism) by a reference to some of his very early writings ("Souvenirs," *Voyage en enfer* [1835], *Agonies* [1838], parts of the *Dictionnaire des idées reçues,* early letters), and a close study of his *Mémoires d'un fou* [1838] and *Smarh* [1839]. Sartre sees these as imaginary works by which the adolescent sought to transcend the problems of his situation, which he describes through biography. *Madame Bovary* should then become intelligible as the successful form of Flaubert's early project and over-all endeavor up to the time of its writing.

It is impossible for a child to become conscious of himself as being bourgeois when he finds himself within his class. This was the case for Gustave Flaubert, especially so, since towards 1830 the bourgeoisie still saw itself as representative of universal man. However, Gustave was not fully integrated into his family as was his older brother Achille. And he did not manage to establish firm bonds of friendship with Alfred Le Poittevin. In his very first writings he rises up against the family (*La Peste à Florence*), the masses (*Un Parfum à sentir*) and mankind as a whole (*La Dernière Heure*); but the concept of the bourgeois (or rather antibourgeois) does not as yet appear in them.

Doctor Flaubert was directly involved with workers only as recipients of his charity, and Gustave was only nine years old at the time of the revolt of the weavers in Lyons. Saint-Marc Girardin's lucid and cynical articles in the *Journal des Débats,*

[39] See above, pp. 100–2, for Sartre's point of view on Realism in *What is Literature?*

which provoked an awareness of being bourgeois in many circles, can hardly have reached Gustave. What he himself remembers is the enthusiasm with which he read *Chatterton.* Its subject is precisely the antagonism of the poet against the bourgeois, and Sartre remarks that "believing that he had found a liberator, he assumes the disdainful gaze of an aristocrat within himself" (*Les Temps Modernes,* No. 240, p. 1928). The entire generation of authors who began to write in the 1820s thought likewise: Chateaubriand, of course Vigny, the author of *Chatterton,* Victor Hugo and Lamartine, among others. The monarchy and aristocracy seemed to raise the poet to a privileged station in life. For the students in the 1830s the voice of these poets is actually that of the past, but of a charming and prestigious one, when compared to the sordid utilitarianism of the bourgeoisie ruling since 1830. "His family's *good characteristics,* which have been his for a long time, he suddenly discovers from the outside as *blemishes* . . . and now he willingly takes on and nourishes with his own resentment the hatred which the ruined aristocrats bear towards his own class" (p. 1933). But at the same time he wishes to succeed in the eyes of those who have given status to his brother Achille: those who practice bourgeois mores. "How does he live his malaise?" asks Sartre. "In order to enlighten ourselves we will have to go through . . . this life from adolescence to death. Then, we will turn back to the years of crisis—1838–1844—which contain in potency all the tendencies of this destiny" (p. 1935).

Flaubert lowers the bourgeois class to the level of petit bourgeois when treating of shopkeepers, grocers and office boys as members of the former. Then, he goes on to practice bourgeois sensibility: to be *distinguished.* The bourgeois is not born different from his workers, as is the aristocrat, but he bases his privileged position on his culture and distinction from their "vulgar" way of life. Caught in this contradiction, Flaubert will write: "I call bourgeois anything that thinks basely."

There is another contradiction in his conception of the class to which he belongs when, to the contrary, he extends the word "bourgeois" to include the entire human species. In 1854, and again in 1867, he makes statements to this effect. When Flaubert looks at his class with the eyes of an aristocrat, he sees it as a particular species; but when he, the proprietor of Trouville, reacts against the political and social demands of republicans and workers, he sees the bourgeoisie as an élite which represents the imperiled universal man. He then reproaches it with not having created a bourgeois order in the image of aristocratic chivalry; whereupon he proposes some sort of dictatorship of talent.[40] Late in his life, the fear of the *Commune* leads him to accept his class unequivocally. Actually, he always had: his often expressed hatred of the bourgeois is only the resentment of a "misunderstood child" (p. 1949).

In the light of the foregoing, how are we to understand Flaubert's lifelong preoccupation with bourgeois stupidity, especially striking in his *Dictionnaire des idées reçues* and *Bouvard et Pécuchet?* Language as a *pratico-inerte* structure infects us with ready-made thoughts, which we learn with the intention of giving voice to our own thoughts. But a certain counter-finality stalks our actions at every step. Briefly, here is Sartre's analysis of how Gustave Flaubert meets this problem within his family.

The nine-year-old writes to his friend: "You're right in saying that New Year's Day is stupid," and further on concludes his letter by confiding that "there is a lady who comes to see daddy and who always tells us stupid things. I'm going to write them down" (No. 241, p. 2114). After a number of other examples of the context in which Flaubert uses the word "stupid," Sartre points to l'abbé Bournisien and Mr. Homais snor-

[40] It is well known that similar contradictions beset Stendhal who, in final analysis, wanted to be neither a Restoration aristocrat nor a New York shopkeeper, and aspired to belong to the "happy few." (See his second and third prefaces to *Lucien Leuwen*.)

ing at the deathbed of Emma, whom both failed to save, as the symbol of ever-triumphant stupidity. To return to the first stupidity noted by Gustave, Sartre sees in it an effort at distancing himself from ceremonial events at which his brother Achille had the privileged role. And there are more basic causes for Flaubert's obsession with prefabricated ideas. The indifference of his morose mother kept him in a state of passivity and simple belief. Worse yet, his father made of him "the family moron," in which opinion Doctor Flaubert found himself further justified by his son's "mediocre" performance in school. Gustave interiorized his father's judgment of himself as inferior; it took him a long time to free himself from his family.

It would seem that a consciousness can sink into thingness as well as into some social concept of the mass-media variety through an inert acceptance of the commonplace. Flaubert's talent for seizing the banal lies in the fact that he hears on the outside what actually speaks in him. His *Correspondence* contains the same clichés in large numbers, and he often adds phrases like "as Mr. Prudhomme [John Doe] would put it," or "to talk like the grocer," when, astonished, he rereads himself. One could go beyond a commonplace statement by seeking a signification which transcends that which it narrowly signifies. This synthetic bent of mind is not that of Flaubert who is rather analytical. Flaubert talks and writes like a bourgeois while mocking himself. In Mr. Homais, Flaubert presents and ridicules his own thoughts (and the rational experimentalism of Doctor Flaubert). Fascination with stupidity, and contempt for it, spring from the fact that it represents a "bogging down" of consciousness into a reified language: "Stupidity is a passive process by which man makes himself inert in order to internalize the impassibility, the infinite depth, the permanence, the total and instantaneous presence of matter" (p. 2128).

It is by becoming a poet, and then an artist, that Gustave

tries to resolve the problems of his childhood in the Flaubert family, but not without an early crisis. Sartre believes that Flaubert's nervous breakdown in January 1844 was the inevitable outcome of a long process which was psychosomatic and which corresponded to Gustave's decision to endure his situation passively: "Flaubert makes himself to the very degree that he is made by the situation and events" (No. 243, p. 197). From 1837 to 1842 the adolescent was concerned with the choice of a career and a severe disappointment in his literary ambitions, and from 1842 to January 1844 each preoccupation becomes particularly oppressive in view of the other.

There is a perfect concordance in what we know of this period from the testimony of Flaubert himself, and the objective changes in his writings between 1837 and 1843, and the "lived experience." Retrospective and contemporary letters to Louise Colet, Chevalier and Louis Bouilhet, and pages of the "Souvenirs" permit one to conclude that Flaubert had abandoned his 1837 concept of literature as the product of inspiration. He was confronted between his sixteenth and seventeenth year by the criterion of "taste" as though by a veritable catastrophe: "the young author remarks impassively that he has lost his verve, his originality, his imagination" (p. 199). This reflection on his work was a reflection on himself. Flaubert still thought of himself as a poet and Sartre draws a parallel with Baudelaire and Mallarmé, to point up the nineteenth-century phenomenon of "critical poetry." In the case of Flaubert, one must seek the specific reasons why this most unreflective of young men turns at sixteen to a reflective attitude.

This internal upset shows in Flaubert's early writings: in a five-year interval pure fiction accounts for only two titles out of a total of about thirteen. Compared to his earlier years this literary output is meager; he himself speaks of his "laziness," a certain creative impotence which appears to him like a personal disaster. Many indications lead one to believe that the doctor Flaubert was also fully aware of his son's crisis, which must have been obvious to others as more than a crisis of inspiration.

Sartre links Flaubert's nervous breakdown to his sudden self-recognition as a member of the bourgeoisie: he comes to the painful realization that if he cannot become the great poet he wishes to be, he must follow a middle-class career. Having established Flaubert's acute concern with his class, Sartre now returns to the beginning of this period. Flaubert is haunted by his "bourgeois being" since his reading of *Chatterton.* The "bourgeois being," this sociological way of being, is, according to Sartre, already "signified" for an unborn child "by a certain field of possibles, rather limited and very clearly structured, which reflects back to him the social demands defined by his class . . . and, finally, by the will of his father" (p. 207). The child will get to know this "structured whole" as an inert demand made on him, and he will view it as his future reality, just as if some finality awaits him. To the older Achille, who identifies himself with his father, this interiorization of his objective "bourgeois being" appears as his great good fortune and as something due to merit. The younger Gustave, however, sees in it nothing but a fatality, which permits him to assume only a particular way of being bourgeois. Once he becomes a notary, his life will be quenched; he feels "his most intimate impressions, his despairs, even his refusals . . . disqualified by his future and present reality" (p. 209). How is he to escape this fatality? His crisis from 1837 to 1844 is a desperate attempt to change his being. He would in fact wish to escape any class conditioning. Like Vigny's Chatterton, Flaubert also considered himself a poet, who would write spontaneously and to whom poetry would actually be a flight from reality and its negation. Sartre shows, by drawing on his "Souvenirs," how Gustave prefers improvisation and inspiration to all else up to his sixteenth year. Then, suddenly, Gustave hesitates, for he cannot believe in God, who is somehow, for him, involved in his concept of poetic creativity.[41] Inspiration is no longer a demand made on him by a given future, but the exuberance of the present. Flaubert must therefore change his future: and in so doing, he becomes an artist, whose creation is the result of his own labors.[42] In a larger perspective, Sartre sees the decline of Romanticism in such an attempt to escape "bourgeois being." [43]

Since Flaubert most often thinks of bourgeois ends as simply human ones, he rejects them all. He had wished, as a poet, to escape from reality; he now wills as an artist the negation of this world. During his crisis years he tries to realize this aim aesthetically in three different ways: first, by a totalization of the universe through interiorization, through the subjective development of the life and death of a protagonist who comes to represent general human experience, and whose passive endurance symbolizes the negation of the world. Second, Flaubert at times develops a protagonist from the start in the light of objective and *a priori* notions, maintaining him in a posture of "explicit overflight" (p. 216), of impassible and stoic refusal to become involved; and this constitutes instead a totalization through exteriorization. Or third, Flaubert has a protagonist adopt an attitude of resentment—as against the other ones of passivity or pride—through which he aims systematically to demoralize the reader into a compelling belief in nothingness.

Flaubert, already at the age of fourteen, had wished to show that life is eternal damnation by describing evil and unhappi-

[41] "Inspiration? Reminiscences, that is all" (Sartre, Preface to Mallarmé, *Poésies*, p. 7).

[42] "Flaubert . . . has definitely constituted Literature as an object by the advent of a work-value: form has become the end-product of a workmanship" (Roland Barthes, *Le Degré zéro de l'écriture*, p. 11).

[43] Sartre has often shown that to an equal degree this was true of the early "aristocratic" Romanticism itself. But since from 1830–48 it assumed bourgeois social aspirations, Sartre is justified in the appraisal just mentioned.

ness everywhere. He embodies this view in *Le Voyage en enfer* (1835) and in *Agonies* (1838). In the earlier work, in final analysis, he passes from philosophy to autobiography: the devil speaks in the first person, and through him the young Flaubert tries to make his scepticism appear as the fruit of experience. He seeks what Sartre calls the "universal singular"—an individual or a situation representative of all (p. 220),—wherein, however, the general risks becoming abstract and the personal broadly general. This external-internal totalization—this mixture of philosophic generalization and autobiographic experience—does not please Gustave when he reads his work one or two years later. In *Agonies* there appears a child full of illusions who moves from faith to despair. But there are also passages which indicate a shift from this "universal singular" to a completely objective totalization in unrelieved pessimism. Flaubert oscillates between these two external totalizations, one perfectly objective, the other only seemingly subjective because the protagonist's ego is so rudimentary. In the former, the protagonist knows the world; in the latter he feels it imposed on him step by step. A month after *Agonies* the distressed adolescent bans all references to himself as author in "La Danse des morts." From 1838 onward, Flaubert sees clearly the two possible approaches to his subject and keeps them apart: *Mémoires d'un fou* is a rigorous attempt at internal totalization just as *Smarh* (1839) will be that of a perfectly objectified, external one.

Flaubert is irritated to the point of exasperation by the *Mémoires*. He resents the fact that he has revealed himself.[44] Yet he does not aim at creating a type, and he never will: according to Sartre, "to the end *Madame Bovary* remains an incomparable individual" (p. 232). What he seeks in the *Mém-*

[44] He handed the only manuscript to his friend Alfred Le Poittevin with a dedication stating that "they contain a soul in its entirety. Is it mine?" and admitting that "the personal impression pierced through the fiction (*Œuvres complètes, Premières Œuvres*, VI, 273).

oires too is a "universal singular," who projects his belief in nothing by a subjective temporalization of disillusionment. The particularity of the narrator is meant to reassure the reader, to interest him; and finally, when it is too late, he realizes that this singular destiny contained the universal, that is, his very own. "Only the meticulous invention and the inflexible organization of a fictional life will permit him to project *a priori* truths under the cover of a spurious contingency" observes Sartre (p. 233), who here goes to the heart of many a reader's gnawing insatisfaction with those brilliant masterworks, *Madame Bovary* and *Sentimental Education.*[45]

Flaubert is so terribly upset with the cost of the experimental writing of his apprenticeship period because he had tried to escape his anomaly as "the family moron" in an intimate novel, the *Mémoires d'un fou,* where he was to become a universal subject, but had actually returned to wounding autobiography. The "I" of the *Mémoires,* of *Agonies,* of *Novembre,* is a "recovery of oneself," but only as an active passivity: "The world *lets itself be suffered* in this subjectivity grasped as a universal milieu" (p. 236). Already at the age of eight, Gustave is disillusioned. Towards himself, the father's malediction is interiorized as disgust for oneself; towards the outside he manifests a belief in nothing. Life in school has not created but only deepened his dispositions. Surprisingly, Sartre considers Flaubert's pessimism not as a product of his history but of his protohistory: at eight he totalizes life in his family; his mother's care left him very early with a lack of appetite, a passive attitude, which in time became a disgust for living, boredom and a belief in nothing. Gustave is not fashioned by a conscious experience but by a process which precedes this experience, a process which conditions him (see p. 238).

However, let me repeat that precisely at the critical point in

[45] Put differently: what Flaubert so rigorously circumscribes is only half of the truth, but that half is true.

his adolescence, Flaubert has come to reflect on himself and to seek the negation of this—and of all—reality in his imaginary work. What leads to the ultimate outbreak of his latent crisis is lack of success in this direction. In the *Mémoires* Gustave could either have described despair as an experience or he could have treated of an objectively desperate reality. But Flaubert still has failed to choose, and the book is supposed both to lead to a conclusion and to present an aprioristic outlook.[46] His thought undermines his story, which falls flat.

This confusion stems from the fact that, in bad faith, he hides his true predicament. In 1842 he will write in *Novembre:* "I was therefore what you all are." Flaubert dissimulates his anomaly in generalizing it; furthermore, he makes his protagonist the victim of the others' cruelty without mentioning even in his intimate novel the real culprits, his parents; finally, "the family moron" is presented as a superior being.[47]

Sartre doubts that the reminiscence of an actual meeting with a young woman in Trouville was originally intended to become part of the *Mémoires.* Instead of the scepticism and boredom which surround it in the rest of the book, we find in this episode a charming adventure, melancholy only because the narrator happened to be too young. It appears as a sudden, unconnected irruption of the present in a book so far written in the past. This true event ends for a time the monotonous ruminations that characterize the greater part of the novel. By including the lyrical Maria episode in the *Mémoires* Flaubert has actually drastically changed his plan.[48]

[46] "So I am going to write the story of my life. But have I lived? I am young" (*Mémories d'un fou,* p. 225). A few pages later the narrator knows enough to affirm: "And everything will give way and collapse into nothingness, and the virtuous man will curse his virtue and vice will clap his hands" (p. 287).

[47] "The imbeciles! They, laughing at me! They, so weak, so vulgar, with such narrow minds; I whose spirit was drowning at the limits of creation" (*ibid.,* p. 280).

[48] In the Pléiade edition of Flaubert's *Œuvres* (II, 461–80), only the Maria episode is published from the *Mémoires.* Indeed, the reader does not in the least

Sartre notes that in Elisa Schlesinger, the Maria of the Trouville interlude, Flaubert sees his own mother, and if he does not *know* it, he at least *understands* something about it.[49] And in the jealousy exhibited towards the end of the episode, the old resentment against his brother finds expression once more. Another fundamental relationship with his family shows itself in a dream in Chapter IV of the *Mémoires,* which must be interpreted as a nightmare masking his fear of castration by his surgeon-father.

In a letter written in 1845 to his sister Caroline, Flaubert declares that "as a result of analyzing myself so much, I don't know at all any more what I am" (cited, No. 244, p. 453). Flaubert "knew" himself at the age of sixteen, at the time of his reflective period in 1837–38, and he actually wished to reduce his particularity to its universal elements through this reflectively gained knowledge of himself. The writings of 1838–42, in their portrayal of a progressive disillusionment, represent a justification of his own failures. Before long, he feels that one cannot know oneself. In the "Souvenirs," he inveighed against himself: "[In spite] of an immense pride I doubt more and more. If you knew the extent of my vanity. What a savage vulture, how it eats at the heart—how alone I am, isolated, distrustful, base, jealous, selfish, fierce" (cited, p. 459). Sartre finds the explanation of Flaubert's pessimism in his cynicism, the shame he feels over his misery, and his meanness.

---

miss the other parts nor see a manifest connection with them when he finds them in a complete edition.

[49] For an interesting elucidation of this point, see *Les Temps Modernes,* No. 244, p. 448. It should be noted that in *Sentimental Education,* Frederic Moreau is attracted by three women (Marie Arnoux, Rosanette and Madame Cambreuse), all older than he is. It is clearly Flaubert's passive childhood that lies at the root of passages such as the following: "Madame Dambreuse closed her eyes, and he was astonished at his easy victory. The tall trees in the garden ceased their gentle quivering. Motionless clouds streaked the sky with long strips of red, and on every side there seemed to be a suspension of vital movements. Then he recalled to mind, in a confused sort of way, evenings like this, filled with the same unbroken silence. Where was it that he had known them?" (Ranous, II, 119).

The artist, consequently, meets defeat. In order to write, he would have to be sincere, he would have to know himself—which he does not want:

The terror of this haunted boy, the unceasing struggle within himself among the determinations of his "selfness"—class being, the Ego of his fundamental intention, the Alter-Ego which the others expose, the Quasi-object of introspection and the reflexive Subject of knowledge—are in 1838 inseparable from his literary failure [p. 460].

Flaubert abandons his inward totalization through a work of art. He now attempts the totalization outward in a kind of *anti-Mémoires,* namely in *Smarh.* In this work, for which *Faust* may have been the inspiration, a man, Smarh, is slowly led by Satan from illusion to absolute scepticism and the mortal sin of despair. The hermit's "experience," his inward totalization, is actually only an element of the cosmic scheme of things.[50] Through the outward movement of Satan, in a consciousness that surveys from above, Flaubert wishes to escape completely from his subjectivity. This is a technique which permits him to assume an attitude of pride and thereby to "desituate" himself, to place himself, in his imagination, outside his true situation.

Already when he was thirteen years old, Flaubert had attempted this "totalization from above" (No. 245, p. 599), and from his fifteenth to his twenty-seventh year he repeats it in *La Danse des morts, Smarh* and the first *Tentation de Saint Antoine.* Each one develops a nightmare and recreates through it the identical totality following the same rules of procedure. Again and again, he desituates himself in order to totalize and totalizes in order to desituate himself. But actually we know that the fictional subject of this "survey" has been created by a

50 "Satan had but to give a last blow, and this wheel of evil which had been crushing mankind since creation would at last come to a stop" (*Smarh, Œuvres complètes,* II, 204).

real subject who is the author of both the imaginary one and whatever he is made to contemplate. If, however, these do not express Flaubert's knowledge of his reality, this is due to his passivity which inhibits him from facing up to his problems as he knows them. Sartre sees "at the very roots of his imagination . . . the pessimism, the misanthropy, the misogyny which are the intentional determinations of his sensibility" (p. 605).

The evil mythical figures whom we encounter in Flaubert's novels are projections of his "religious instinct," his superstitions, his mysticism, his lost faith,[51] his predilection for the fetish and the idol. All of these lead invariably to absolute evil, which is the inevitable conclusion of every one of his works, for this is the meaning he gives to his *Lebenswelt*—his "lived world." His art is a way of objectifying his *Weltanschauung:* his lived world and his imaginary one have this meaning in common. In the first case, his outlook unifies his real experience; in the second, it produces his imaginary world. The result is that the imaginary situation is less varied and more rigorous than the real one; the contingency and ambiguity of life become an inflexible aesthetic necessity, which, it is true, he has not as yet consciously formulated in his adolescence, but towards which he moves by trial and error during these crucial years. Yet already in his fifteenth year, he struggles step by step against improvisation, for it would contradict what he has discovered as "good taste." This aesthetic criterion actually represents what he sees as the meaning of his life, and it is what he wishes to impress on his work. Flaubert's beauty is the perfection in malice, it is a balm on his wound, on his festering resentment. His beauty is a process of demoralization. It will lead to the inimitable "tone" of *Madame Bovary:* he refuses the very sympathy he elicits.

In 1838 Flaubert read Rabelais and Byron in such a way as

[51] While Goethe has Faust and Marguerite saved in the end, Flaubert damns Smarh.

to see in them admiringly "the only two who have written with the intention of harming the human race." [52] In 1839 he states: "I despise men too much to do good or evil to them" (cited, p. 612). Actually, however, he is sadistic; he expresses his appreciation of the Marquis de Sade (whom he may not have read) and dreams of being Nero, "the greatest poet" (*La Danse des morts,* cited, p. 614). The young author of *Smarh* aims to "harm mankind" by leading his readers to despair.

As Flaubert makes himself an artist, he tends to realize his dreams, to move from his fantasies, conceived in deep resentment against his family, his class, and people in general, to actions affecting others.[53] In *Smarh* a holy hermit, the objectification, as it were, of every man at his best, is made by Satan to lose himself in the throes of abjection and evil. With this totalization in exteriority, Flaubert downgrades the finite by means of the infinite and the real by the imaginary, and both mysticism and artistic creation are intertwined in what Sartre calls "the syncretism of Flaubert" (p. 619).

Flaubert will continue to hold on to both the truth and imaginary transposition, to a surgeon's scalpel and to lyrical evasion, to life's dolorism and impotence and to the power of words. In *Madame Bovary* Flaubert describes with painstaking realism the emotional involvement of a character in a small world, and succeeds in impressing on us his view of the world at large. Also, since Emma Bovary is an expression of the rigorous totalization possible only in imagination, she has more density of being in his scheme of evil than "the real Emmas who suffer and weep in a hundred villages," and has become an archetype, thus constituting a link between the microcosm and macro-

[52] Letter of September 15 to Ernest, *Correspondance,* I, 29, cited in *Les Temps Modernes,* No. 245, p. 612.

[53] Sartre points to this passage from a letter to Louise Colet written as late as November 1851: "It is beautiful to be a great writer, to hold men in the frying pan of one's sentences and to make them jump like chestnuts. It must make one deliriously proud to feel that one weighs upon humanity with all the weight of one's idea" (cited, *ibid.,* p. 619).

cosm. She is beautiful because she represents something imaginary, a creation of being in a void. "She fulfills in an illusory way by non-being our non-satisfaction and reveals obscurely something that cannot be articulated and remains inconceivable" (p. 625).

Long before reaching maturity, Flaubert had to seek his solution in a severe adolescent crisis. In the *Mémoires,* he had failed to desituate himself in an inward totalization. But in *Smarh,* he feels triumphant in his refusal of masochism and reflective stocktaking, in its replacement by pride, sadism and the exercise of a satanic mandate. Determined by his father to the role of the younger child and to a bourgeois station in life and directed by his mother's care to a passive activity, Flaubert tried to free himself not in revolt but in alienation, in art: the artist is the son of his masterwork. The author of *Smarh,* which represents a macrocosm—the author's *Weltanschauung*—feels that he has at last found a way out. It is that of a counteralienation, the replacing of one finality by another one, the counterposing to his bourgeois being of a being-for-art.

This was his illumination of December 1838, and so he started to write *Smarh* with elation, but as he proceeded it gave way to bleak disappointment. The *praxis* of writing deflated his vision of the artist into its gratuitous, contingent and everyday reality. In vain did he struggle to replace his real being by an imaginary one; at best he would be a bourgeois who wrote. He was anguished at the thought of the necessary and yet impossible transubstantiation. The disappointment with the failure of *Smarh* was also specifically literary. He had wanted to write his masterpiece, since he had to create like a genius to belie his family's opinion of him. Yet he was far from ready and undermined his very effort by his ambitions to reach so high. On every page, his being—petit bourgeois or genius—is put to a test. From day to day, from month to month, in 1838, in 1839, he alternately hopes and despairs until at its completion he notes its failure when he writes that no reader will be demoralized by *Smarh.* He tells himself a year later: "You thought of yourself as a little Goethe. . . . The best advice I can give you is to stop writing." [54] Indeed, he had hardly written anything since *Smarh,* excepting a supposedly humorous version of it, *Les Funérailles du docteur Mathurin,* with which he is equally dissatisfied.

His morale is wounded to the point of physical distress. His father prescribes tranquillizing drugs, and when, in December 1840, Gustave has himself dismissed from the *lycée,* he sends him off to the Pyrénées for a cure and then to Corsica in the company of a doctor. In Paris Flaubert sees his former professor Gourgand who encourages him in his literary vocation. But in vain, for between the fall of 1840 to 1842 Flaubert does not write. He suffers physically his disappointment as an author and his lucid pessimism, the conflict of his singularity and his class determination: genius or petit bourgeois.

Through it all, Flaubert holds on to his fundamental idea that the world is hell and he holds on to the outwardly directed objectifying totalization of his presentation in *Smarh.* However, he comes to believe that his literary failure lies in a paucity of characters and episodes, and, especially, he runs up against the problem of language. Since childhood, language had seemed brought to him by the others; hence his unusual concern with commonplace notions and stupidity.[55] And yet he himself has to mediate with words the distance between his inner sensibility and the materiality of things on the outside. "[Words] *should be capable* of rendering the singularity of a thing, its shape, its fabric and its framework" (p. 653), they should be able to represent ontological knowledge. Flaubert becomes an observer in order to capture a particular essence of a thing in words. Beyond this, it is not only on words that this

[54] Entry of February 28, 1840, in his "Souvenirs," cited in *ibid.,* p. 646.
[55] See above, pp. 240–41.

"musician of genius" (p. 654) relies; he seeks to express the ineffable in a melody, in a particular way of saying things, in style.

> Style, a strange mixture of materials and intentions, does not fail to *say,* but, in order to realize those abstract significations which then only serve as references, it awakens in each term through all the others the multiplicity of significations which interpenetrate one another and uses them together—those which refer back to the darkness of childhood and those which designate external objects—so as to capture in the reality sought some of its secret opacity; it brings out through a hundred different devices the musical or visual value of words so as to make of them the *analogies* of imaginary presences;[56] it plays on a pace, a stop, a new start, a rhythm in order to have us *live* a feeling which language can only name [p. 657].

Before 1838 Flaubert considered style to be the apt ending of a moving and pathetic story. The failure of *Smarh* leads him to deepen his understanding of literature, to fuse content and form: "the beauty of writing becomes the absolute *means* of expression" (p. 657). He will later admit as much when he writes to Louise Colet that "there are neither beautiful nor ugly subjects . . . , style being of itself alone an absolute manner of seeing things."[57] This absolute manner represents his absolute point of view (a survey from above) and is the product of his belief in absolute evil: *the world is hell.* But as an abstraction it cannot be plausibly articulated in language, although it can become persuasive in style. In the same letter, Flaubert wrote this celebrated sentence: "What I would like to write is a book about nothing . . . where the subject would be almost invisible, if that could be." Sartre points out that he is writing such a book at the time of his letter: it is *Madame Bovary,* the almost invisible theme of which is: *the world is*

[56] See above, pp. 19–22, for Sartre's conception of analogy in his *Psychology of Imagination.*

[57] Letter of January 16, 1852, cited in *Les Temps Modernes,* No. 245, p. 658.

hell. Flaubert now recognizes that in his aesthetics words as signs convey information, but that the meaning of a work as a whole lies in its formal beauty of style.[58] Henceforth he will be careful not to serve up either mere information or incoherent beauty.

There were at the time, writes Sartre, only two young men concerned with creating modern literature, Baudelaire and Flaubert. They knew that the author could no longer rely on anything. A belief in literary gifts or poetic inspiration would be like falling back on God. Flaubert, who thinks of himself as asocial and refuses objective determinations, realizes with anguish that he is the only creator, and also the only objective judge of his work whom he respects. In judging *Smarh* the young man prepares *Madame Bovary.*

> Softness of fabric, half-shades, refinements, precision, rhythm, condensed style, unity: aren't these the qualities one generally recognizes in this novel, and don't we know that they are *acquired?* [pp. 664–65].

Genius, which no longer appears to him as a gift, now becomes for him a doubtful struggle. Mostly with himself, since every sentence discloses to him his *exis,* his way of being, and he has to control rigorously both his vulgar provincialism and his masochistic lyricism. This modern author has to write without models and he writes against himself, for he is bourgeois and insincere. In a characteristic reading of Buffon he would say that "all long patience is genius."

It is easy to see why Sartre would get thoroughly involved in Flaubert's problems. For the critic, to as great a degree as this bitter Realist of the last century, is terribly concerned with his

[58] Thus, also *Sentimental Education,* a downheartening and successfully demoralizing work if ever there was one, is uplifting through its formal perfection. And this does not mean that there is a dichotomy between form and content: in beauty we approach the imaginary value in-itself-for-itself, which imposes on us here the "necessity" of the evolution and outcome of Moreau's life; and this necessity, for all its sad banality, satisfies our need for coherence.

class determinations. Both have been destined before birth, as Sartre would now formulate it, to follow a career as petit bourgeois of some standing, and both have chosen literary creation as their way out of this determination. Of course, the author of *The Words* has been able to face up to disillusionment in good faith and has abandoned the pursuit of his being-for-art, while Flaubert had, as early as the *Mémoires d'un fou,* refused the road to self-knowledge.

In his Flaubert articles, Sartre has perfected his method of existentialist biography. Written after the *Critique,* they offer an analysis of social structures as they insinuate themselves into family life and become interwoven with its relationships. In so doing, Sartre has in no way renounced the findings of the ontology and the existential psychoanalysis he had developed in *Being and Nothingness.* There now is, to be sure, a considerable concern for the "proto-historic" class determination of an individual which limits the field of his choices. But there is not any suggestion of mechanistic causal relationships between the situation into which an individual is born and his ultimate reaction to it. The forward step that Sartre has taken is to include more of the outside world, of its historical and social structures, into the situation confronting the child, and to discover in the world of Flaubert the specific ways in which he lived them, that is, interiorized and exteriorized them from the point of view of his project. The proof of the efficacy of Sartre's method lies in the fact that it makes worthless juvenilia yield an understanding of the mature Flaubert heretofore suspected but never explicated.

The Flaubert articles, though fragmentary, are essential, for in having focused on the years of Flaubert's acute crisis, Sartre has been able to satisfy his primary concern, which was to locate the adolescent's choice of being as an author and as a man. This is the vantage point in life which has always interested Sartre, in *Nausea,* in *The Flies,* in his creative works generally, as in his critical and philosophic writings. For with this knowledge, gained mainly through a regressive and analytical study, one is now equipped to move forward progressively and synthetically to a comprehension of Flaubert's mature works.

At the time of the publication of the *Critique,* Sartre wrote an introduction to a reedition of Paul Nizan's *Aden, Arabie.* A critic has noted "the almost heart-rending tone of the preface" [59] and explains it by an awareness of the problem of scarcity left unresolved in the *Critique.* One should add that if need and other ominous aspects of international life connected with it seem insoluble, this is primarily due to an acute political question: how to harness for human purposes the immense economic and technological potential available in our time. Indeed, with the outbreak of World War II, Sartre had definitely taken an attitude of refusal of his bourgeois past, and of commitment towards "socialism," which had long been exemplified to him by Nizan, his friend for two decades. In the domain of both politics and committed literature, as Jean-Albert Bédé, a fellow student at the Ecole Normale and at the time a close friend of both Nizan and Sartre, sees it,

> this career . . . precedes and, to a considerable degree, dominates that of Sartre—as the result of an emulation which still continues and of which there are few examples in the history of ideas.[60]

Sartre's avowed purpose in the Preface is twofold. He wants to speak of the author and to rehabilitate the man who said no to the Stalin-Hitler pact and as a result was excommunicated by the French Communist Party to which he had belonged for twelve years. The fact that, though shaken, he had acquiesced in silence to the Moscow trials did not save him:

[59] Alphonse de Waehlens, "Sartre et la Raison dialectique," p. 91.
[60] Bédé, "Paul Nizan," p. 311.

They planned the obliteration of Comrade Nizan. An exploding shell had struck him, among other places, on the nape of the neck, but this liquidation satisfied no one. It was not enough that he ceased to live; he must never have existed.[61]

But his work—four novels and two essays—does exist, and Sartre wishes to bring it to the attention of today's young readers.

Aden, Arabie, this outcry against "a condensation of Europe, only white hot" (p. 111), is partly an anti-novel debunking the travel novel, partly an essay on man.[62] For his one-year stay in a colony had not provided Nizan with any kind of exotic or personal escape but had only confirmed him in his deepest gloom. Upon his return to France he took the road of blind commitment. In his Preface, Sartre actually speaks little of this, Nizan's first book, referring instead, for his portrait of Nizan, largely to *Antoine Bloyé,* his more completely personal novel, dealing as it does with the life of his parents, especially his father.

Nizan interiorized the conflicts of his old parents; his mother's "Breton bigotry" (p. 99) and his father's "betrayal" of his working-class background when he became a head clerk. Nizan was at various times royalist and dandy, and he talked seriously of entering an order or converting to Protestantism; but finally he chose to throw in his lot with those "who had not succeeded," "these men without importance" (cited, p. 115), whom his father had left behind. But he also loved his father and wanted to identify himself with him. His father had suffered from his advance in position for he then felt isolated from his former fellow workers. Nizan, a witness of his father's solid attachments to these people in the past and of his father's

61 Sartre, "Paul Nizan" (Preface to *Aden, Arabie*), *Situations,* pp. 82–83.

62 On the Europeans of Djibouti, for instance: "All of them also go around in circles, running into the invisible walls of their destiny, going through the same motions at the same time as the Englishmen on the Asian side, racing their cars in the evening towards the gardens of Ambouli, where couples whose members are always interchangeable go to console themselves" (*Aden, Arabie,* p. 143).

decline, decided to cross the lines backwards. He lived his conflict, not without a "moral laceration," [63] and with the fear of solitude and death in his heart. It was, as it were, "the death agony of an old man gnawing the life of a very young man" (p. 107).

His literary work was part and parcel of his total revolt: "His books wanted to displease: that is their great merit" (p. 84). He was the first of the "angry young men"; he pointed to the true situation at a time of illusions. For him, at the beginning of everything, there is refusal, and he said no to the end.

> But he said that love was real and that we were prevented from loving: that life could be real, that it could bring forth a real death, but instead, they make us die even before we are born [p. 109].

Sartre was not ready to understand his friend in the Twenties and Thirties, though now he writes in retrospect that at fifteen Nizan knew what mattered in life. Nizan entered the Communist party (just as he had founded a family) to escape his solitude, but he knew that even in commitment there is no salvation.[64] Furthermore, Nizan knew that he could not cross class lines. Sartre writes that Nizan "saw in them [the communist intellectuals], in himself, *petits bourgeois* who had taken sides with the people." And Sartre adds as his own opinion that "between a Marxist novelist and a skilled worker, the gap isn't filled" (p. 116).

We are here coming up against an anxiety which agitated both Nizan and Sartre equally, if at different periods in their lives, and which neither has overcome even though Nizan had said, as reported above by Sartre, all that can be said and, given his opinions, had done all that can be done. There just cannot be a proletarian culture,[65] an intellectual cannot become a

[63] Bédé, "Paul Nizan," p. 312.

[64] See also Maurice Merleau-Ponty, *Signes*, p. 41.

[65] No other than Leon Trotsky pointed out that, historically, each ruling class needed centuries to form its own culture, and that the working class would at

worker, and a worker becomes a petit bourgeois as he cultivates himself. And while, broadly speaking, the petite bourgeoisie has been the instrument of the crimes of our time, East and West, it is no crime to be an enlightened petit bourgeois. Such was almost the entire Russian intelligentsia, such were practically all who preceded them from Euripides and Plato onward, in the endeavor of "preparing man" (p. 112).

By his commitment Nizan represented a temptation for Sartre just as Camus by his independence.[66] In his letter to the editor of *Les Temps Modernes* which led to the break with Sartre,[67] Camus had spoken of Sartre, of Merleau-Ponty and perhaps of Nizan when he noted that "it is a case of repentance with these intellectuals who want to atone for their bourgeois origins, even at the price of contradiction and of doing violence to their intelligence." [68]

Sartre's preoccupation with history was no more extraneous to his writing than it was to the writing and the very lives of Eluard, of Desnos, of Vercors and the other authors whose words are carved on the walls of the Paris Monument of the Deportation, alongside those by Sartre: "The choice each one made of himself was authentic because it was made in the face of death." [69] What form was Sartre's commitment to take in the postwar years? " 'If you want to engage yourself,' writes a young imbecile, 'what are you waiting for? Join the Communist Party' " [70] observes Sartre wryly in rejecting a simplistic

---

most govern for decades in order to make way for a socialist society. (See his *Littérature et Révolution,* pp. 160–61.) If anything, Trotsky's forecast has been far too optimistic concerning the extent or the mere possibility of proletarian rule.

66 The fact that Camus lacked independence with regard to the policy of *Algérie française* does not alter the weight of his criticism, but extends it to himself.

67 See above, pp. 118–23.

68 *Les Temps Modernes,* VIII (August 1952), 329.

69 "La République du silence," *Situations,* III, 12.

70 *What is Literature?* p. xvii.

solution. Let us recall a truism about Sartre's endeavor which is sometimes lost sight of: his has been a search in the course of which he has scrupulously guarded his freedom from encroachments from any quarter.

Committed literature for Sartre not only means freedom of commitment but also calls for genuinely literary standards:

> Good sentiments incline towards academicism; if one wants to communicate a legitimate indignation to the reading public, the message must above all be easy to decipher; one then subordinates the problems of art to the false security [of formalism]; . . . one adopts the most legible kind of writing, which is necessarily a former style that has become conventional.[71]

The debate on commitment in literature which Sartre had provoked with the publication of *Les Temps Modernes* and more particularly of *What is Literature?* came to a boil at the "East-West Colloquium on the Contemporary Novel" in Leningrad in 1963. The spokesman for Socialist Realism, Leonid Leonov (speaking in the wake of Simonov who likened the author of a book to the pilot of a plane), declared simply that "form is governed by the practical aim of the artist, the port of arrival that every serious author ought to foresee in advance." [72] Alain Robbe-Grillet noted with astonishment the similarity of the criticism leveled against the anti-novel in the East to that voiced in the West.[73] He had stated his position already before leaving for Leningrad when he declared that "the calling in question of the world . . . can only be accomplished by form and not by a vaguely social and political

[71] "Le Peintre sans privilèges," *Situations,* IV, 366. Neither in theory nor in fact is there any justification for the kind of criticism often leveled at Sartre—for example, by Cranston (*Jean-Paul Sartre,* p. 99): "The final criterion [of Sartre's literary criticism] is thus strictly speaking, neither literary nor psychological: it is political." Already the adjective psychological, rather than philosophical, condemns Cranston's reading of Sartre as uninformed.

[72] "Pourquoi les occidentaux vivent-ils à l'enseigne du 'tout est permis'?" p. 48.

[73] See "L'Ecrivain, par définition, ne sait où il va, et il écrit pour chercher à comprendre pourquoi il écrit," pp. 63–65.

anecdote" and that "literature acts upon revolutions, but in an unforeseeable and unaccountable way." [74]

It may at first seem surprising that it is the Sartre of "scarcity" and of *praxis* rather than the one of the project and ontological freedom, who, in Leningrad, ceased to insist on overt political commitment on the part of the author. But in the *Critique* Sartre had understood *praxis* as the project totalizing itself in the world:

> A novel is the work of a total man and . . . it cannot be good if it is not total. A novel can be total in many ways. Kafka has written thin volumes which treat only of particular and petit bourgeois problems. But if one reads them in depth, one discovers that totality which a new and modern novel should always aim at reaching. . . . It matters little whether literature is called committed or not: it is so necessarily [in] the totality of today's man. . . . Something of the period must be reflected one way or another in his work.[75]

Sartre here seems to echo a statement made at the Colloquium by Robbe-Grillet,[76] but he actually sets up a criterion for good literature to which that author has turned his back: the imbuing of a fragment, even a small detail, of prose with the totality one is.[77] Sartre has further clarified his thought on committed literature and reached what would seem a definitive position, in his talk at a symposium in Paris on *What can Literature do?* [78] Since meaning is given to life by a unifying consciousness of it, in a literary work it stems from the totality represented by the author, who cannot but include an acute concern for the disaster threatening man and, possibly, his own

[74] Robbe-Grillet as cited by Pierre Fisson, "Un portrait-interview," p. 3.

[75] "Un Bilan, un Prélude," p. 84.

[76] "Certainly, the novelist is committed—but he is so no matter what, and neither more nor less than all other men," Robbe-Grillet, "L'Écrivain," p. 63.

[77] In this respect it may be possible to compare much of the anti-novel (notably that of Robbe-Grillet and of Butor) with the impassible Parnasse, an interlude between Romanticism and Naturalism, both equally generous.

[78] Published as *Que peut la littérature?* (1965).

inability to do anything about it. "Only it is not necessary, it is sometimes not even desirable, that all these preoccupations take the shape of a reality expressly designated in the work" (p. 124). What is imperative, however, is that "the person about whom one speaks to us, who is at once the other and ourselves, be immersed in this universe and that he be able to realize freely this seizure of significations." This intelligibility is not a matter of concepts for the reader—any more than for the author or his characters—but "[the author] will speak to him with the density of a style, with a manner of being, of putting him in situation, which must itself be obscure" (p. 126). If the author is successful, the reader will have lived a moment of freedom, a moment of escape from alienation and oppression. This implicit—one is tempted to write "natural"—rather than explicit, overt and willful manner of literary commitment seems definitive for Sartre. For it at last avoids the normative and *a priori* approach to a work of fiction, in favor of the unfolding of an intrinsic quality, that of the author's consciousness of being in the world.

Since the author communicates this moment of awareness of alienation and oppression—and hence distance from them—to his readers, Sartre had felt that "at the heart of the aesthetic imperative we discern the moral imperative." [79] Yet Sartre, like Nizan before him, has now realized that we are not saved by literature any more than by politics.[80] And Sartre considers that his own evolution since the writing of *Nausea,* as described in *The Words,* has culminated in finally abandoning his aim to found an ethics, while nonetheless continuing to work for the liberation of man.

It is now possible to consider a serious objection to Sartre's existentialism which Georges Poulet has formulated as follows:

[79] *What is Literature?* pp. 56–57.

[80] See "Jean-Paul Sartre s'explique sur *Les Mots,*" Interview by Jacqueline Piatier, p. 13.

But the task which Sartre imposes on man is perhaps unrealizeable. It actually consists in providing a justification, by means of his own actions, for an existence unjustifiable by itself. How could this be possible if not by creating *ex nihilo* the value of his actions? Sartrian existentialism can only culminate in an ethics whose object would be to prove that the *good* can be derived from *nothing*. That is almost the position of a God who would have to create himself. A morality that is its own cause! [81]

Sartre, who does deny man a first cause and an ultimate purpose, certainly does not claim to justify existence. And value—the in-itself-for-itself (ultimately: God)—is to him, as we know, an ontological illusion. But freedom and commitment are nonetheless rooted in our facticity and contingency. While these are not first or final causes, neither can they be called "nothing"; and imperatives drawn from them are therefore not drawn *ex nihilo*. Even though Sartre has finally abandoned his aim to develop his own version of value, a normative ethics, he has established a valid ethical imperative, negatively, in his condemnation of the "spirit of seriousness" (which denies contingency) and, positively, in his injunction to commitment (through which we recognize our ontological and anthropological facticity). Sartre seeks in the *praxis* of committed literature, in philosophy and in literary criticism, a disclosure in the light of his dictum: "Faire et en faisant se faire" ("To create and while creating create oneself"). [82]

[81] "La Nausée de Sartre," *Etudes sur le temps humain*, III, 235–36.
[82] Preface to Mallarmé, *Poésies*, p. 14.

Conclusion

THE VALIDITY OF LITERATURE AND THE ROLE OF LITERARY CRITICISM

The great adversary of Nietzsche is idealism. The error which vitiates everything since Socrates and Plato is the distinction of the intelligible world from the sensible world. Christianity is only a "Platonism for the people." But the world does not refer back to anything else. Nietzscheanism represents above all this denial of ulterior worlds.[1]

Sartre is one of those philosopher-writers who, like Pascal, Kierkegaard, Heidegger and others before him, have returned to what Husserl called "das urpräsentierbare Sein"[2]—the being that can be seized as it is originally.

More than any other, Sartre has bridged the dichotomy civilization has cultivated between sensation and thought. To the student steeped in traditional idealist philosophy, who might ask whether one can think nausea, he would reply, as did Merleau-Ponty, that "the world is not because I think, but what I live."[3] The prereflective precedes the reflective consciousness of the world, but it is certainly not divorced from it. "There is only intuitive knowledge. Deduction and discursive

[1] Jean Lacroix, "Nietzsche," p. 9. [2] *Ideen,* II, 163.

[3] *Phénoménologie de la perception,* p. xii. Sartre tells us ("Itinerary of a Thought," p. 46) that all his life he tried "to provide a philosophical foundation for realism . . . to give man both his autonomy and his reality among real objects, avoiding idealism without lapsing into mechanistic materialism." See also above, p. 45.

argument, incorrectly called examples of knowing, are only instruments which lead to intuition." [4]

From the start, Sartre adopted and radicalized Husserl's *epoché,* his phenomenological suspension of all presuppositions, both as a modern Cartesian "methodical doubt" and an original "how to conduct one's reason rightly," in which phenomenological description appears as a particular aspect of literary description.[5] As a result, one of Sartre's first criteria for good literature is that it describe rather than postulate.

Yet Sartre has not dispensed in the least with the achievements of classical philosophy. As a matter of fact, his mature position can be understood as a synthesis of Kierkegaard and Hegel, of Husserl and Marx, who are integrated through some fundamental innovations. Still, it is precisely his systematic philosophy that is characterized by the use of phenomenological description throughout, and the reliance on literature and his own practice of literature and of literary criticism as concomitant to his philosophy.

For, on the whole, in good literature the sensible is linked to the intelligible; knowledge is acquired intuitively, free from presuppositions; not general, conventional explanations, but original descriptions, lead to a concrete *Lebenswelt.*[6] In this context, the following much-quoted passage by one of Husserl's great literary contemporaries bears repetition:

The grandeur of real art . . . is to rediscover, grasp again and lay before us that reality from which we live so far removed and from which we become more and more separated as the formal knowledge which we substitute for it grows in thickness and impervious-

[4] *Being,* p. 172.

[5] In the sense Wittgenstein had in mind when he wrote that "we must do away with all explanation and description alone must take its place" (*Philosophical Investigations,* No. 109). But contrary to Wittgenstein, Sartre transcends phenomenological description to seek theoretical comprehension. Examples of this are given throughout, especially in the *Saint Genet* and the "Flaubert."

[6] Husserl thus designates the prescientific experience of the world (*Krisis,* p. 81).

ness—that reality which there is grave danger we might die without ever having known and yet which is simply our life, life as it really is, life disclosed at last and made clear, consequently the only life that is really lived, *that is literature.*[7]

A philosopher described Sartre's philosophy as one "rooted in experience and directed towards the analysis of experience," of experiences which are "paradigm cases" for him.[8] But there are, beyond these, individual phenomena which are irreducible to philosophy as a coherent body of thought. Sartre therefore relies on literature to complement philosophy and on literary criticism to mediate between literature and philosophy.

Sartre found or founded in literature vertigo and anguish as the experience of man's freedom; man's gaze as the revelation of the other, interiorized in shame when dominated, in pride when dominating; the privileged moments of a choice of being or of a profound change in direction as "paradigm cases" of the project and *praxis,* either authentic in a spirit of contestation or in bad faith in the "spirit of seriousness." Literature is also the medium in which description of the act of living discloses knowledge. Sometimes a literary "becoming" has the weight of a comprehensive philosophical or theological demonstration. Roquentin feels that life acquires a greater density of being when he hears the voice of commitment. In short, in literature an imaginary prereflective and reflective experience precedes philosophy, just as existence precedes essence. And since Sartre —by his reliance on literature—has been able to produce a systematic existentialist philosophy, this constitutes, in turn, a validation of literature.

However, as has been said, only part of *le monde vécu* can be integrated into a philosophical system. Beyond this, we meet the indefiniteness of "lived experience" and the infinite partic-

[7] Proust, *Remembrance of Things Past,* II, 1013. For the italicized phrase, missing in the Blossom translation, see Pléiade, III, 895.

[8] James M. Edie, "Introduction" to Pierre Thévenaz, *What is Phenomenology?* p. 167.

ularity of each man. Baudelaire's style of life, Genet's peculiar sainthood, and Flaubert's search for the absolute in style can only be understood through existentialist biography, that is, in a study which examines highly complex and unique individual attitudes, irreducible to any generalization. But they can be described and comprehended in literature, where, in the words of Proust, there are as many worlds as there are authors.

Sartre's evolution shows a remarkable degree of consistency; it is the story of an unfolding, not of changes in direction.[9] His career as a literary critic follows by a few years the publication of his phenomenological monographs. In the latter, he expelled interiority from consciousness and established the distinction between perception and imagination. He was one of the early enthusiastic readers of Dos Passos because that author dispensed with inner life, and, in turn, his discovery of Faulkner's "disloyal" temporality foreshadowed the development of his own ontological temporality in *Being and Nothingness.* In his other early reviews Sartre treats of Giraudoux's latent Aristotelianism, Ponge's psychoanalysis of things, Mauriac's *a priori* essentialism, Camus's concept of absurdity from the point of view of reason, and the problem of language as that of the recuperation of being. In the style of a work, its structure, its temporality, its semantic field, its tone or its rhythm, Sartre seeks to detect the metaphysics of an author and judges it according to his own. For from the outset Sartre used literary criticism as a mediation between his philosophy and literature.

He expanded his thought in his phenomenological ontology, which permitted him to define man's project as a variant of value and aesthetic beauty as value. Commitment, arising from contingency and facticity, brought him to the need and the promise of a normative ethics. So far, modifying Freud through his existentialist psychoanalysis, Sartre had described the inau-

[9] Bédé had already pointed out during the early stages of this development that it was likely to lead to a unified "edifice." (See "Sartre, Jean Paul," pp. 722–23).

thenticity of the spirit of seriousness and asked only that one recognize one's contingency.

With the first issue of *Les Temps Modernes* Sartre, aroused by the war and the Resistance movement, manifested his involvement with social issues. Its "Présentation" announced as its aim the foundation of a synthetic anthropology. Later issues featured *What is Literature?* with its definition of aesthetic pleasure and of committed literature, and a series of articles on literary criticism in character with his existentialist ontology and his new concern for history.

With the *Baudelaire* and the *Saint Genet* Sartre created what is actually a new genre: existentialist biography. Following the elaboration of an existentialist anthropology in the *Critique,* Sartre could expand and perfect his biographical criticism in the Flaubert articles. It remained the history of an author's consciousness, but it now gave greater weight to his family and social conditioning as a child. Sartre fully developed his regressive-progressive and analytico-synthetic method of research: a man's life is the endeavor to unify his world in a totalizing *praxis* in which he develops his initial project.

In the 1960s, through his article on Nizan, his address to the Leningrad Colloquium, his participation in the Symposium on "What can Literature do?" and through various other articles and interviews, a modified position on commitment emerged. What should matter to prose authors is not some overt political intervention, Sartre now held, but an awareness of the total human situation, manifested in their work to the degree that it belongs there intrinsically.

The concept of commitment called for a normative ethics, which Sartre had been intending to formulate over the last thirty years. But following *The Words,* he had to recognize that such a formulation is contrary to the open-endedness of human existence, as he had consistently described it: knowledge does not precede living, only *praxis* is disclosure.

The role of literary criticism as a dynamic correlation between literature and philosophy is in many respects originally and peculiarly Sartrian.[10] Sartre did not, in spite of his *tabula rasa* point of departure in philosophy, discard any of the criteria of literary criticism to be derived from the humanistic disciplines, but he centered them on his own philosophical system. In this critical reflection on an author's work as the expression of his total existence, Sartre penetrates to the underlying metaphysics. Sartre can be a rewarding reader, ready to recognize and adopt valid discoveries in a literary work or to criticize them from the point of view of his existentialist criteria. We know that one approaches beauty as density of being and that, to the contrary, the presence of an internal or omniscient narrator, or of characters who do not act or who exist only in the past, or of an illusory inner life, denotes a lack of being. On the other hand, Sartre has often reminded us that, when all is said, there remains in art a certain irreducibility to any general criteria: "In the greater writers, . . . in Gide, in Claudel, in Proust, one finds the real experience of man, a thousand directions." [11] Such authors represent an authentic experience,[12] which cannot be disregarded. Sartre's literary criticism is a guide, a method of research, but not an *a priori* system to be imposed on original thought. To him, literary criticism is in a permanent evolution, moving back and forth from philosophy to the lived world of the author, so as to renew, to complement, to enlarge, to deepen and to explicate one by the other.

Sartre's philosophy and literary criticism exist as the antidote to most Anglo-American philosophy, preoccupied, in the words of one critic, "with the analysis of language and with problems

[10] Of course, there were philosopher-critics before Sartre. The difference is one of content and of the degree of integration. In this vein, Norman Torrey reminds us that "another tenet of literary humanism is the belief that 'through fiction we arrive at a higher reality' " (*The Spirit of Voltaire*, p. 272).

[11] *What is Literature?* p. 168.

[12] Let us also recall Merleau-Ponty's "a simple tale can signify the world with as much 'depth' as a philosophical treatise" (*Phénoménologie de la perception*, p. xvi).

in the theory of knowledge," philosophers to whom "philosophy [is] a dialogue between philosophers, unbroken by reference to anything outside philosophy." [13] One might perhaps say that nonexistentialist philosophy as a whole is more dominated by the tradition of its own past than is literature, thanks to its "belletristic" freedom.[14] Taking reflection on experience as its point of departure, Sartrian literary criticism is a free and unending dialogue between the two disciplines in which he seeks a unification of many branches of knowledge, and to which he brings the criteria developed in his philosophy.

Success in one's critical endeavor is reached, by his own standards, when one has the intuition of having attained irreducibility and thus advanced to an understanding of a work and an author that explicates the greatest number of phenomena. This is exactly what Sartre has achieved: he has "reduced" traditional categories in many fields while integrating them into his concept of the original choice of being.

Acknowledgement of Sartre's importance has come in many ways. He is one of the very few living authors to have been placed on the now discontinued *Index Librorum Prohibitorum.* And he is perhaps the only one who, even when he was *persona grata* in Moscow, remained practically unpublished in the Soviet Union. Another kind of acknowledgment were the

[13] Charles Frankel, "Solitude, Silence and Sincerity," p. 3. At the philosophers' convention in New York in 1969 an observer put it this way: "When critical philosophers point their finger to reality, orthodox philosophers study the finger."

[14] Lukacs noted: "Literature offers numerous examples of authors influenced in their personal ideas by [capitalist] fetishism, who are to a large degree able to shed them in their literary creation. In other words, these authors manage to represent, in their works, human relations as such, in spite of their individual ideas that run contrary to them. But in philosophy, where first principles are themselves called into question, the object of study cannot exert such a salutary influence" (*Existentialisme ou Marxisme,* p. 30).

Lukacs actually provides us in this passage with an excellent explanation for the phenomenon occurring especially in the Soviet Union, where a fetishized Marxism—which, precisely, does not reflect anyone's "individual ideas"—prevents any progress in philosophical thought while literature continues to thrive more or less clandestinely.

dynamite attacks against his home during the Algerian war. But he is also considered acidly provocative in circles less certain of their values, which to him is the saving grace of his success. It is surprising that praise often comes from avowed adversaries. Thus Karl Jaspers wrote:

> I have gained the greatest respect for Sartre. He is not only a thinker and brilliant analyst of phenomena; he has gained an unusually wide audience for this philosophy thanks to his creative writing. . . . There is no existentialism. There is Sartre.[15]

What Jaspers fails to mention is that for Sartre (as much as for Heidegger, though in a more lucid manner) literary criticism is an integral part of his creative writing and his philosophy. Another interesting and at first rather startling appreciation recognizes his uniqueness:

> He is the Saint Augustine of an atheistic century: the same dialectical power, the same relentlessness, the same fervor which the saint brought to bear in situating himself in the light of God, Jean-Paul Sartre brings to bear in situating himself in his absence.[16]

Sartre's first impetus to write came from a passion to understand what he was to others. In the process he often had to think against himself,[17] and, in tried and true phenomenological fashion, he came, as has no one before him, to understand those of whom he himself was conscious: the others.[18] In either case, in the words of a perceptive reader of Sartre, "we can no longer formulate a general truth about ourselves which shall encompass us like a house." [19] The most we can do is to emulate Sartre's lack of illusions, his lucidity, his wager of commitment, and his example of someone who "by inventing his own issue, invents himself." [20]

15 "Der Philosoph in der Politik," p. 29.

16 Robert Kanters, "De Sartre à Beauvoir," p. 4.

17 "I came to think systematically against myself, to the extent of measuring the obvious truth by the displeasure it caused me" (*The Words,* p. 158).

18 "Sartre and Pagniez were united by their mutual passion for understanding people" (Beauvoir, *Prime,* p. 33).

19 Iris Murdoch, *Sartre, Romantic Rationalist,* p. 78.

20 *What is Literature?* p. 287.

BIBLIOGRAPHY

SELECTED BIBLIOGRAPHY OF JEAN-PAUL SARTRE'S WORK

1923

"L'Ange du morbide," short story, *Revue sans Titre,* a student publication.

1924–1928

"Défaite." Unpublished novel.

1929

A Letter quoted in "Enquête auprès des étudiants d'aujourd'hui. Correspondance," *Nouvelles Littéraires,* VIII (February 2, 1929), 10.

1931

"Légende de la vérité," *Bifur* (June 8, 1931), pp. 77–96.

1936

"La Transcendance de l'ego, Esquisse d'une description phénoménologique," *Recherches Philosophiques,* VI (1936), 85–123 (Paris, Vrin, 1965).

The Transcendence of the Ego. An Existentialist Theory of Consciousness. Translated by Forrest Williams and Robert Kirkpatrick. New York, The Noonday Press, 1962.

L'Imagination. Paris, Alcan, 1936 (Paris, Presses Universitaires de France, 1963).

Imagination. A Psychological Critique. Translated by Forrest Williams. Ann Arbor, The University of Michigan Press, 1962.

1937

"Le Mur," *Nouvelle Revue Française,* XLIX (July 1937), 38–62 (in Le Mur).

The Wall and Other Stories. Translated by Lloyd Alexander. New York, New Directions, 1948.

1938

"La Chambre," *Mesures,* III (January 15, 1938), 119–49 (in Le Mur).

The Room, in The Wall and Other Stories.

"Sartoris," *Nouvelle Revue Française,* L (February 1938), 323–28 (in Situations I).

"William Faulkner's Sartoris," in Literary and Philosophical Essays. Translation by Annette Michelson. New York, Collier Books, 1967.

"A propos de John Dos Passos et de '1919,'" *Nouvelle Revue Française,* LI (August 1938), 292–301 (in Situations I).

"John Dos Passos and 1919," in Literary and Philosophical Essays.

"Intimité," *Nouvelle Revue Française,* LI (August, September 1938), 187–200, 381–406 (in Le Mur).

Intimacy, in The Wall and Other Stories.

"La Structure intentionnelle de l'image," *Revue de Métaphysique et de Morale* (October 4, 1938), pp. 543–609 (in L'Imaginaire).

"La Conspiration" (by Paul Nizan), *Nouvelle Revue Française,* LI (November 1938), 842–45 (in Situations I).

La Nausée. Paris, Gallimard, 1938.

Nausea. Translated by Robert Baldick. Harmondsworth, Middlesex, Penguin Books, 1965.

1939

"Une Idée fondamentale de la phénoménologie de Husserl: l'Intentionnalité," *Nouvelle Revue Française,* LII (January 1939), 129–32 (in Situations I).

"M. François Mauriac et la Liberté," *Nouvelle Revue Française,* LII (February 1939), 212–32 (in Situations I).

"François Mauriac and Freedom," in Literary and Philosophical Essays.

"La Chronique de Jean-Paul Sartre" (V. Nabokov's La Méprise; D. de Rougemont's L'Amour et l'Occident; Ch. Morgan's Le Fleuve étincelant), *Europe,* VII (June 1939), 240–49 (the first two in Situations I).

"A propos de Le Bruit et la Fureur. La Temporalité chez Faulkner," *Nouvelle Revue Française,* LII and LIII (June, July 1939), 1057–61, 147–51 (in Situations I).

"On The Sound and the Fury: Time in the Work of Faulkner," in Literary and Philosophical Essays.

Esquisse d'une théorie des émotions. Paris, Actualités scientifiques et industrielles, 1939 (Paris, Hermann, 1960).

The Emotions. Outline of a Theory. Translated by Bernard Frechtman. New York, The Wisdom Library, 1948.

Le Mur. Paris, Gallimard, 1939.

The Wall and Other Stories.

1940

"M. Jean Giraudoux et la Philosophie d'Aristote. A propos de Choix des élues," *Nouvelle Revue Française,* LIV (March 1940), 339–54 (in Situations I).

"Jean Giraudoux and the Philosophy of Aristotle," in Literary and Philosophical Essays.

Bariona. Typescript; Paris, Elisabeth Marescot, 1967.

L'Imaginaire; psychologie phénoménologique de l'imagination. Paris, Gallimard, 1940.

The Psychology of Imagination. Translated by Bernard Frechtman. New York, Washington Square Press, 1966.

1943

"Explication de L'Etranger," *Cahiers du Sud,* XXX (February 1943), 189–206 (in Situations I).

"Camus' The Outsider," in Literary and Philosophical Essays.

"Aminadab ou du fantastique considéré comme un langage" (by M. Blanchot), *Cahiers du Sud,* XXX (April, May 1943), 299–305, 361–71 (in Situations I).

"Aminadab or the Fantastic Considered as a Language," in Literary and Philosophical Essays.

"Les Mouches," *Confluences,* III (April–May 1943), 371–91 (a fragment, in Théâtre, Vol. I).

The Flies. Translated by Stuart Gilbert. New York, A. A. Knopf, 1948.

"Un Nouveau Mystique," (on G. Bataille), *Cahiers du Sud,* XXX (October, November, December 1943), 783–90, 866–86, 988–94 (in Situations I).

L'Etre et le Néant. Essai d'ontologie phénoménologique. Paris, Gallimard, 1943.

Being and Nothingness. An Essay of Phenomenological Ontology.

Translated by Hazel E. Barnes. New York, Philosophical Library, 1956.

1944

"Aller et Retour" (on Brice Parain), *Cahiers du Sud,* XXXI (February–March, April–May 1944), 117–33, 248–70 (in Situations I).

"Departure and Return," in Literary and Philosophical Essays.

"Hommage à Jean Giraudoux," *Voici la France de ce mois* (New York, March 1944), p. 15.

"A propos du Parti pris des choses," *Poésie* (July, October, November, December 1944) (in Situations I, 245–93).

"Paris sous l'occupation," *La France Libre* (November 1944), pp. 9–18 (in Situations III).

"L'Homme ligoté" (on Jules Renard), *Messages* (Geneva), No. 2 (1944), pp. 51–62 (in Situations I).

"La République du silence," *Lettres Françaises* (1944) in Situations III).

1945

"Un Collège spirituel," *Confluences* (Lyon, January–February 1945), pp. 9–18 (in Baudelaire).

"Qu'est-ce qu'un collaborateur?" *La République Française* (August–September 1945), pp. 14–17 (in Situations III).

"Présentation," *Les Temps Modernes,* I (October 1945), 1–21 (in Situations II).

"La Nationalisation de la littérature," *Les Temps Modernes,* I (November 1945), 193–211 (in Situations II).

"Portrait de l'antisémite," *Les Temps Modernes,* I (December 1945), 442–70 (in Réflexions sur la question juive).

L'Age de raison. (Les Chemins de la liberté, Vol. I.) Paris, Gallimard, 1945.

The Age of Reason. (The Roads to Freedom, Vol. I.) Translated by Eric Sutton. New York, A. A. Knopf, 1947.

Le Sursis. (Les Chemins de la liberté, Vol. II.) Paris, Gallimard, 1945.

The Reprieve. (The Roads to Freedom, Vol. II.) Translated by Eric Sutton. New York, A. A. Knopf, 1947.

Huis Clos. Paris, Gallimard, 1945 (in Théâtre, Vol. I).

No Exit, and Three Other Plays. Translated by Lionel Abel. New York, Vintage Books, 1956.

1946

"Forgers of Myths: The Young Playwrights of France," *Theatre Arts*, XXX, No. 6 (June 1946), 324–35.

Lecture at the Centre de culture de l'amitié française, published in Les Grands Appels de l'homme contemporain. Paris, Editions du Temps Présent, 1946.

"Matérialisme et Révolution," *Les Temps Modernes*, I (June, July 1946), 1537–63, 1–32.

"Materialism and Revolution," in Literary and Philosophical Essays.

"Présentation" (special issue on the United States), *Les Temps Modernes*, I (August–September 1946), 193–98 (in Situations III).

"Introduction" to Charles Baudelaire, Ecrits intimes. Paris, Editions du Point du Jour, 1946 (in Baudelaire).

L'Existentialisme est un humanisme. Paris, Nagel, 1946.

Existentialism and Humanism. Translated by Philip Mairet. London, Methuen, 1957.

"La Liberté cartésienne," preface to Selections from Descartes, Geneva, Traits, 1946 (in Situations I).

"Cartesian Freedom," in Literary and Philosophical Essays.

"Les Mobiles de Calder," *Collection d'Art Moderne de la Galerie Carré*, No. 3 (Paris), 1946 (in Situations III).

Morts sans sépulture. Lausanne, Marguérat, 1946 (in Théâtre, Vol. I).

The Victors, in Three Plays. Translated by Lionel Abel. New York, A. A. Knopf, 1949.

La Putain respectueuse. Paris, Nagel, 1946 (in Théâtre, Vol. I).

The Respectful Prostitute, in No Exit and Three Other Plays.

Réflexions sur la question juive. Paris, Gallimard, 1946.

Portrait of the Anti-Semite. Translated by Erik de Mauny. London, Secker & Warburg, 1948.

1947

"Qu 'est- ce que la littérature?" *Les Temps Modernes,* Vols. II, III (February, March, April, May, June, July 1947) (in Situations II, 55–330).

What is Literature? Translated by Bernard Frechtman. New York, Harper Colophon Books, 1965.

"Introduction" to the catalogue of the David Hare exhibit, Paris, Galerie Maeght, 1947.

"Lettre-préface" to Francis Jeanson, Le Problème moral et la Pensée de Sartre. Paris, Editions du Myrte, 1947, pp. 13–14.

"Préface," Nathalie Sarraute, Portrait d'un inconnu. Paris, Gallimard, 1947 (in Situations IV).

"Nathalie Sarraute," in Situations. Translated by Maria Jolas.

"La Responsabilité de l'écrivain," in *Les Conférences de l'UNESCO*. Paris, Fontaine, 1947, pp. 57–73.

Baudelaire. Paris, Gallimard, 1947.

Baudelaire. Translated by Martin Turnell. New York, New Directions, 1967.

L'Homme et les Choses (on Francis Ponge). Paris, Seghers, 1947 (in Situations I).

Les Jeux sont faits. Paris, Nagel, 1947.

The Chips Are Down. Translated by Louise Varèse. Boston, Prime Publishers, 1965.

Situations I. Paris, Gallimard, 1947.

Théâtre, Vol. I. Paris, Gallimard, 1947.

1948

"La Recherche de l'absolu" (on Alberto Giacometti), in *Les Temps Modernes,* III (January 1948), 1153–63 (in Situations III).

"Conscience de soi et Connaissance de soi," *Bulletin de la Société Française de Philosophie* (April–June 1948), pp. 49–91.

"Entretien sur la politique" with David Rousset, *Les Temps Modernes,* III (September 1948), 385–428 (in Entretiens sur la politique).

"Introduction" to the Catalogue of the Giacometti exhibit. New York, Pierre Matisse Gallery, 1948.

"Orphée noir," introduction to Léopold Sédar-Senghor, Anthologie de la nouvelle poésie nègre et malgache de langue française. Paris, Presses Universitaires de France, 1948 (in Situations III).

"Jean-Paul Sartre répond à ses détracteurs," Pour et Contre l'existentialisme. Paris, Atlas, 1948.

"Preface" to The Respectful Prostitute, in Art and Action, New York, 1948.

L'Engrenage. Paris, Nagel, 1948.

Les Mains sales. Paris, Gallimard, 1948.

Dirty Hands, in Three Plays. Translated by Lionel Abel. New York, A. A. Knopf, 1949.

Situations II. Paris, Gallimard, 1948.

Visages, preceded by Portraits officiels. Paris, Seghers, 1948.

1949

"A propos de la politique de M. Sartre" (a reply to Mauriac), Le Figaro Littéraire, March 7, 1949.

"Drôle d'amitié" [first chapter of the projected La Dernière Chance, Les Chemins de la liberté, Vol. IV], in *Les Temps Modernes,* No. 49 (November 1949), 769–806, and No. 50 (December 1949), 1009–39.

Entretiens sur la politique. With David Rousset and Gérard Rosenthal. Paris, Gallimard, 1949.

La Mort dans l'âme (Les Chemins de la liberté, Vol. III). Paris, Gallimard, 1949.

Troubled Sleep (The Roads to Freedom, Vol. III). Translated by Gerard Hopkins. London, H. Hamilton, 1957.

Nourritures. Paris, Damase, 1949.

Situations III. Paris, Gallimard, 1949.

1950

"Les Jours de notre vie" with Merleau-Ponty, *Les Temps Modernes,* V (January 1950), 1153–68.

"A propos du mal," *Livres de France* (Paris, June 1950), pp. 13–14.

"Préface," Louis Dalmas, Le Communisme yougoslave depuis la rupture avec Moscou. Paris, Terre des Hommes, 1950.

"Préface," Juan Hernanos, La Fin de l'espoir. Paris, Collection des Temps Modernes, 1950 (in Situations VI).

"Préface," René Leibovitz, L'Artiste et sa conscience; esquisse d'une dialectique de la conscience artistique. Paris, Arche, 1950 (in Situations IV).

"The Artist and his Conscience," in Situations. Translated by Benita Eisler. Greenwich, Conn., Fawcett Publications, 1966.

"Préface," Roger Stéphane, Portrait de l'aventurier. Paris, Sagittaire, 1950 (in Situations VI).

1951

"Gide vivant," *Les Temps Modernes,* VI (March 1951), 1537–41 (in Situations IV).

"The Living Gide," in Situations.

Le Diable et le Bon Dieu. Paris, Gallimard, 1951.

The Devil and the Good Lord and Two Other Plays. New York, A. A. Knopf, 1960.

1952

"Réponse à Albert Camus," *Les Temps Modernes,* VIII (August 1952), 334–53.

"Reply to Albert Camus," in Situations.

"Préface," Mallarmé, Poésies. Paris, Gallimard, 1952.

Saint Genet, Comédien et Martyr. Œuvres complètes, Vol. I. Paris, Gallimard, 1952.

Saint Genet, Actor and Martyr. Translated by Bernard Frechtman. New York, Mentor Books, 1964.

1953

"Commentaire" on L'Affaire Henri Martin. Paris, Gallimard, 1953.

1954

"Préface," Henri Cartier-Bresson, D'une Chine à l'autre. Paris, Delpire, 1954 (in Situations V).

"Introduction" to Jean Genet, The Maids, Deathwatch. New York, Grove Press, 1954.

Les Peintures de Giacometti. Paris, Editions Pierre à Feu, 1954.

"The Paintings of Giacometti," in Situations.

Kean. Paris, Gallimard, 1954.

Kean, based on the Play by Alexander Dumas, in The Devil and the Good Lord and Two Other Plays.

1956

"Pour répondre à l'appel des écrivains hongrois," *Le Figaro Littéraire* (November 10, 1956), p. 10.

Nekrassov. Paris, Gallimard, 1956.

Nekrassov, in The Devil and the Good Lord and Two Other Plays.

Les Sorcières de Salem (after the play by Arthur Miller). Paris, Gallimard, 1956.

1957

"Questions de méthode," *Les Temps Modernes,* XII (September, October, 1957), 338–417, 658–97 (in Critique de la raison dialectique).

Search for a Method. Translated by Hazel E. Barnes. New York, A. A. Knopf, 1963.

"Le Séquestré de Venise," *Les Temps Modernes* (November 1957), 761–800 (in Situations IV).

"The Prisoner of Venice," in Situations.

1958

"Préface," Henri Alleg, La Question. Paris, Editions de Minuit, 1958.

"Préface," André Gorz, Le Traître. Paris, Editions du Seuil, 1958 (in Situations IV).

"Of Rats and Men," in Situations.

1960

"Albert Camus," *France Observateur,* No. 505 (January 7, 1960) (in Situations IV).

"Albert Camus," in Situations.

"Avant-Propos," Paul Nizan, Aden, Arabie. Paris, Maspéro, 1960, pp. 9–62 (in Situations IV).

"Paul Nizan," in Situations.

Critique de la raison dialectique. Paris, Gallimard, 1960.

Cuba. New York, Ballantine Books, 1960.

Les Séquestrés d'Altona. Paris, Gallimard, 1960.

The Condemned of Altona. Translation by Sylvia and Georgia Leeson. New York, Random House, 1963.

1961

"Beyond Bourgeois Theatre" (Lecture at the Sorbonne, 1961), translated by Rima Drell Reck, *Tulane Drama Review* (Spring 1961) (in Theatre in the Twentieth Century, edited by Robert W. Corrigan, New York, Grove Press, 1963, pp. 131–40).

"Le Peintre sans privilèges" (on Lapoujade), *Médiations,* No. 2 (2d Quarter 1961) (in Situations IV).

"Préface," Frantz Fanon, Les Damnés de la terre. Paris, Maspéro, 1961 (in Situations V).

1964

"Jean-Paul Sartre s'explique sur Les Mots," Interview with Jacqueline Piatier, *Le Monde* (April 18, 1964), p. 13.

"Un Bilan, un Prélude" in "Colloque Est-Ouest de Leningrad sur le roman contemporain," *Esprit,* XXXII (July 1964), 80–85.

Les Mots. Paris, Gallimard, 1964.

The Words. Translated by Bernard Frechtman. Greenwich, Conn., Fawcett Publications, 1966.

Situations IV, Portraits. Paris, Gallimard, 1964.

Situations V, Colonialisme et Néo-colonialisme. Paris, Gallimard, 1964.

Situations VI, Problèmes du marxisme, Vol. I. Paris, Gallimard, 1964.

1965

"L'Écrivain et sa langue," *Revue d'Esthétique,* XVIII, Nos. 3–4 (1965), 306–34. Interview with Pierre Verstraeten.

Speech at symposium. Que peut la littérature? Paris, L'Inédit 10/18, 1965, pp. 107–27.

Situations VII, Problèmes du marxisme, Vol. II. Paris, Gallimard, 1965.

1966

"Anthropologie et Philosophie," *Cahiers de Philosophie,* Nos. 2–3 (February 1966), pp. 3–12.

"La Conscience de classe chez Flaubert," *Les Temps Modernes,* XXI (May, June 1966), 1921–51, 2114–53.

"Flaubert: du poète à l'artiste," *Les Temps Modernes,* XXII (August, September, October 1966), 197–253, 423–81, 598–674.

"Saint Georges et le Dragon," *Arc,* No. 30 (n.d., dépôt légal: 4th Quarter 1966), pp. 35–50.

"Jean-Paul Sartre répond," *Arc,* No. 30, pp. 87–96.

Les Troyennes (after Euripides). Paris, Gallimard, 1966.

1967

"Mythe et Réalité du théâtre," *Le Point,* No. 7 (January 1967).

1968

"Les Bastilles de Raymond Aron," Interview with Serge Lafaurie, *Le Nouvel Observateur* (June 19–26, 1968), pp. 26–29.

"La Nouvelle Idée de mai 1968," Interview with Serge Lafaurie, *Le Nouvel Observateur* (June 26–July 2, 1968), pp. 21–24.

1969

Interview. "Itinerary of a Thought," *New Left Review,* No. 58 (November–December 1969), pp. 43–66.

Les Communistes ont peur de la révolution. Paris, Les Editions John Didier, 1969.

GENERAL BIBLIOGRAPHY OF WORKS CITED *

Abel, Lionel. "Metaphysical Stalinism," *Dissent* (Spring 1961), pp. 137–52.

—— "The Genius of Jean Genet," *The New York Review of Books,* I (October 17, 1963), 7–8.

Aron, Raymond. "Sartre's Marxism," *Encounter* (London, June 1965), pp. 34–39.

Audry, Colette. "La Vie d'un philosophe," *L'Express* (March 11, 1964), p. 34.

* Works mentioned but not cited are not listed.

BIBLIOGRAPHY

Ayer, A. J. Language, Truth and Logic. London, Gollancz, 1949.

Baker, Carlos. "The Relevance of a Writer's Life," *The New York Times Book Review* (August 20, 1967), pp. 2 and 31.

Barnes, Hazel E. Humanist Existentialism (a revised edition of The Literature of Possibility). Lincoln, The University of Nebraska Press, 1959.

—— "The Optimism of World Denial," *The Colorado Quarterly,* XII (Summer 1963), 5–26.

Barthes, Roland. Le Degré zéro de l'écriture. Paris, Gonthier, 1957 (1964).

Bataille, Georges. La Littérature et le Mal. Collection Idées, Paris, Gallimard, 1957 (1967).

Baudelaire, Charles. Œuvres complètes. Paris, Gallimard, Pléiade, 1963.

—— Baudelaire: A Self-Portrait. Selected Letters. Translated by Lois Boe Hyslop and Francis E. Hyslop, Jr. London, Oxford University Press, 1957.

—— The Flowers of Evil and Other Poems. Translated by Francis Duke. Charlottesville, University of Virginia Press, 1961.

—— Intimate Journals. Translated by Christopher Isherwood. Hollywood, Marcel Rodd, 1947.

Beauvoir, Simone de. La Force de l'âge. Paris, Gallimard, 1960. The Prime of Life. Translated by Peter Green. Cleveland, Meridian Books, 1966.

—— La Force des choses. Paris, Gallimard, 1963. Force of Circumstance. Translated by Richard Howard. New York, G. P. Putnam's Sons, 1965.

—— Pour une morale de l'ambiguïté. Paris, Gallimard, 1947 (1965).

Bédé, Jean-Albert. "Sartre, Jean Paul," Columbia Dictionary of Modern European Literature. New York, Columbia University Press, 1947, pp. 722–23.

—— "Paul Nizan," *The Romanic Review,* LVIII (December 1967), 310–13.

Blanchot, Maurice. "L'Echec de Baudelaire," *L'Arche,* III (February 1947), 80–91.

Blin, Georges. Le Sadisme de Baudelaire. Paris, Corti, 1948.

Boros, Marie-Denise. "La Métaphore du crabe dans l'œuvre littéraire de Jean-Paul Sartre," *PMLA,* LXXXI (October 1966), 446–50.

Brée, Germaine, ed. Camus. A Collection of Critical Essays. Englewood-Cliffs, Prentice-Hall, 1962.

Brée, Germaine and Margaret Guiton. The French Novel. New York, Harcourt, Brace and World, 1962 (1957).

Burnet, J. Early Greek Philosophy. London, Black, 1930.

Butor, Michel. "Toute invention est critique," *L'Express* (June 11, 1964), pp. 24–25.

Camus, Albert. "Lettre au directeur des Temps Modernes," *Les Temps Modernes,* VIII (August 1952), 317–33.

Cormeau, Nelly. L'Art de François Mauriac. Paris, Grasset, 1951.

Cranston, Maurice. Jean-Paul Sartre. New York, Grove Press, 1962.

Cumming, Robert D. "The Literature of Extreme Situations," in Aesthetics Today. Cleveland, Meridian Books, 1961, pp. 377–412.

—— ed. The Philosophy of Jean-Paul Sartre. New York, Random House, 1965.

Doubrovsky, Serge. "Jean-Paul Sartre et le Mythe de la raison dialectique," *Nouvelle Revue Française,* IX (September, October, November 1961), 491–501, 687–98, 879–89.

Edie, James M. "Introduction" to Pierre Thévenaz: What is Phenomenology? Chicago, Quadrangle Books, 1962, pp. 13–92.

Eliot, T. S. Selected Essays, 1917–1932. New York, Harcourt Brace, 1932.

Ellevitch, Bernard. "Sartre and Genet," *The Massachusetts Review,* V (Winter 1964), 408–13.

Ellrodt, Robert. Les Poètes métaphysiques anglais. Paris, Corti, 1960.

Esslin, Martin. "Jean Genet: A Hall of Mirrors," *The Theatre of the Absurd,* pp. 140–67. Garden City, New York, Anchor Books, Doubleday, 1961.

Feuerlicht, Ignace. "Camus's L'Etranger Reconsidered," *PMLA,* LXXXVIII (December 1963), 606–21.

Fields, Madeleine. "Voltaire et le Mercure de France," *Studies on Voltaire and the Eighteenth Century,* XX (1962), 175–215.

Fisson, Pierre. "Portrait-Interview" ("Moi Alain Robbe-Grillet . . ."), *Le Figaro Littéraire,* XVIII (February 23, 1963), 3.

Flaubert, Gustave. L'Education sentimentale. Œuvres, Vol. II. Paris, Gallimard, Pléiade, 1952. Sentimental Education. Translated by Dora Knowles Ranous, London, Brentano's Ltd., 1923.

Flaubert, Gustave. Mémoires d'un fou. Œuvres complètes, Premières Œuvres, Vol. VI. Paris, Librairie de France, 1923.

—— Smarh. Œuvres complètes, Vol. II. Paris, Librairie de France, 1923.

"La France s'interroge devant le roman américain," *Le Monde,* Sélection hebdomadaire (April 6–12, 1967), pp. 10–11.

Frankel, Charles. "Solitude, Silence and Sincerity," *The New York Times Book Review* (November 3, 1963), pp. 3 and 50.

Genet, Jean. Les Bonnes. Sceaux, Pauvert, 1954 (1946). Paris, Barbézat, 1963.

—— Le Condamné à mort. Œuvres complètes, Vol. II. Paris, Gallimard, 1951 (1938–45).

—— Haute Surveillance. Paris, Gallimard, 1949.

—— Journal du voleur. Paris, Gallimard, 1949.

The Thief's Journal. Translated by Bernard Frechtman. New York, Bantam, 1965.

—— Miracle de la rose. Œuvres complètes, Vol. II (1943).

—— Notre Dame des Fleurs. Œuvres complètes, Vol. II (1942).

—— Our Lady of the Flowers. Translated by Bernard Frechtman. New York, Bantam, 1964.

—— Poèmes. Paris, Barbézat, 1948.

—— Pompes funèbres. Œuvres complètes, Vol. III (1949).

Gide, André. Les Faux-Monnayeurs. Paris, Gallimard, 1951 (1925).

Grisoli, Christian. "Les Chemins de la liberté" (interview with Sartre), *Paru,* No. 13 (December 1945), pp. 11–17.

Hahn, Otto. "L'Œuvre critique de Sartre," *Modern Language Notes,* No. 80 (May 1965), pp. 347–63.

Hegel, Georg Friedrich. Vorlesungen über die Aesthetik. Berlin, Duncker und Humblot, 1843.

Holz, Hans Heinz. "Sartres 'Kritik der Dialektischen Vernunft,'" *Merkur,* No. 164 (Munich, October 1961), pp. 969–80.

Husserl, Edmund. Ideen zu einer Reinen Phänomenologie und Phänomenologischen Philosophie, Vols. I and II. Hague, Martinus Nijhoff, 1950 (1913 and 1928). Ideas (I). Translated by W. R. Boyce Gibson. New York, Collier Books, 1962.

—— Die Krisis der Europäischen Wissenschaften und die Transzendentale Phänomenologie. Hague, Martinus Nijhoff, 1954 (1935–36).

Hytier, Jean. "L'Époque contemporaine de 1919 à nos jours," Histoire de la littérature française illustrée, ed. Bédier, Hazard, Martino. Paris, Larousse, 1949, II, 415–64.

Jaspers, Karl. "Der Philosoph in der Politik," *Der Monat,* XV (Berlin, April, 1963), 22–29.

Jeanson, Francis. "Albert Camus ou l'âme révoltée," *Les Temps Modernes,* VII (May 1952), 2070–90.

—— "Pour tout vous dire," *Les Temps Modernes,* VIII (August 1952), 354–83.

—— Le Problème moral de la pensée de Sartre. Paris, Editions du Myrte, 1947.

—— Sartre. Les Écrivains devant Dieu, Paris, Desclée de Brouwer, 1966.

Jourdain, Louis. "Sartre devant Baudelaire," *Tel Quel,* Nos. 19 and 21 (Autumn 1964, Spring 1965), 70–85, 79–95.

Kaelin, Eugene. An Existentialist Aesthetic, The Theories of Sartre and Merleau-Ponty. Madison, The University of Wisconsin Press, 1962.

Kanters, Robert. "De Sartre à Beauvoir," *Le Figaro Littéraire* (January 23–29, 1964), p. 4.

Knight, Everett W. Literature Considered as Philosophy, The French Example. New York, Macmillan, 1958.

Lacroix, Jean. "Nietzsche," *Le Monde* (August 25, 1966), p. 9. [A review of Jean Granier's Le Problème de la vérité dans la philosophie de Nietzsche. Paris, Editions du Seuil, 1966.]

Leonov, Leonid. "Pourquoi les occidentaux vivent-ils à l'enseigne du 'tout est permis'?" *Esprit,* XXXII (July 1964), 41–49.

Loy, J. Robert. Diderot's Determined Fatalist. New York, Columbia University Press, 1950.

Lukacs, George. Existentialisme ou Marxisme? Paris, Nagel, 1948.

McPhee, John. "Profiles. A Roomful of Hoving," *The New Yorker,* XLIII (May 20, 1967), 49–137.

Mallarmé, Stéphane. Œuvres complètes. Paris, Gallimard, Pléiade, 1961.

Malraux, André. Les Noyers de l'Altenburg. Paris, Gallimard, 1948.

Marcuse, Herbert. "Existentialismus: Bemerkungen zu Jean-Paul Sartres L'Etre et le Néant," in Kultur und Gesellschaft 2. Frankfurt, Suhrkamp, 1965, pp. 49–84. Originally published (excepting last chapter) in *Philosophy and Phenomenological Research,* VIII (March 1948), 309–36.

—— One-Dimensional Man. Boston, Beacon Press, 1964.

Marcuse, Ludwig. "Der Künstler und die Ideologie," *Der Monat* (Berlin, October 1961), pp. 14–19.

Marx, Karl. "Zur Kritik der Hegel'schen Rechtsphilosophie," in *Deutsch-Französische Jahrbücher* (Paris, 1844), Marx-Engels Gesamtausgabe. Frankfurt, Marx-Engels Archiv, 1927, pp. 607–21.

Mendel, Sidney. "From Solitude to Salvation: A Study in Regeneration," *Yale French Studies,* No. 30 (n.d.), pp. 45–55.

Merleau-Ponty, Maurice. Phénoménologie de la perception. Paris, Gallimard, 1945.

—— Signes. Paris, Gallimard, 1960.

Montaigne, Michel de. The Complete Essays. Translated by Donald M. Frame. Stanford, Stanford University Press, 1965.

Murdoch, Iris. Sartre, Romantic Rationalist. New Haven, Yale University Press, 1960 (1953).

Nizan, Paul. Aden, Arabie. Paris, Maspéro, 1960 (1932).

O'Brien, Justin. "Albert Camus: Militant," *Columbia University Forum,* IV (Winter 1961), 12–15 (in Camus. Englewood Cliffs, N.J., Prentice-Hall, 1962).

Peyre, Henri. Jean-Paul Sartre. Columbia Essays on Modern Writers, New York, Columbia University Press, 1968.

—— ed. Baudelaire, A Collection of Critical Essays. Englewood Cliffs, N.J., Prentice-Hall, 1962.

Picon, Gaëtan. "La Littérature du XXe siècle," Histoire des Littératures. Paris, Gallimard, Pléiade, 1958, III, 1249–1363.

—— "La Poésie au XIXe siècle," Histoire des Littératures. Paris, Gallimard, Pléiade, 1958, III, 887–997.

Poulet, Georges. Etudes sur le temps humain. Paris, Plon, 1964.

Proust, Marcel. Swann's Way, Part I. Translated by Scott-Moncrieff. London, Chatto and Windus, 1955.

—— The Past Recaptured. Translated by Frederick A. Blossom. In Remembrance of Things Past, II, New York, Random House, 1932.

—— A la recherche du temps perdu, III. Paris, Gallimard, Pléiade, 1954.

Robbe-Grillet, Alain. "L'Ecrivain, par définition, ne sait où il va, et il écrit pour chercher à comprendre pourquoi il écrit," *Esprit,* XXXII (July 1964), 63–65.

Romains, Jules. Les Hommes de bonne volonté. Paris, Flammarion, 1946.

Rougemont, Denis de. L'Amour et l'Occident. Paris, Plon, 1939.

Rousseaux, André. "Le Baudelaire de Sartre," *Le Figaro Littéraire* (March 31, 1947), p. 2.

Sarraute, Nathalie. L'Ere du soupçon. Paris, Gallimard, 1956.

Schaff, Adam. A Philosophy of Man. New York, Monthly Review Press, 1963.

Sédar-Senghor, Léopold, ed. Anthologie de la nouvelle poésie nègre et malgache. Paris, Presses Universitaires, 1948.

Shattuck, Roger. "Genesis of the Artist," *The New York Times Book Review* (March 12, 1967), pp. 4–18.

Simon, Ernest. "Descriptive and Analytical Techniques in Maupassant's *Pierre et Jean*," *The Romanic Review*, LI (February 1960), 45–52.

Simon, Pierre-Henri. "Œuvres complètes de Charles Baudelaire," *Le Monde*, Sélection hebdomadaire (May 25–31, 1967), p. 11.

Sontag, Susan. "On Style," *Partisan Review*, XXXII (Fall 1965), 543–60.

Thody, Philip. Jean-Paul Sartre, A Literary and Political Study. New York, Macmillan, 1960.

—— "Sartre as a Literary Critic," *London Magazine*, VII (November 1960), 61–64.

Torrey, Norman. The Spirit of Voltaire. Oxford, The Marston Press, 1963 (1938).

Trotsky, Leon. Littérature et Révolution. Paris, Juillard, 1964 (1924).

Valéry, Paul. "Au sujet de Stendhal, Préface pour Lucien Leuwen," Œuvres complètes de Stendhal. Paris, Champion, 1927, VI, i–li.

—— Œuvres, Vols. I and II. Paris, Gallimard, Pléiade, 1957 and 1960.

Van Baelen, Jacqueline. Rotrou, Le Héros tragique de la révolte. Paris, Nizet, 1965.

Van Tieghem, Philippe, ed. Voltaire, Contes et Romans. Paris, Rocher, 1930.

Vietta, E. Versuch über die Menschliche Existenz in der Französischen Philosophie. Hamburg, Hauswedell, 1948.

Waehlens, Alphonse de. "Sartre et la Raison dialectique," *Revue Philosophique de Louvain*, LX (February 1962), 79–99.

Wittgenstein, Ludwig. Philosophical Investigations. New York, Macmillan, 1960.

INDEX

INDEX

INDEX

INDEX

INDEX

INDEX

INDEX

INDEX

INDEX

INDEX

INDEX

INDEX

INDEX

INDEX

INDEX

INDEX